International Security and Gender

NICOLE DETRAZ

polity

First published in 2012 by Polity Press

Polity Press
65 Bridge Street
Cambridge CB2 1UR, UK

Polity Press
350 Main Street
Malden, MA 02148, USA

ISBN-13: 978-0-7456-5116-3 (hardback)
ISBN-13: 978-0-7456-5117-0 (paperback)

A catalogue record for this book is available from the British Library.

Typeset in 10.5 on 13 pt Minion
by Servis Filmsetting Ltd, Stockport, Cheshire
Printed and bound in Great Britain by the MPG Books Group

The publisher has used its best endeavors to ensure that the URLs for external websites referred to in this book are correct and active at the time of going to press. However, the publisher has no responsibility for the websites and can make no guarantee that a site will remain live or that the content is or will remain appropriate.

Every effort has been made to trace all copyright holders, but if any have been inadvertently overlooked the publisher will be pleased to include any necessary credits in any subsequent reprint or edition.

For further information on Polity, visit our website: www.politybooks.com

Contents

Acknowledgments

International Relations has fascinated me since my first year as an undergrad. I would like to start by thanking all who make this field so captivating. I cannot imagine studying anything else. I would specifically like to thank the community of feminist security scholars for producing important and thought-provoking work. You have been the most welcoming and supportive collection of people that I could ever hope to interact with. Thanks for allowing me to join in the engaging conversations that you are having. Your work has been and continues to be an inspiration to me.

Along the way I have had a wonderful community who have encouraged me and enabled this research on international security and gender. I want to start by thanking all of my professors who challenged me to think critically about IR. I also want thank my department at the University of Memphis for being so supportive of my work. From having in-depth discussions about ontology and epistemology, to comparing notes about the writing process, to going with me to get cupcakes, you all help me in countless ways. Thanks in particular to Sera Babakus, Gira Joshi, and Chad Wallace for research help.

Additionally, several people provided source suggestions, general feedback, or comments on outlines and earlier chapter drafts. Thanks to Soumita Basu, Keri Brondo, Catia Confortini, Caron Gentry, Annica Kronsell, Jennifer Lobasz, Megan MacKenzie, Swati Parashar, and two anonymous reviewers. In addition, I am extremely thankful to Laura Sjoberg for answering numerous emails, providing comments, and generally being one of the most supportive people I have ever met. The feedback from all of you made the final product better; however I accept any errors as my own.

Finally, I owe an enormous thank you to Louise Knight and David Winters at Polity Press for all of their hard work on this book at each stage of the process. Thanks for your professionalism, encouragement, and continued commitment to the project.

1

Understanding Gender in Security Debates

The Arab Spring is a term used to refer to the series of uprisings that took place in several states in the Middle East and North Africa in 2010–2011. This movement captured the attention of the general public, policy experts, and security scholars. We heard about peaceful and violent protests, the actions of state security forces, the activities of "insurgent groups," and discussions by the United Nations Security Council. Each of these elements has ties to security. In the global news, we hear stories daily about domestic-level conflicts around the world, about wars and tensions between states, about ideas like cyber-security and social security. This broad list highlights the fact that security is an idea with multiple meanings. Security is a uniquely important concept in the modern world. Common understandings of security range from inter-state war and conflict studies to a concern for well being at an individual level. Security has historically been one of the most fundamental topics of concern for international relations (IR) scholars. Largely since the end of the Second World War, scholars have worked to define and understand security in the global community. Throughout its existence, security studies has been marked by competing definitions of security. Ronnie Lipschutz (1995: 8) argues "there are not only struggles over security among nations, but also struggles over security among notions. Winning the right to define security provides not just access to resources but also the *authority* to articulate new definitions and discourses of security, as well." This quote suggests that the ways in which we define security have important implications for the scholarly and policy realms.

Security is an idea that governments typically take very seriously, so calling something a security issue often results in increased attention and resources being channeled in the direction of the "security issue." To demonstrate how important security has been for both states and IR scholarship, we can examine the concepts of *high politics* and *low politics*. Within IR, high politics has always been the exclusive realm of security, while low politics includes things like economics, social issues, and the environment. In the hierarchy of issues states face, security is at the top, while all other issues are placed beneath it. The term high politics is illustrative of the central place security has had for scholars and policymakers. Asking questions and problematizing this concept contributes to making scholarship and policymaking more reflexive. It causes us to step back and examine our assumptions about both the definition of security and also the way security policy is formulated and carried out. An important component of problematizing security is understanding the host of connections between security topics/concepts and gender.

What is Gender?

This book draws on feminist scholarship in order to explore how security and gender intersect. Much important insight into the connections between gender and security has come from feminist scholars, who approach the issue from a variety of perspectives. Feminism is best thought of as a large umbrella term which contains a range of subcategories. In other words, there are a great many feminisms. What holds them together is the goal of revealing and challenging widespread inequality in society. Most feminists focus specifically on inequality in the form of women's subordination; however, this is typically part of a broader concern about how multiple forms of inequality intersect. Feminists will have different ways of understanding the sources of this inequality as well as different suggestions for how to deal with them, but at their root they all seek an international community in which people are not discriminated against because they are identified as women or men.

Gender is the central, uniting concept for feminist scholars. According to Marysia Zalewski (1995: 339) "the driving force of feminism is its attention to gender and not simply to women. To be sure, for many feminists the concern about the injustices done to women because of their sex is paramount, but the concept, nature and practice of gender are key." Gender can be defined as a set of socially constructed ideas about what men and women ought to be. This definition has a few important pieces; firstly the idea of social construction. Rather than gender roles and assumptions being deterministic entities, they directly come out of a society's expectations. Gender characteristics are cultural creations passed on through socialization (D'Amico and Beckman 1994; Eisenstein 2007). The process of gender socialization begins at birth, if not before, for many children. When a child is born, it is identified as a boy or girl. A friend or family member may buy a blue outfit and a truck for a new baby boy or a pink outfit and a doll for a new baby girl. This reflects what society tells them is an "appropriate" item for a boy or a girl. While there is nothing natural about these gifts, gender roles become so ingrained in society that they take on the appearance of being natural or "normal." This means when individuals act in ways that defy these gender norms they are seen as being unnatural. It is also important to note that gender identity is expected from society. Individuals are identified as boy or girl even if they themselves do not feel comfortable with those identities.

The second piece of the definition refers to the difference between gender and sex. Peterson and Runyan (1999: 30) point out:

> Because models of appropriate gender behavior vary, we know that femininity and masculinity are not timeless or separable from the contexts in which they are observed. Thus, gender rests not on biological sex differences but on *interpretations* or constructions of behavior that are culturally specific and may or may not have anything to do with biological differences.

The term "sex" is typically used to describe biological differences between people understood to be men and people understood to be women (Sjoberg and Gentry 2007). Gender describes the socially constituted differences between these same groups. "Masculinities and femininities are made up of behaviour expectations, stereotypes, and rules which apply to persons because they are understood to be members of particular sex categories" (Sjoberg and Gentry 2007: 6). To go back to the earlier example, there is nothing biologically determined about the sex category of male that would necessarily be associated with the color blue. There is no evidence that the color blue is associated with testosterone production. Instead, blue is simply one of a number of shades possible for painting a room or dying fabric. It is because of *gender* that some societies associate blue with masculine babies and pink with feminine babies.

There has been a general lack of attention to gender in IR scholarship. More importantly, much IR scholarship continues the assumption that gender differences are deterministic; that men and women really do exhibit dichotomous characteristics. Helen Kinsella (2003: 296) argues "by insisting on a definition of sex and gender as if their conceptions are *already* settled and natural categories – indeed, empirical categories – one completely misses the politics and power of conceptual definition and the relationship of concepts to understanding. Categories and concepts are not neutral." Not all feminists agree on what this means for future scholarship. Where disagreement often comes into play is in discussions of what should be done about this and the consequences that are likely to follow.

Gender analysis challenges the reduction of people to simplistic assumptions about their identity based on a set of socially constructed expectations. Men are one thing and women are another. This disregards the complexity of individuals. Moreover, it tends to assume that generalizations can be made across cultures with regard to the characteristics and experiences of members of gender groups. Some feminists from the global South in particular have critiqued this position and argued this reduces the agency of women who are often viewed as "victims" (Mohanty 2003; Sedghi 1994). This critique is also extended to feminists who disregard the complexity of experiences across the globe, including differing experiences based on race, class, sexual orientation, etc. Peterson and Runyan (2010: 7) explain that "[i]ntersectional analysis holds that there are no generic women and men; our gender identities, loyalties, interests, and opportunities are affected by intersecting and cross-cutting gender, race, class, national, and sexual identities. Whereas some parts of our identities may confer privilege, others may serve to disadvantage us." For example, a straight, white, middle-class woman in France can have very different experiences, challenges and perspective than a gay, Arab, lower-class woman in Jordan. To imply the fact that both are women makes them equal in the larger group of gender is to deny the complexity of the world.

That being said, gender is an important concept in IR because of its role is shaping inequalities in society. In every society, traits and characteristics associated with masculinities are more highly valued than those associated with femininities. This affects both how institutions in society look, and the differential access of men and women to these institutions. Ann Tickner (1992: 7) claims "gender difference has played an important and essential role in the structuring of social inequalities in much of human history and that the resulting differences in self-identifications, human understandings, social status, and power relationships are unjustified." This relates to the concept of *patriarchy*. Cynthia Enloe (2004: 4) explains "patriarchy is the structure and ideological system that perpetuates the privileging of masculinity." Many different types of social structures and institutions can be patriarchal. For example, when an institution is said to require people who are "rational," "level-headed," or "decisive," as is the case with many powerful Western institutions including public office, powerful corporations, etc., the institution is privileging characteristics associated with masculinities. Most feminists discuss patriarchy because patriarchal systems marginalize that which is associated with female, leading to the marginalization of women themselves. Both men and women are instrumental in supporting patriarchal systems and their continuation. Feminist scholars do not argue all men actively support the marginalization of women while women are innocent victims in this process. Patriarchy is a deeply rooted process that works in both seen and unseen ways.

In sum, gender refers to a set of socially constructed expectations about what men and women ought to be. Gender is distinct from biological sex, and includes a set of criteria about how people *should* be. IR scholarship has been slow to incorporate gender and gender concerns in a significant way. This is unfortunate because of the role patriarchy has in structuring institutions in ways that value that which is masculine over that which is feminine.

What is Security?

There is not a single, agreed-upon definition of security that exists within academic circles. In fact, scholars have remarked that security is an extremely complex concept, and the literature on security reflects a wide variety of views (Buzan 1991; Buzan and Hansen 2009; Steans 2006). At a very basic level, security refers to a condition of being "protected, free from danger, safety" (Der Derian 1995: 28). While this definition of security does not identify who or what is being protected, it is important to think about security by asking both what is the referent object of security, and what are the necessary conditions for security.

Countries, or *states* in IR terminology, have historically been the principal subject of security scholarship. Traditional security scholarship is conceptualized as the study of the threat, use, and control of military force (Nye and Lynn-Jones 1988; Walt 1991). Many security scholars assume conflict between states is always a possibility and the use of military force is a key component to the maintenance of security for states. This means it is the state that has been seen as the legitimate actor to define security, to create security policy, and to enforce security policy, often through the military. This idea of security is typically referred to as *national security* or *state security*. The term national security comes from the idea that it is the security of the nation, or the state more accurately, that is dominant. Most international relations scholarship understands a distinction between the terms *state* and *nation*. A state is an entity with a distinct territory and government (e.g. France). A nation is a group tied together through common language, history, ethnicity, etc. (e.g. the Kurds). While there is some attention given to other entities in traditional security studies, the focus tends to come back to the state. This is because all states in the international system are considered to be important actors to include in analyses of security. This includes states from the global North and global South. The North/South labels can be problematic, but they are used as a way to highlight the different positions dominant states and non-dominant states have within the international system. It is used as a category of analysis to point out differing power relationships and systems of marginalization.

The fact that the state has been the key actor associated with "security" has particular implications both for the position of states in the international system, and for the way security is studied and carried out. Many scholars argue that states have typically benefitted from being seen as the sole providers of security and the object that needs to be secure. In fact, the identity of states as providers of security has been a large part of the international community for centuries (Campbell 1998). States derive legitimacy from this role of state security provision. This implies that the states'association as the protectors of security gives it a particular authority. It is understood as legitimate for states to use deadly force as long as that force is deployed in the name of state security. The security label also comes with certain policy expectations. Lene Hansen (2006: 35) claims "security discourses are thus characterized by a dual political dynamic: they invest those enacting security policies with the legitimate *power* to undertake decisive and otherwise exceptional actions, but they also construct those actors with a particular *responsibility* for doing so." This means we tend to see an obligation for some actor, often the state, to address security issues or "fix" them.

During the past few decades, these conceptions of security have been challenged by scholars wishing to problematize, or contest, state security's position as the dominant view of security in IR as well as those wishing to include new elements into security discourses such as economics and the environment (Buzan 1991; Barnett 2001). These moves have been discussed as broadening and deepening security studies. In a widely cited discussion of the evolution of security scholarship, scholars Keith Krause and Michael C. Williams (1996: 230) identified the trends of *broadening* "to include a wider range of potential threats" and *deepening* to include "moving either down to the level of individual or human security or up to the level of national or global security." Other voices have called for an *opening* of the security agenda. Annick Wibben (2008) argues that opening the security agenda entails discussing the meaning(s) of security. This includes questioning why appeals to security remain so powerful in both IR scholarship and policymaking.

These moves toward broadening and deepening security were propelled forward in a meaningful way in the 1990s. When the Cold

War ended, there was a radical shift in the way the public and the academy viewed security. The familiar security threat of the Soviet Union was now gone, and it was not immediately clear who or what would replace it. Once traditional notions of security become questioned and perhaps more open to interpretation, room is made for the inclusion of previously neglected additions to security. This is where notions like economic security, human security, and environmental or ecological security come into play. As the perceived threats to state security receded, many security scholars, and the security community in general, began to accept the idea that there might be non-military threats to state security. This implies that, while the target of concern for security scholars may have remained the state, the nature of the threat shifted from being solely military to something else. Several new threats to security were identified as central to the preservation of state security during the early 1990s. Among these were threats associated with environmental damage (environmental security), energy availability (energy security), the lack of sufficient stores of food (food security) and an array of difficulties associated with the global South including the possibility of failed states and transboundary crime (Barnett 2001).

During roughly the same time period, there were calls to move the focus away from the security of states and direct it to people in general. These moves resulted in concepts like *human security* and *environmental security* being debated by multiple actors. In particular, the human security narrative was the result of members of the international community using the context of the end of the Cold War to shift the focus away from states as the primary referent of security and bring the focus to individuals. This reflects a deepening of security because it moved the discussion of security down to the level of people. This was important because it served as a direct threat to traditional ideas of security. The relationship between human security and traditional security will be taken up in Chapter 5.

Additionally, fields like critical security studies (CSS), the Copenhagen School, and feminist security studies have emerged as a challenge to traditional security scholarship. Ken Booth (2005: 16), a key CSS scholar, explains the field as "concerned with the pursuit of critical knowledge about security in world politics. Security is conceived comprehensively, embracing theories and practices at multiple levels of society, from the individual to the whole human species." Three central concepts of CSS are security, community, and emancipation, suggesting a radically different way to understand security in IR. Richard Wyn Jones (1999: 160) argues the main task of CSS scholars is to attempt to undermine the existing hegemonic security approaches. The Copenhagen School, associated most closely with scholars Barry Buzan, Ole Wæver, and Jaap de Wilde, has outlined the process of *securitization* for society. They explain that securitizing, or presenting something as an existential threat, prompts a strong reaction from the state and often results in "emergency" measures being justified. "The invocation of security has been the key to legitimizing the use of force, but more generally it has opened the way for the state to mobilize, or to take special powers, to handle existential threats" (Buzan et al. 1998: 21). These scholars challenge traditional notions of security by highlighting the discursive power of security and calling attention to how security language has important impacts on the ground. Along with feminist security studies, which will be discussed below, CSS and the Copenhagen School are examples of communities of scholars who challenge mainstream security definitions and policymaking.

Threats and Vulnerabilities

Threat and *vulnerability* are two terms commonly discussed in connection with both traditional notions of security and expanded versions. P. H. Liotta (2005: 51) explains that a threat is "*identifiable, often immediate, and requires an understandable response . . . A threat, in short, is either clearly visible or commonly acknowledged.*" A security threat is often understood to be an entity or phenomenon that undermines the safety and continued existence of the state. Threats are something to be acted swiftly upon in order to eliminate them and maintain security. An example would be if an enemy's army was marching toward a state's borders, that state would marshal its own forces to meet them.

Vulnerability is a broader concept than threat. A general definition of vulnerability is the liability to suffer damage in a potentially dangerous event (Gaillard 2010). These events can be natural, economic, political, etc. Vulnerabilities are not as clearly defined as threats, but can include disease, hunger, unemployment, crime, social conflict, etc. (Liotta 2005). In a discussion of security in most forms, it is necessary to identify potential threats and vulnerabilities. The sources of threats and vulnerabilities will vary for different types of security, however. For example, the sources of threats in environmental security will come from things like increased competition over natural resources or damage from natural disasters rather than military might of a state. Most scholars wishing to problematize the idea of state security argue we must be concerned with both threats and vulnerabilities.

The inclusion of vulnerabilities and alternative threats into a discussion of security is not, however, viewed by all as a positive move. For example, in a widely read critique of the notion of environmental security, Daniel Deudney (1990: 194) claims "if all large-scale evils become threats to security, the result will be a *dedefinition* rather than a *redefinition* of security." Wæver (1995) offers another warning, claiming that expanding the notion of security may actually serve to strengthen the hold the state possesses over more areas. His logic is that since security issues have traditionally been seen as the purview of the state, identifying threats other than military ones as security threats will give the state greater control over more issues. Securitization means "the issue is presented as an existential threat, requiring emergency measures and justifying actions outside the normal bounds of political procedure" (Buzan et al. 1998: 24). State-sponsored solutions may or may not be the optimal resolution for each problem.

In sum, security studies has a long history within IR, but has seen some important changes in recent years (Buzan and Hansen 2009; Collins 2007; Williams 2008). These changes include the addition of elements that have not historically been understood as high politics. There are those who enthusiastically welcome these additions as challenges to state-centric, military security scholarship. Alternatively, there are those who see these additions as either watering down the concept of security past the point of effectiveness, or as unnecessarily militarizing or securitizing issues that are better addressed through a different discourse. Each of these shifts in security studies can be understood by using gender lenses. As will be discussed below, using gender lenses to view a topic results in asking particular questions and challenging dominant understandings of definitions and discourses.

Gender and Security

Several feminist scholars analyze the specific linkages between gender and security. These feminist authors often claim "security must be analyzed in terms of how contemporary insecurities are being created and by a sensitivity to the way in which people are responding to insecurities by reworking their understanding of how their own predicament fits into broader structures of violence and oppression" (Tickner 2001: 47). Feminists are often suspicious of statist versions of security that treat the survival and well being of institutions as more important than the survival and well being of individuals (Hudson 2005; Tickner 2001). Additionally, feminist security scholars specifically seek to understand the unique security situations of women and men. Most acknowledge that both women and men are often negatively impacted by war and conflict; however these impacts are typically gendered. Rather than assume conflict or war impacts everyone similarly, or even that it impacts the marginalized in the same ways, feminist security scholars conclude that all stages of conflict are gendered- and this often serves to make women more vulnerable than men to security threats. Feminist security studies concentrate on the ways world politics can contribute to the insecurity of individuals, especially individuals who are marginalized and disempowered (Enloe 2000; 2007; 2010; Reardon and Hans 2010). This is in contrast to traditional security approaches that have typically evaluated security issues either from a structural perspective or at the level of the state and its decisionmakers. There is a tendency in this literature to look at what happens during wars as well as being concerned with their causes and endings (Riley et al. 2008; Tickner 2001).

There is a danger, however, in a simplistic analysis that automatically views women as victims in times of war. This volume calls for a more nuanced understanding of the particular experiences of women and men during times of conflict. This caution is echoed by many feminists who argue against simplistic notions of peaceful women and aggressive men. The automatic connection of women with an uncomplicated definition of peace has worked to devalue both women and peace. A project that unquestioningly asserts an association between women and peace may actually serve to disempower women by defining them in opposition to the ideas security studies considers most crucial, specifically strategizing for and fighting in wars (Tickner 2001). Still, many feminists who engage in security studies do focus on particular issues and abuses women often face during war or conflict. These include rape in war, military prostitution, refugees (many of whom are women and children), and more generally issues about civilian casualties. Additionally, there has been increased attention paid to the place and experiences of women as political and military leaders, soldiers, revolutionaries, and terrorists.

This book explores gendered understandings of security rather than simply the roles and responses of women in the security debate. As mentioned above, gender can be defined as a set of socially constructed ideas about what men and women ought to be. Gender analysis involves examining gender-based divisions in society and differential control of/access to resources. This is different from an approach seeking to bring women into an analysis, which can isolate women from the broader socio-cultural context in which behavioral norms are embedded. Therefore, this book will not only explore the particular position of women and men within the context of security, but also investigate the objects of study and the specific language used in the present security discussions for examples of gendered implications.

Why Study Women?

Like most feminist scholars, I see the inclusion of gender in my analysis to mean both men and women are important subjects of study. In order to understand how gender "works" in the world, it is essential to include the socially constructed categories of men and masculinities as well as the socially constructed categories of women and femininities in our analyses. It is also essential to recognize that there are multiple genders. "Race/ethnicity, class, sexuality, and other cultural variations shape gender identities and performances" (Peterson and Runyan 2010: 3). Terrell Carver (2003: 290) claims "it is often difficult to persuade men that they have any gender or that gender is of any relevance or interest, other than as something that women do, about women. . ." On the contrary, gender stereotypes have profound implications for men as well. This is particularly the case when we examine something like expectations of masculine behavior. Traits associated with masculinities in many societies include being active, displaying reason, being political beings, etc. (Peterson and Runyan 1999). These are constraining standards to live up to, and many men face ridicule when they fall short of achieving masculine ideals.

This book will address both masculinities and femininities with regard to international security; however, there will be a great deal of attention paid to the experiences of women. While most feminists are careful to stress that both men and women need to be included in any analysis, the experiences of women often have something important to tell us. This is particularly true for a book about international security. In many facets of international security, women participate on the margins. Shedding light on the ways they experience international security issues allows us to go beyond the typical discussions and topics of concern. With regard to the effects of war on women specifically, Ann Tickner (2001: 51) explains:

> By looking at the effects of war on women, we can gain a better understanding of the unequal gender relations that sustain military activities. When we reveal social practices that support war and that are variable across societies, we find that war is a cultural construction that depends on myths of protection; it is not inevitable . . . The evidence we now have about women in conflict situations severely strains the protection myth; yet, such myths have been important in upholding the legitimacy of war and the impossibility of peace. A deeper look into these gendered constructions can help us to understand not only some of the

causes of war but how certain ways of thinking about security have been legitimized at the expense of others, both in the discipline of IR and in political practice.

This underscores that looking at both the experiences of men *and* women are important, even if we have to probe the margins in order to get a complete picture. For example, there is often an assumption that war is a "man's business," yet women have played an active role in fighting and supporting wars throughout history (Mazurana et al. 2005). It is interesting to reflect on the roles of women during times of war, during peacebuilding initiatives, in the face of environmental conflict; and the widely held assumption that these roles are nonexistent or at least less important than the roles of men. The assumption that women are not actively involved in security issues relates to the marginalization of women's experiences in general. Marginalization is linked to exclusion and discrimination. When groups are marginalized in (or by) society, they are excluded from spheres of power and decisionmaking. This exclusion makes discrimination against them fairly easy to achieve. If their voices are not counted as important and heard throughout the process of policymaking, then it is simple to leave them and their concerns on the margins. When groups are excluded "several forms of discrimination occur, such as limited access to government services or high-profile political roles, discriminatory access to higher-education institutions such as medical and engineering schools, and limited access to resources such as agricultural products and social welfare" (D'Costa 2006: 131). For these reasons, it is important to give particular attention to the experiences of men and women in our analyses of security.

Analyzing Security Through Gender Lenses

Like much feminist work, this book casts a wide net of scholarship and draws on several different literatures including general security studies, feminist security scholarship, and work specifically on human security, peacekeeping, terrorism/militancy, and environmental security. Following the work of Cynthia Enloe (2007), the book uses a feminist curiosity to ask questions that often remain unasked in mainstream security scholarship. Enloe (2004: 3) claims "[a]ny power arrangement that is imagined to be legitimate, timeless, and inevitable is pretty well fortified. Thus we need to stop and scrutinize our lack of curiosity. We also need to be genuinely curious about others' lack of curiosity – not for the sake of feeling self-satisfied, but for the sake of meaningfully engaging with those who take any power structure as unproblematic." Using a feminist curiosity to examine international security involves asking questions like "Why have certain definitions of security, war, and terrorism been dominant within security studies?" "Who benefits and who suffers when traditional definitions are used?" "How can definitions be rethought in ways that reduce inequality and encourage security for people in their daily lives?"

One way to explore the connections between security and gender is to examine security issues through gender lenses. We can think about gender lenses like the different lenses of a camera. As any photography buff knows, there is a vast array of camera lenses to choose from. Some lenses allow for wide views, some for intense close-ups, while others filter out certain colors. If we take a picture with one lens, particular elements of a scene will come to light. For example, if we take a picture of a beach with a wide-angle lens we can see much more of the scene than would be possible with a regular lens. Because of this, the pictures taken with each lens will look different. The wide-angle shot will show the entirety of the scene including a broad expanse of white sand, a long row of beach chairs with umbrellas, and crowds of people swimming, lying on the sand and walking along the water. The regular lens will give more detail to a smaller area, including a couple sitting under a big red umbrella with two children building a sandcastle a few feet from the clear blue water. In much the same way, using gender lenses allows us to view different elements of gender as we explore a particular topic. Peterson and Runyan (1999, 2010) have popularized the idea of examining topics in international relations through gender lenses. They argue that gender lenses allows us to examine issues in ways that go beyond what is typically visible and present in IR scholarship. Steans (2006: 30) claims that to use gender lenses "is to focus on gender as a particular kind of power relation, and/or to trace out the ways in which gender is central to understanding international processes and practices in international relations. Gender/feminist lenses also focus on the everyday experiences of women as women and highlight the consequences of their unequal social position."

It is important to stress the plural in the idea of gender lenses in order to highlight the fact that there are multiple elements of gender that can inform IR scholarship. If we use a gender lens that is also sensitive to class issues in order to understand the recent global economic downturn, our analysis will focus on issues like the North–South differences in the "feminization of poverty." Additionally, if we use a gender lens that is also sensitive to sexual orientation, we can better understand the differences of experience "motherhood" may have for a straight single-mother versus a lesbian couple who faces discrimination when they try to adopt a child. It is important to understand gender with regard to a variety of topics, including international security, and it is important to do this in a way that acknowledges the complexity of people's perspectives and experiences. As conceptualizations of security shift and broaden, it is imperative that gender informs the discussion. By using gender lenses, this book can identify the ways gender is currently incorporated in security issues, as well as the ways gender can be incorporated in security studies into the future.

Each of our understandings of security has important ties to gender. This book provides an introduction to the links between gender and security by analyzing some of the key issues and topics within security studies through gender lenses. The book challenges narrow ideas of security and provides an alternative conceptualization that seeks to broaden and deepen understandings of security. This book is premised on the idea that there are multiple ways scholars, policymakers, the media and other actors discuss and understand security issues. In other words, there are a variety of *security discourses* at play. Discourses can be thought of as "specific ensembles of ideas, concepts and categorization that are produced, reproduced and transformed in a particular set of practices and through which meaning is given to physical and social realities" (Hajer 1995: 45). This definition suggests that discourses are constantly evolving entities that are shaped over time. Political debates are typically informed by multiple discourses, although certain discourses may become more dominant than others as coalitions of actors succeed in promoting their preferred understanding of the world. As certain discourses take hold, some types of policy responses may become more or less viable and the interests of some groups may be served more than others (Bäckstrand and Lövbrand 2005; Cohn 1993; Haas 2002; Hajer 1995; Litfin 1999).

The goals of the book are twofold. First, I want to illustrate that concepts and topics within security studies look different when we examine them through gender lenses. Incorporating gender into security studies pushes us to ask different questions and broaden our sphere of analysis. Second, I want to show that this broadened sphere of analysis offers a more holistic understanding of security that reflects reflexive scholarship and benefits the process of policymaking. Gender analysis reveals multiple forms of insecurity that people experience daily, many of which are absent in traditional security scholarship. It also demonstrates some of the gendered consequences of using existing discourses of militarization, peacekeeping, terrorism, human security, and environmental security.

An idea tied to this second goal is to reflect on the emancipatory potential that gender lenses offers when linked to key themes and topics in security studies. The idea of emancipation features in much feminist scholarship and beyond. The work of Ken Booth (1991: 319), a leading figure in critical security studies and the Welsh School, or Aberystwyth School, is particularly useful when thinking about the concept and potential of emancipation. He claims emancipation is:

> The freeing of people (as individuals and groups) from the physical and human constraints which stop them carrying out what they would freely choose to do. War and the threat of war is one of those constraints, together with poverty, poor education, political oppression and so on. Security and emancipation are two sides of the same coin. Emancipation, not power or order, produces true security. Emancipation, theoretically, is security.

Booth (2007: 115) later explains:

> . . . to practise security (freeing people from the life-determining
> conditions of insecurity) is to promote emancipatory space
> (freedom from oppression, and so some opportunity to explore
> being human), and to realize emancipation (becoming more
> fully human) is to practise security (not against others, but with
> them).

In order to consider emancipation along these lines, it is necessary to
be clear about the security narratives involved. Security in these terms
does not refer to state security, or the protection and maintenance
of the state, but rather has much more in common with notions of
human security. There are various definitions of human security, as
will be discussed in Chapter 5; however, they each shift the focus of
security to people. This approach to emancipation suggests a concern
with the ability of people to freely make choices.

Examining emancipation through gender lenses requires reflexive
scholarship which highlights the various ways that constraints to the
achievement of security are gendered (Basu 2011). It also requires
an acknowledgment that a path to security will include getting past
socially constructed gender identity (Hudson 2005; Tickner 2002).
When our actions and the interpretations of our actions are guided
by gender norms, this constrains and limits our ability to freely
choose what to do and how to be. Choice is also constrained by
gender through widespread gender inequity that persists across most
societies. Finally, it requires particular attention to both marginalization and agency when examining obstacles to emancipation. Just as
it is unhelpful to lump all men with war and all women with peace,
so too is it unhelpful to assume men have a clear path to emancipation while women do not. It is essential to recognize the complex
ways obstacles to emancipation manifest in society and overlap with
categories of race, class, ethnicity, sexuality, etc. It is also important
to recognize how marginalization and the silences that accompany marginalization present unique challenges for emancipation.
Lene Hansen (2000: 287) reminds us to pay particular attention to
instances "when insecurity cannot be voiced, when raising something
as a security problem is impossible or might even aggravate the threat
being faced." This makes the goal of incorporating the voices of marginalized actors especially important, but problematic at the same

time. The idea of "giving voice" makes many feminists uncomfortable, as it is associated with simplistic assumptions about the agency of Northern women and the passivity of Southern women (Wibben 2011). For these reasons, it is not necessary to "give voice" in order to think about emancipation and security, but rather it is necessary to make space for multiple interpretations and perspectives on freedom and choice.

Some scholars have critiqued the concept of emancipation for being universalist and utopian. Critics of universalism "express concerns about the dangers of forcing others to be free, denying the legitimacy of difference, and imposing values that are ultimately Western in philosophical origin" (McDonald 2009: 121). Feminists have also expressed concern about the extent to which the individual should be/can be the ultimate referent of security practices. Laura Sjoberg (2011: 119) argues security as emancipation "requires us to categorize individuals such that we can see what their identities demand they be emancipated from. Each of these critical approaches suggests categorization and distinction among and between individuals essential for 'emancipation.'" There is a concern that these distinctions may have the potential to silence people and groups. These critiques and concerns are important and essential to consider when exploring the connections between security and gender. They remind us of the importance of engaging with the idea of emancipation in a way that avoids oversimplification and acknowledges the complexity of sources of insecurity more broadly.

This book strives to highlight how feminist interpretations of central issues and concepts within security studies intersect with the goals of emancipation. Laura Shepherd (2010: xx) defines emancipation as "freedom from tyranny or oppression, the production of autonomy." Emancipation is consistent with removing sources of insecurity. These sources of insecurity can stem from various sources and processes. The goal of an emancipatory project is to remove sources of insecurity in order to allow people to make choices freely. This exercise requires acknowledging that theorizing about emancipation is not static, but rather requires understanding certain contexts and particular circumstances that will change over time (Basu 2011; Steans 1998). Strategies for emancipation require frequent analysis and rethinking so they reflect changing conditions and power structures. None of this is to suggest emancipation is easy or even to suggest it has a definite endpoint of achievement. Sources of insecurity are often deeply entrenched within society and can even stem from a person being associated with a particular category, such as a gender, race, or class (Sjoberg 2011). While acknowledging the difficulty of this enterprise, feminist IR projects of this kind act as a point to begin larger conversations about how to engage in scholarship and policymaking that is guided by an overall goal of human well being. Security and emancipation are conceptualized as processes rather than defined end points (McDonald 2009).

Outline of the Volume

The remainder of the book is divided into five chapters which explore various topics of security, and a brief conclusion. Chapter 2 will examine the gendered elements of militarization and militarism for society. Each of these concepts is typically associated with elements of security, and each has been criticized for playing a role in legitimizing violence as a way of resolving conflicts. They are also linked to the establishment of power relationships and hierarchies in the global community. Additionally, each of the terms is typically understood to be associated with males and masculinities. Both state and non-state institutions that are heavily militarized are frequently made up largely of men, led by men, and infused with similar types of masculinities. This chapter examines some of the important consequences militarization and militarism have for society with a particular focus on how these consequences are gendered.

Chapter 3 explores gender as it relates to peacekeeping and peacebuilding. Security studies have moved away from a narrow focus on war and conflict to the study of peace. The international community has increasingly embraced the idea of encouraging peace between adversaries, even in some instances if the actions taken towards this goal violate state sovereignty. The concepts of both peacekeeping, or the potential use of military force to maintain peace between two potential foes, and peacebuilding, or striving to rebuild society in the aftermath of conflict or peacekeeping, have become relatively popular among both security scholars and policymakers. This chapter explores the role of women in peacekeeping and peacebuilding efforts, as well as gendered elements to the overall conceptualization of these important security topics.

After the Cold War, the definitions and scope of security studies shifted. The remaining chapters reflect this shift by examining topics that are part of an expanded or at least altered idea of security. A major shift in security studies, particularly in the post-9/11 period, is a rise in attention to terrorism. Chapter 4 looks at the connections between gender and terrorism. It asks questions about why terrorists are often portrayed as angry, radical, non-white, young men and what the implications of this portrayal are. It explores the various terrorism discourses that are used by states, militant groups, and the media to claim that terrorism scholarship and counterterrorism policymaking must be informed by reflexive understandings of what motivates people to engage in violence.

"Human security" represents another avenue of expansion in recent security scholarship. The idea of human security refers to the security of people rather than states. According to a 1994 United Nations report there are several dimensions of human security, and each of these has important links to gender. The book's fifth chapter explores how the discussions about human security's potential to broaden and deepen security debates have largely left gender out of the equation. Some scholars have welcomed notions of human security as a way of avoiding state-centered ideas of security. However, many feminists have cautioned that human security must still consistently take into account gender and gender-based inequalities. The chapter examines topics associated with human security through gender lenses, including human trafficking and global health.

Chapter 6 continues the trend of examining the broadening and deepening of security scholarship through an exploration of the connections between gender, security, and the environment. Scholars and policymakers have recently used concepts of "environmental security" to link the ideas of traditional security scholarship to the environment. Some have viewed these connections as a positive way to highlight the serious threats that environmental degradation raise for both people and states, while others view them as another example of loading down the idea of security with conceptual baggage. This chapter will assess the terrain of the security and environment debate, and address the inclusion of gender into this debate. The chapter will address the theoretical and practical implications of ignoring the gendered aspects of security and the environment through an examination of climate change as a security issue with unique gender connections.

Incorporating gender into security debates requires rethinking some of the key assumptions and concepts of security scholarship and policymaking. The book's conclusion expands on these ideas by arguing that integrating gender involves examining how security debates are gendered, as well as exploring the unique experiences of men and women in security situations. The conclusion draws together discussions from previous chapters around the theme of the shifts that come with including gender into security scholarship. The chapter includes sections on some of the social and policy implications of gendered security concepts, as well as including commentary on possible future directions for security scholarship and the links to gender.

Gender fundamentally alters the way we understand traditional and evolving security concepts. Looking at security issues through gender lenses involves asking new questions and conceptualizing key concepts in alternative ways. The book argues the necessity of including gender into discussions and evaluations of security and security concerns. Security scholarship has shifted from being narrowly concerned with state security and war to broadly considering a host of security threats and issues. Each of these elements of security scholarship has a unique relationship with gender – or socially constructed ideas about what men and women ought to be. Security debates exhibit gendered understandings of key concepts, and these gendered assumptions and understandings benefit particular people and are often detrimental to others, particularly as they influence the process of policymaking. The title of the book reflects the idea that security is an overarching concept with implications for the entire international community. International security is not used here to refer only to the removal of threats at the international level, but rather is intended to convey the goal of thinking about security from the level of humans to the entire globe. For this reason, the chapters will draw on examples and perspectives from both the global North and South. Through these perspectives we can reflect on the implications of rethinking security in ways that reveal the central location of gender.

2
Gendered Militarization and Militarism

Military spending has increased in several regions in recent years, including in Latin America and the Caribbean. Two recent reports on military spending in this region issued by the Stockholm International Peace Research Institute (SIPRI) evaluated the practice with regard to issues like transparency, democratic accountability, and trade-offs between these expenditures and spending on other areas like education and healthcare (Bromley and Solmirano 2012; Perlo-Freeman 2011). The focus of these reports suggests that the institute was interested in evaluating the range of impacts military spending has on society. Along with military spending, and the role of the military in society, researchers have studied the broad concepts of militarization and militarism. These are important phenomena that exist across the international system. From military parades to battle-oriented video games and beyond, we can spot evidence of militarization and militarism if we know what we are looking for. Feminists and other critical IR scholars have called attention to the presence and impacts of these concepts, and argued that they are important not just for academics thinking about the world, but because of the myriad consequences of the phenomena for how we live our lives. These concepts are typically associated with elements of security. There are vocal and often powerful voices who claim that militarization is the best path for achieving security. In fact, for some IR scholars and policymakers, behaving in a militarized way is taken for granted. It is simply what people and states do.

Many feminist scholars are critical of militarization and militarism because of the range of impacts they have on societies. They criticize the role played by the ideas in legitimizing violence as a way of resolving conflicts. They also critique militarization and militarism for establishing power relationships and hierarchies in the global community. These feminists argue it is essential to explore these ideas through gender lenses because they are often understood to be associated with males and masculinity, and these associations can have important implications for power structures and security at an individual or personal level. In particular, masculinity has been normalized and regularized throughout the history of most military institutions. These associations with masculinity have important implications for women's place in and relationships with institutions associated with militarization. In some instances, women can be invisible in these institutions even when they are present. This chapter explores these issues by asking such questions as what is militarization and militarism, what is the role of the state in processes of militarization, how does militarization relate to ideas of hegemonic masculinity, and what are some of the gendered consequences of militarization around the world? The United States and the US military are interesting places to examine militarization due to the fact that the US military is a large institution that has, until recently, been engaged in two inter-state wars. This chapter will highlight various facets and consequences of militarization using examples from the US, but will also incorporate examples from around the globe. Examining these questions through gender lenses offers an important perspective on the general concepts of militarization and militarism as well as the impacts of these ideas for society. It also reveals some potential avenues for emancipation through shifting away from militarization as a driving force in security studies and practice.

Militarization and Militarism

Many critical security scholars have addressed the concepts of militarization and militarism because they have been such popular ideas within security scholarship and policymaking. In particular, feminist scholars have worked to critically reflect on the definitions of the terms and how they shape the world in which we live. Shepherd (2010: xxiii) defines *militarization* as "the process by which beings or things become associated with the military or take on military characteristics." Similarly, Enloe (2000: 3) claims:

> Militarization is a step-by-step process by which a person or a thing gradually comes to be controlled by the military *or* comes to depend for its well being on militaristic ideas. The more militarization transforms an individual or a society, the more that individual or society comes to imagine military needs and militaristic presumptions to be not only valuable but also normal. Militarization, that is, involves cultural as well as institutional, ideological, and economic transformations.

Both of these definitions stress that militarization is best understood as a process; while *militarism* can be understood as the belief that military solutions to problems are the most appropriate. Militarism is displayed when individuals adopt militaristic attitudes in their own lives and view global and local problems as problems to be addressed by the military. Militarization and militarism are related ideas. Militarism is an important component of militarization.

Militarization is a process that centrally features the military as an institution, but also goes beyond it. Obviously there is a great deal of militarization evident in military organizations around the world; however it exists in civilians and civilian institutions as well. Militarization and militarism require the compliance of many within a population in order to thrive. This means that both men and women have been complicit in the support of militarization (Enloe 2000). Militarization can occur slowly, spreading across generations, but can also often occur rapidly in the aftermath of a particular crisis event. Many scholars and commentators have noted a noticeable spike in militarization in the United States after the terrorist attacks on September 11, 2001 (hereafter referred to as 9/11), including militarization of police forces (Balko 2011) and even higher education (Giroux 2008). In this time period, many citizens (both military personnel and civilians) demonstrated an attitude that favored military retaliation and the preservation of "security" at all costs. This is not to say that all Americans exhibited evidence of militarization during this time or after it, far from it. In fact, there were protests and dissenting voices which strongly opposed a militaristic reaction to the attacks. Despite these voices, however, the days following 9/11 saw a dramatic rise in both discourses of nationalism and militarization as a whole (Agathangelou and Ling 2004). This will be discussed further in Chapter 4.

We see evidence of militarization in multiple spheres of everyday life. Militarization is evident at overarching levels – as when military values and logic influence government policies, national values and even identities – to lower levels – with the language we use to communicate with each other, elements of popular culture, and the functioning of our education systems (Enloe 2000). Evidence of militarization can show up in both expected and unexpected places. An important facet of militarization and militarism is the way that they become naturalized over time. They are processes that take place without many of us taking notice.

Militarization and the State

The process of militarization is intricately tied to the state. It is often the state that is the major champion of militarization and militaristic values in a society. Many states were founded as a result of military conquest or postwar territorial changes (Enloe 2000). Typically, the violence carried out by state militaries is considered legitimate violence. Veterans of military campaigns are often highly respected and their sacrifices honored in national commemorations and ceremonies. Military cemeteries are often important symbols of the state. Individuals who have a record of military service are often better positioned for running for political office or gaining appointment to high-ranking government positions. In most states, Departments or Ministries of Defense are key government bodies (Kirk 2008). All of these trends point to the fact that as states are closely associated with their militaries and defense institutions in general, they are major forces for advancing militarization in society. In fact, when militarism is evident in a society (i.e. individuals seeing military solutions to problems as the most appropriate solutions) it is the state that typically undertakes the military exercises envisioned as appropriate.

Not only is there a close association between the state and its military, but the military/defense institution is unlike any other institution in society. Militaries have a close relationship to most central elements of the state, and are typically regarded as essential to the maintenance of the state. This position leads to the military being a very powerful entity in many states. Enloe (2000: 46) explains:

> [The military] can keep secrets; it can create its own court system; it can conscript the labor it needs; it can own or control vast complexes of research and manufacture; it can be exempted from laws requiring nondiscrimination; it can run its own universities; it can back up its policy directives with tanks; it can form its own alumni associations; it can operate its own hospitals; it can have its own representatives placed in the government's overseas embassies. The military branch of government is not interchangeable with that government's labor ministry or its environmental protection agency, even if they too wield the state's authority and spend the public's money.

This unique position and status of the military within states means both states and the military can benefit from militarism.

Militarization is also typically related to issues of nationalism/ national identity. Because most states in the present international community have relatively diverse populations, they can benefit from presenting an idea of a singular national identity. This national identity is typically associated with patriotic songs and stories, and national symbols like flags. Many of these songs, stories, and symbols are militarized – invoking images of a glorious past where forces of the state were strong (Tickner 2001). For example, many national anthems depict battles, conflicts, or victorious episodes of the state's past. While this might seem trivial, it is part of a larger sense of what makes a state a state. These images are often invoked in the days after a national crisis as a way to give comfort and direction. These images, however, are not often associated with women. The heroes alluded to in patriotic stories are most frequently male (Tickner 1992). "This produces a 'gendered nationalism' in which only men who forged a nation in blood get to define what that nation is, regardless of whether women spilled blood for it or on its altar as (fewer) combatants or (many) noncombatants, and regardless of the many other contributions that women make to (re)producing and sustaining the life of a nation" (Peterson and Runyan 2010: 146). It is important that this sense of strength and military security is what societies use for national identity, and it is important that it is typically associated with men and masculinity. It gives us a clue that militarization and militarized masculinities are deeply ingrained in many societies.

It is interesting to reflect on the fact that thus far in this section, I have written about the state as if it were a singular entity. This is a common way to think about states in IR; however it is not without its problems. Discussing states as unitary actors masks agency and simplifies a complex story. If we consider this with regard to security, it is easy to think of the behavior of France or Germany in the Second World War without taking into account that it is people, men and women, who make decisions about war and conflict. Problematizing security and asking questions about power relations, etc. allows us to understand these complexities. "By bringing into focus the people who decide to make war and who organize and populate 'the state' and the 'state system', a gender lens restores human agency in and therefore responsibility for war" (D'Amico 2000: 106).

This close link is particularly evident in those countries in which there is a strong association between citizenship and military service. The concept of *martial citizenship* refers to this relationship between citizenship and soldering. Like militarization and national identity, militarization of citizenship relates to who is considered "true" citizens – true Israelis or true South Africans, etc. Martial citizenship "suggests that *real* citizens are soldiers, and, conversely, that only soldiers are *real* citizens. This model of martial citizenship has prompted groups excluded from political power within a state to seek 'full citizenship' by entering the armed forces" (D'Amico 2000: 105). These excluded groups include women, gays and lesbians, and marginalized populations within a state. There are several questions raised about this strategy, including whether these groups can achieve full membership in militarized organizations if they are regarded by the institution as lacking the characteristics associated with military masculinities.

Military Masculinities

Military and defense organizations are often said to reinforce hegemonic masculinity. "Hegemonic masculinity refers to a particular set

of masculine norms and practices that have become dominant in specific institutions of social control . . . Hence, hegemonic masculinity
is a set of norms and practices associated with men in powerful social
institutions" (Kronsell 2005: 281). As this quote suggests, the notion of
hegemonic masculinity is premised on the fact that there are multiple
masculinities and femininities in each society. R.W. Connell (1995: 44),
a well-known scholar of masculinities, claims "masculinities are config-
urations of practice structured by gender relations. They are inherently
historical; and their making and remaking is a political process affecting
the balance of interests in society and the direction of social change."
Masculinities interact with each other, and with the various femininities present in a given place. Some masculinities are more highly valued
in society, thus hegemonic masculinity is that version of masculinity
associated with the powerful, the successful, the dominant. Hegemonic
masculinity is taken as the "natural" set of characteristics displayed by
those who rise to the premier positions within society. In the global
North, it is typically associated with white, upper-class straight men.
Subordinated masculinities are exhibited by those who lack one, some,
or all of these privileges (Peterson and Runyan 2010).

   Much feminist work focuses on particular types of masculinities
that have been normalized and regularized throughout the history
of most military institutions (Duncanson 2009; Enloe 2000; Higate
2003; Hopton 2003; Kovitz 2003). Military masculinities are plural
because, like masculinity in general, there are differences in the
masculinities associated with different contexts of military service
(combat versus peacekeeping, etc.) and particular branches of militaries. For example, Paul Higate (2003: 31–32) describes the multiple
masculinities he experienced during his service in the British Royal
Air Force as a personnel administrator. He claims:

> Although perceived as less masculine than that of the army, my
> military social universe was nonetheless significantly influenced
> by close contact with military men and rather less women, and my
> views were concomitantly shaped in line with the more extreme
> ideologies of military masculinity.

The most commonly identified militarized masculinity requires individuals to be violent enough to kill if asked, yet they must also be

willing to subordinate themselves to hierarchy and authority. This militarized masculinity is reinforced through repetition (drilling) and reward. Sandra Whitworth (2008: 111) explains "[t]he contemporary practices of boot camp are remarkably similar across most modern state militaries, and they involve the same sets of practices, whether focused on male or female recruits. It is a tightly choreographed process aimed at breaking down the individuality of the recruits, and replacing it with a commitment to and dependence upon the total institution of which they are now a part." One facet of this drilling is reinforcing standards deemed appropriate for the institution, including standards of masculinity. Characteristics associated with militarized masculinity, like toughness and lack of emotion, are rewarded and characteristics not associated with masculinity are punished. Anuradhu Bhagwati, a former US Marine who left at the rank of Captain, explains her experience by saying: "Marine boot camp is so infamous because it succeeds in making killers out of the most timid human beings, and not just killers, but killers who love just how tough and badass they've become" (cited in Shigematsu et al. 2008: 95).

Tickner (2001: 57) argues "[w]hile the manliness of war is rarely denied, militaries must work hard to turn men into soldiers, using misogynist training that is thought necessary to teach men to fight. Importantly, such training depends on the denigration of anything that could be considered feminine; to act like a soldier is not to be 'womanly.'" Several scholars have suggested that since it is often difficult to get people to risk their lives to fight in armies, ideas of masculinity are used to encourage people to enlist (Goldstein 2001; Tickner 2001). Over time, many cultures have developed gender norms that equate "manhood" with military service and toughness under fire. The military then becomes an obvious place for those wishing to prove their manhood. While there are other avenues available in society to demonstrate hegemonic masculinity, some feminists argue that the military remains a likely venue for this purpose for those men who do not belong to the ranks of the white, wealthy, and heterosexual (Peterson and Runyan 2010). Whether or not individuals who attempt to fit into hegemonic masculinity through these means are successful is a different story. Maria Baaz and Maria Stern

(2009: 499) assert that militarized masculinities "rarely resonate with soldiers' sense of self, lived experiences, or with the actual conditions of militarized men's lives. The fragility and indeed impossibility of militarized masculinity therefore requires continual concealment through the military institutional practices, and in the individual expressions of such masculinity . . . such efforts are often fraught with failure."

Militarized masculinities must therefore be reinforced because of their frequent disconnect with lived experiences. An important element in this is the portrayal of the military as "protector." Within this discourse women and children are discussed as particularly vulnerable elements of the population that need protection. Militaries as overwhelmingly masculine institutions are committed to a discourse of the protection of the state, and its most vulnerable people. Feminist scholars have routinely criticized this discourse because of its essentialist and misleading nature. Many refer to the idea of a "protection racket" to highlight the problematic nature of this assumption (Sjoberg and Peet 2011; Wilcox 2009). The protection racket refers to the situation in which "women are promised protection from wars by men who then take credit for protecting them, while not actually doing so" (Sjoberg and Peet 2011: 167). Because of this pervasive depiction of women in need of protection, the introduction of women into military service can be unsettling for the dominant discourses that serve as the foundation of military organizations. If women are helping to do the protecting on equal footing as men, then who is the vulnerable population that needs protection? Additionally, how do we think about militarization, military masculinities, and military institutions in light of the fact that in many instances these processes and institutions are actually responsible for enhancing insecurity rather than providing protection?

Consequences of Militarization

There are a multitude of consequences of militarization for society. These range from narrowing the terms of a debate to the exclusion that accompanies the process of "othering" perceived enemies. In terms of narrowing the terms of a debate, militarism implies that military solutions to problems are acceptable and the most appropriate. What does this mean for non-military options? To use the example of the US in the days after 9/11, there was a loud group of voices calling for a military response to the event before there was a clear idea about where a military response would be targeted. Alternative voices calling for debate about underlying causes of terrorism and larger impacts of the last few decades of US foreign policy were not the ones most frequently heard on television and talk radio during that time period. Within militarized societies, non-military options are regarded as fine for low-politics issues, but not for *security* issues. This narrowing of debates about appropriate security policies is regarded as deeply problematic for individuals who feel that probing what is taken for granted is the only way to genuinely understand and address the complexities of issues that have been placed under the security heading.

Another consequence of militarization is the exclusion that accompanies the process of othering perceived enemies. Militarization implies an inside and an outside, an us and a them, a remover of threats and a source of threats. It "relies on making other peoples appear different or threatening, making their lives seem expendable, and making their deaths seem inevitable or even desirable" (Lee 2008: 57). Military organizations spend a considerable amount of time and energy distinguishing between the heroic fighters and the enemy. This enemy, no matter who, is routinely dehumanized in order to keep soldiers feeling justified in their actions of waging war against a clearly unworthy "other" (Peterson and Runyan 2010). Often this process of dehumanization is accomplished by feminizing the enemy to feel superior to them. This is a process seen the world over, in both Northern and Southern states. An often cited example of this process is the array of cartoons in the days leading up to both the first Gulf War and the 2003 Iraq invasion in which Saddam Hussein was portrayed as having a US missile aimed at his backside. Likewise, there have been several images manufactured of Osama bin Laden depicting him suffering anal rape (Jackson et al. 2011). This joking depiction of rape was intended to signal US dominance over Iraq and Al-Qaeda in the upcoming conflicts. While some may argue these cartoons are simply light-hearted jokes, many feminists disagree. They claim it is indicative of deep-seated processes at work within society that both trivializes rape and reinforces the idea that feminization is a useful tool for making an enemy "the other." If an enemy is associated with feminine qualities and fails to live up to dominant forms of masculinity, then they are legitimate targets for aggression (Cohn 1993).

Another example of this process was the portrayal of Tutsis during the 1994 Rwandan genocide. In the years just before the genocide, Hutu extremists disseminated propaganda depicting Tutsis as less than human. Documents like the "Hutu Ten Commandments," a tract circulated widely and read out at public meetings, portrayed Tutsi women as deceitful temptresses and Tutsis in general as greedy and a threat to the country (Anderlini 2007). This othering took place at high levels in the Rwandan government. In June 2011 the former Minister for Family and Women's Affairs during the genocide, Pauline Nyiramasuhuko, was sentenced by the International Criminal Tribunal for Rwanda to life in prison for her role in the genocide, particularly for the ordering of the rape of women and girls (Simons 2011). She was accused of using her ministerial powers against Tutsi women and helping to create Hutu militias in Butare, her home district. She was found guilty of genocide, crimes against humanity, and war crimes. This conflict is an extreme example of the othering of an enemy and the horrible consequences that can stem from this process.

Militarization does not impact everyone in the same way. Some communities are more directly impacted by militarization than others. For example, many poor communities find themselves being given special attention by military organizations when militarization is evident. These poor communities are seen as recruiting grounds for new soldiers necessary to fight the next battle, conflict, or war (Enloe 2010). Gina Pérez (2006) claims that in these working-class communities, like Puerto Rican communities around Chicago in the US, the military is understood by many to be an important avenue of social mobility for families and households with limited resources. One way the military becomes seen this way is by using schools as recruiting grounds. Pérez (2006: 54) argues "the military insinuates itself in the daily lives of the urban poor through schools, through promises of economically secure futures for impoverished and working-class families, and with assurances that values such as discipline, loyalty, and tenacity will translate into better youth, families, personal success, and secure economic futures." This quote suggests that the military is seen/portrays itself as a way both to economically advance in society and to acquire characteristics that are highly valued in most Western societies, and are typically associated with masculinity – characteristics like discipline, loyalty, and tenacity.

Gendered Consequences of Militarization

Using gender lenses enables the examination of the various ways the consequences of militarization are gendered. Both the example of othering Iraqis and the othering that took place before and during the Rwandan genocide demonstrate that gender can play a powerful role in this process. The latter demonstrated that the depiction of an enemy's women can play an important role in larger patterns of propagating an image of an evil enemy. Additionally, the voices of women versus men typically look different in societies where militarization is deeply embedded. Enloe (2004: 128) explains the process by saying:

> When any policy approach is militarized, one of the first things that happens is that women's voices are silenced. We find that when the United States touts any military institution as the best hope for stability, security, and development, the result is deeply gendered: the politics of masculinity are made to seem "natural," the male grasp on political influence is tightened, and most women's access to real political influence shrinks dramatically.

Women are rarely heavily represented in institutions associated with militarization. Armed forces and Departments/Ministries of Defense tend to be dominated by male voices rather than the voices of women. For liberal feminists, who seek equal representation of men and women, this is problematic simply because of its lack of parity. For more critical feminists, this is problematic because it reinforces standards of masculinity and femininity. It becomes routine to think men are militaristic and aggressive so they are the "natural" choice to fill these roles. On the flip side, women are peaceful and passive so they don't belong in militarized institutions. The fact that men form the bulk of these institutions is regarded as natural simply by virtue of the fact that they form the bulk of these institutions.

It is also important to consider the gendered nature of those negatively impacted by war and conflict. While it is true fewer women die as soldiers on battlefields, women, along with children, make up significant numbers of civilian casualties and refugees. By the 1990s, 9 out of 10 individuals who died as a result of direct and indirect consequences of war were civilians. This is particularly true in countries of the global South (Sutton and Novkov 2008). Some of the gendered impacts of war stem from the various positions women occupy in society. Women who are widowed because of war, along with female victims of landmines and female refugees, are particularly vulnerable to poverty, prostitution, and human trafficking (Hynes 2004). The aftermath of war and conflict also has gendered impacts that relate to the diverse roles women play in society. Some feminist scholars have examined how militarization jeopardizes the environment as well as the health of individuals. These consequences pose a particular burden on those women who have a role as caregivers. Sutton and Novkov (2008: 17) explain "[m]ilitarized violence and war have decimated agricultural and forest lands, water and fuel supplies, and basic infrastructure in war-torn countries, especially in developing areas, which negatively affects rural women engaged in subsistence production to ensure their families' survival."

Another important consequence of militarization with gendered impacts is military spending. If militarism means that military solutions are regarded as most appropriate, then defense institutions will rank high in national priorities. Currently, the US spends far more on their military than any other state in the international system. In terms of world military expenditure for 2010, the US represented around 43 percent of the total. The next largest spender is China, which accounts for around 7 percent of the total (SIPRI 2011). Some feminist scholars have tried to call attention to the gendered consequences of privileging military spending over other domestic sectors. If there is only so much money to go around, some projects and policies will receive less funding than others. For instance, between 1980 and 1985, a significant period for the Cold War, US spending on domestic social programs and support to low-income, often female-headed families was drastically cut while military spending dramatically increased. These policy priorities were particularly acute for black and Hispanic female-headed families (Steans 2006). Beyond simply involving tradeoffs on which government policies receive the most funding, these priorities also impact what kinds of jobs are created in a state. Women tend to be employed in sectors like health care, education, and consumer industries much more frequently than in the defense sector. That means they do not benefit from job creation in this industry in the same way men may (Anderson 1999). It may be for these reasons that a recent study has found that within democratic states, as the proportion of women in national legislatures increases, defense spending decreases (Koch and Fulton 2011). While we must be careful not to essentialize and assume that all women have the same motivations as public servants, this study includes some interesting findings about the presence of women in legislatures and the direction of military spending.

Still other consequences of militarization directly relate to the ways various women interact with military institutions in very personal ways. Issues of wartime rape, sexual misconduct and domestic abuse, and militarized prostitution are major topics of concern for scholars who ask questions about gender and militarization. These issues are all examples of gendered consequences of militarization that directly impact people's bodies, and most frequently women's bodies. Bodies matter in international relations in general, and security studies in particular. Shepherd (2010: 6) claims "global politics is studied and practiced by gendered bodies." Similarly, Jill Steans (2010: 84) explains "women's bodies are central to 'boundary drawing' and 'identity fixing' practices" which have wide-ranging impacts. Security for some refers explicitly to protecting bodies from harm, as will be discussed in Chapter 5. These ideas of "human security" have the individual as their primary referent. For these notions of security, violence against bodies is a basic source of insecurity. Wartime rape, militarized prostitution, and domestic abuse and violence are each

areas of insecurity at an individual level that are connected to processes of militarization.

Wartime Rape

Throughout much of the history of security studies, the issue of
wartime rape was blurred into the array of destruction and negative
consequences that went along with violent confrontation (Baaz and
Stern 2009). Policymakers have often considered wartime rape as
an unfortunate side-effect of conflict as a whole. Enloe (2000: 108)
explains "[t]he women who suffer rape in wartime usually remain
faceless as well. They merge with the pockmarked landscape; they are
put on the list of war damage along with gutted houses and mangled
rail lines. Rape evokes the nightmarishness of war, but it becomes just
an indistinguishable part of a poisonous wartime stew called 'lootpil-
lageandrape.'" This trend is being reversed as rape during wartime is
a topic of study many feminist security scholars have written about in
recent years. There are different types of rape that occur during war
and violent conflict, including rape at the hand of individuals or small
groups of soldiers, and systematic rape as a weapon of war. Rape is a
phenomenon that accompanies multiple types of war, including
religious, revolutionary, and war between states (Brownmiller 1975).
While men do suffer wartime rape (Zarkov 2001), it is largely women
who experience this consequence of violent conflict.

Throughout history rape has been seen as "a reward for the victorious soldier" and as "a means of destroying the social fabric of the
conquered population by driving a wedge between polluted females
and emasculated males" (Hansen 2001: 56). Baaz and Stern (2009)
explain that soldiers are aware of these differences. Interviews with
soldiers from the Democratic Republic of the Congo (DRC) reveal
that rapes are often divided into the categories of "lust rapes," or those
resulting from the perceived biological sexual urges of men, and "evil
rapes," or those arising "to humiliate the dignity of people" (Baaz and
Stern 2009: 495). Both of these categories exhibit gendered ideas of
people, processes, and circumstances. For the soldiers interviewed,
the category of "lust rapes" was typically viewed as more socially

acceptable, and in some instances was not viewed as "real" rapes. This traces back to the soldiers' descriptions of the "(hetero)sexually potent male fighter" (Baaz and Stern 2009: 505). Several interviewees explained that men had a natural sexual drive which required satisfaction from women whose role it is to satisfy those urges.

According to the soldiers, "Evil rapes" demonstrate gendered ideas of humiliation and weakness. Wartime rape has been understood as a specific tactic for striking at the heart of an enemy's justification for fighting. This refers to the idea that wars are fought *for* women and children *by* the heroic men. If an enemy suffers the rape of their women, then this can be read as a strike against their masculinity. They were unable to protect the very people they are fighting for (Sjoberg and Peet 2011).When systematic rape is consciously used as a weapon of war it is intended to create disorder at the most basic levels of society (MacKenzie 2010). Systematic wartime rape thus has two functions, first to neutralize women as threats, and second to weaken men's resolve to fight by "dirtying" their women. At the same time, wartime rape is used to decimate an ethnicity or enemy culture by impregnating women with "alien" seed or keeping them from reproducing altogether. This category is consistent with the idea of "genocidal rape" as it is defined in international law. The various forms of wartime rape are seen as an effective strategy for perpetrators because the act has long-term and wide-ranging impacts. These extensive impacts include stigmatization and marginalization not only for the victim of the rape but also for her family, including any offspring resulting from the attack.

The strategy of systematic rape has taken different forms depending on the conflict, but is evident as far back as the Crusades, to the First World War with the rapes committed as the Russian Army marched to Berlin, to the Second World War with the sexual slavery of Jewish women for Nazi soldiers and the enforced institutionalized rape of "comfort women" by the Japanese army, in the Bosnian war with the Serb rape camps, and in the Rwandan genocide with the rape of Tutsi women, sometimes instigated by Hutu females (Brownmiller 1975; Eisenstein 2008). Although rape as a weapon of war is a very old phenomenon, it is a topic that members of the international community have had to confront in the 1990s and 2000s, particularly in the aftermath of the wars in the former Yugoslavia and the genocide in Rwanda. These conflicts saw mass rape on a scale that was largely unthinkable in the international community. It has been estimated that as many as 20,000 to 50,000 women were sexually assaulted during the war in Bosnia (Lee 2008), and as many as 250,000 women were raped during the atrocities in Rwanda (Tickner 2001).

Another recent example of widespread wartime rape took place during the 1991 to 2001/2002 civil war in Sierra Leone. A 2002 report by Physicians for Human Rights estimated as many as 215,000 to 257,000 women and girls in Sierra Leone may have been subjected to sexual violence during the conflict. The term "sexual violence" refers to "any violence, physical or psychological, carried out through sexual means or by targeting sexuality" which includes rape (Denov 2006: 320). Because of the social stigma that goes along with sexual violence, it is likely many cases of rape were not reported during and after the conflict, leading many to believe the actual number of women who experienced wartime rape was actually higher. Displaced women and girls were particularly at risk for sexual assault. Research indicates that 50 percent of all female refugees, 75 percent of all females abducted during the conflict and 75 percent of former girl soldiers, abducted children and "unaccompanied children" were raped (MacKenzie 2010). Megan MacKenzie (2010: 203) has argued that rape was an effective tool of war in this case because it violated several norms, including norms associated with marriage and the family left over from the days of British colonization. "Marriage and paternity laws, as well as patriarchal norms that define women as inferior or as property *give meaning* to rape as a violation not only of a female body but also of embedded and engrained social norms linked to national identity and security." Her argument is that when "normal politics" are disrupted by conflict, marriage and paternity laws are weakened and so women's bodies become sites of struggle for control. Several studies have demonstrated a pattern of abducted women and girls being called "bush wives." "This disturbing trend demonstrates that some men who committed sexual violence saw the act in terms of gaining property and gaining consistent access to a woman's body" (MacKenzie 2010: 212). Not only was sexual violence in this case described in terms associated with marriage, but some victims were actually pressured to marry their rape perpetrators in the post-conflict period (Coulter 2008; Denov and Maclure 2006). Many women and girls, because of shame and stigmatization, were encouraged to marry their rape perpetrators in order to escape disgrace in the community for themselves and their families.

Another powerful example of the coping and aftermath of wartime rape comes in the story of discourses of nationhood in Bangladesh after the 1971 war of independence (*Muktijuddho*). It is estimated around 200,000 women (a conservative estimate) were raped during the nine-month conflict in which East Pakistan broke from West Pakistan to become Bangladesh (Roy 2010). Pakistani soldiers and their local collaborators are accused of committing the majority of the crimes, although there are reports that some Bengali women were raped by forces fighting on their own side (Brownmiller 1975). These widespread abuses formed an important part of the backdrop of the story of independence for Bangladesh. There have been several accounts published about the ways in which narratives of nationhood were closely associated with women's bodies in Bangladesh. Nayanika Mookherjee (2008) claims the imagery of "mother nation" that was so strongly tied to women's bodies required reconciliation with the context of widespread rape during the war. One of the first ways the new state tried to do this was to refer to the women as "war-heroines" (*birangonas*) who should be reunited with their husbands or married off (Brownmiller 1975; Mookherjee 2006; 2008). Susan Brownmiller (1975: 83) explains "[i]maginative in concept for a country in which female chastity and . . . isolation are cardinal principles, the 'marry them off' campaign never got off the ground. Few prospective bridegrooms stepped forward, and those who did made it plain that they expected the government, as father figure, to present them with handsome dowries." Due to the hesitancy of society to accept the "war-heroines," they typically faded from public attention as individual figures. Mookherjee (2008: 45) argues that nationalist discourses were built around "respectable, self-sacrificing mother, wife and . . . idealized woman" rather than *birangonas*. The women who were used as symbols of the new state were mostly those of the middle classes who lacked the stigma of rape. When *birangonas* do appear, they are transformed into respectable and mothered figures who are discussed in terms of how they must be cared for. "Rape of women is therefore collapsed into the ravaging of nature and of the mother-nation. Class aesthetisization, valorization of motherhood and the feminization of the beauty of nature together produce a suitable narrative to contain the history of rape" (Mookherjee 2008: 51). In the cases of both Sierra Leone and Bangladesh the use of language is important. The tendency to use the label "bush wives," refusing to label women and girls soldiers, referring to raped women as national heroines linked to mothering – all point to attempts to portray women in a certain light which typically conforms to traditional standards of femininities.

The long-term consequences that stem from rape are often conceptualized as social or private matters rather than as sources of significant state insecurity. Despite this perspective, wartime rape, including forced prostitution, has been illegal under international law for several decades. It is acknowledged as illegal under the 1949 Geneva Conventions and the 1977 Protocols (Goldstein 2001), and more recently in 1998 under the Rome Statute which created the International Criminal Court (which entered into force in 2002). Some credit the events in Bosnia and Rwanda and the response of feminist activists to these events with highlighting the fact that rape was a direct violation of women's human rights that should be treated at the level of torture as an instrument of warfare (Peterson and Runyan 2010). Article 7 of the Rome Statute discusses "crimes against humanity," which is defined as an act "committed as part of a widespread or systematic attack directed against any civilian population, with knowledge of the attack." The Article specifically includes rape as a crime against humanity along with "sexual slavery, enforced prostitution, forced pregnancy, enforced sterilization, or any other form of sexual violence of comparable gravity" (Rome Statute 1998). Many see this codification as progress toward getting steps taken to stop rape as a weapon of war throughout the international community. However, some caution against the ways wartime rape has been treated in international law, particularly when it has been explicitly linked to the family. MacKenzie (2010) argues that many legal responses to rape centered on the family, which could actually serve to lessen the impact of international law on the issue. She explains that each of the "references to the family implies that sex is a part of the natural family unit and that rape is an assault on the entire unit . . . Furthermore, collapsing sex and the family together into the private and domestic spheres distances them from both the political sphere and what might be considered security priorities" (MacKenzie 2010: 209).

Military Prostitution

Another link between sex and militarization is seen with military prostitution. Prostitution is a complex issue for feminist analysis (Outshoorn 2004). Prostitution can be defined as an exchange of sex for material goods, such as money, food, etc. On one hand, prostitution can result in abuse of women (particularly as a result of human trafficking outlined in Chapter 5) and can emerge out of unequal power relationships between men and women. Within this camp some argue all prostitution is exploitative, largely exploitative of women since the majority of research and activism on prostitution revolves around heterosexual prostitution. These voices stress unequal power distributions within society and argue that women who engage in prostitution rarely have a completely free choice in the matter. On the other hand, many women knowingly enter into the sex trade and resent being portrayed as victims (Lobasz 2010). This camp argues we must view prostitution with women's agency in mind. These voices claim we must not paint all women who engage in prostitution with the same brush but rather understand the specific situations of prostitution around the world. Looking at prostitution through gender lenses requires acknowledging agency where it is present as well as where it is absent.

The case of military prostitution seems to be a complex case among discussions of prostitution, however. Military prostitution largely involves women selling sexual services to soldiers. These civilian women necessarily have an unequal relationship with soldiers. Prostitutes are often stigmatized within society, while soldiers, depending on the country, can be lauded and seen as acting on behalf of the state. This unequal relationship is compounded in the situation of soldiers seeking prostitutes in foreign countries. Soldiers are often wealthier and in a position of authority over the local population. Additionally, some local women may turn to prostitution because of economic hardships and loss of livelihood stemming from war and conflict, the very war and conflict that the foreign soldiers are involved with in some instances (Hynes 2004). Enloe (2000: 70–71) argues there are several conditions that promote organized prostitution:

> (1) When large numbers of local women are treated by the government and private entrepreneurs as second-class citizens, a source of cheapened labor, even while other women are joining the newly expanded middle class. (2) When the foreign government basing its troops on local soil sees prostitution as a "necessary evil" to keep up their male soldiers' fighting morale. (3) When tourism is imagined by local and foreign economic planners to be a fast road to development. (4) When the local government hosting those foreign troops is under the influence of its own military men, local military men who define human rights violations as necessary for "national security."

This list illustrates the important intersections between militarization, othering, marginalization, and prostitution.

Prostitution around permanent and temporary military bases has an extremely long history. In most cases prostitution around military establishments is conducted with active involvement by the military command. Joshua Goldstein (2001: 342) explains:

> . . . military commanders have often encouraged, or directly organized, prostitution to service their armies. The Roman empire operated a system of brothels for its armies. The Spanish army invading the Netherlands in the late sixteenth century trailed "400 mounted whores and 800 on foot" who were like "troops" commanded by appointed officers. The word "hooker" comes from US Civil War general Joseph Hooker, whose Army of the Potomac was accompanied by "Hooker"s girls." In World Wars I and II, French and German armies set up systems of military-supervised brothels.

This quote demonstrates the lengthy history of military commanders consciously providing prostitution for service members. Acquiring information on military policy on prostitution is difficult, largely because many militaries do not acknowledge they have policies relating to prostitution. In several cases policy on prostitution is discussed in terms of "health" policy, demonstrating the often discussed link between prostitution, sexually transmitted disease (STD), and the military (Enloe 2000).

Research about prostitution around US military bases in Asia reveals the extent to which military policy about health relates to women's bodies (Lee 2007; Moon 1997; Zimelis 2009). In 1945, the US arrived in southern Korea to accept the transfer of power from Japan. Since that time there has been a significant presence of US military personnel in the country. Also during that time there has been a back and forth exchange of both formal and informal policy about prostitution designed to service US soldiers (Moon 1997). It is estimated that more than one million women have served as sex providers for US military personnel since the Korean War (Tickner 2001). Prostitution is a major source of income for small villages, or "camptowns," around US military bases. Key elements of the system of camptown prostitution can be traced to Korea's experience with colonial rule, particularly but not exclusively colonial rule by Japan as discussed above. Currently, domestic prostitution is officially illegal in Korea; however the government has a history of tacitly condoning and actually regulating prostitution around US military bases (Lee 2007). In her in-depth analysis of the role of prostitution in US–Korean relations, Katharine Moon (1997: 1–2) says the following about US military-oriented prostitution in Korea "It is a system that is sponsored and regulated by two governments, Korean and American (through the US military) . . . As this study reveals, both governments have viewed such prostitution as a means to advance the 'friendly relations' of both countries and to keep US soldiers, 'who fight so hard for the freedom of the South Korean people,' happy."

Women working in the "entertainment industry" in demarcated spaces known as Special Tourism Districts must be registered and are subject to regular examinations for sexually transmitted diseases. Through these examinations, foreign policy gets played out at the level of women's bodies. The driving fear is that STDs will be transmitted to soldiers rather than there being a primary concern for the health of the prostitutes themselves. With these kinds of policies, "security" is conceptualized as entailing the policing of borders as well as bodies. The threat to security comes from the other that soldiers seek out during their deployment.

This othering of military prostitutes plays out in multiple ways. The women who work in the Special Tourism Districts are regarded differently, and some say less, than those most other women in Korea. Some argue camptown women are differentiated within society from those women who do not have sexual contact with soldiers, which is good for Korean national pride. Lee (2007: 454) claims the Korean government has "successfully ghettoized the [camptowns] as buffer zones that prevent US soldiers from entering Korean society and prohibit ordinary Koreans, especially 'respectable' Korean women, from interacting with US men, while reaping the economic benefits that the US military presence and the sex trade serving foreign soldiers provide." Related to this, Moon (1997) claims the *kijich'on* women, or military camptown women, serve as an unwelcome reminder about the precarious security situation South Korea has found itself in since the Korean War's end. It is a reminder of the perceived necessity of US military presence in South Korea, and the assumed price that must be paid for US assistance.

Gwyn Kirk (2008: 30) argues it is not only ideas about the security relationship that shapes US–Korea relations, but also "Korean and US officials' shared beliefs about the soldiers' sexuality [that] have led to policies that ensure the availability of women in bars and clubs near US bases. Racist and sexist assumptions about Asian women – as exotic, accommodating, and sexually compliant – are an integral part of these arrangements." While some argue these stereotypes persist, the nationality of the prostitutes has been changing in recent years. Since the mid-1990s it is largely Russian and Filipina women who work as "entertainment workers" in the camptowns around US military bases (Zimelis 2009). Despite the nationality, women who engage in prostitution around military bases experience the militarization of health and social policy in their daily lives. The fact that military prostitution persists with so much regularity suggests assumptions about men's sexual needs also persist among both men and women. Additionally, this assumption has actually been the basis of military policy at various points in history.

In cases of forced prostitution there is a blurring between militarized rape and military prostitution. The case of forced prostitution on behalf of the Japanese military during the Second World War has come to be widely discussed as a shocking example of the ties between states, their militaries, and women's bodies. In the early 1990s, stories broke in the Western media about the Japanese imperial army's forced mobilization of an estimated 200,000 Asian women to serve as prostitutes during the Second World War. These women were euphemistically called "comfort women" (Enloe 2000). While the examples of forced prostitution during the Second World War are high profile, there was a long history of Japanese policy on Korean prostitution previous to this period. As far back as 1915–1916, a few years after Japanese annexation of Korea, there was formalization and systematization of licensed prostitution (Lee 2007). Na Young Lee (2007: 458) explains:

> After the annexation of Korea, the Japanese colonial government ordered prostitutes in Seoul to have STD exams twice a week and dispatched public medical doctors to 186 regional facilities for this purpose. As a result, 27,539 Korean women were forced to have these examinations in 1911 and 50,904 in 1915. To avoid the dreadful experience of STD checks, many women stopped working temporarily, some fled to the countryside, and others overdosed on opium.

Between 1932 and 1945 Japanese troops had access to "comfort stations" in Japan, Korea, China, and other territories in the Japanese empire. "Comfort women" came to be understood as essential supplies for the military with their key function being to keep up the morale of the troops. They were seen as tools for the use of the military. For example, when the women were transported on military ships they were listed as "military supplies" rather than as individuals with names and identities (Soh 2001).

When the US media picked up the story of "comfort women" in the 1990s there often appeared to be undertones of othering or suggestions that this forced prostitution was evidence of Japan's brutal behavior. There were buried suggestions that nothing in US history resembled the atrocities committed. In particular, the Second World War has often been portrayed in American cinema as a virtuous war against a barbaric other. Films about the Second World War typically depict a plucky band of young soldiers fighting for ideals like freedom and justice. Unsavory issues like rape and military prostitution are rarely discussed. Contrary to this portrayal, it is estimated as many as 17,000 women were raped by American servicemen in Europe between 1942 and 1945 (Williams 2009), and military prostitution is reported to be an ongoing activity in which US soldiers engage (Zimelis 2009). It is important to note that wartime rape and militarized prostitution are two very different gendered phenomena; however they are both important consequences of militarization that women have experienced around the world. While we must understand the issue of military prostitution as a complex one involving both women with agency and women who get caught up in the process due to their marginalization in society, it is an important example of a consequence of militarization that plays out directly at the level of women's bodies.

Sexual Misconduct and Domestic Abuse

Like the others in this section, domestic abuse and sexual misconduct in the military are serious concerns for those wishing to understand some of the gendered consequences of militarization. Recent studies have shown that in the United States, the rates of domestic violence are 3 to 5 times higher in military couples than in comparable civilian ones (Kirk 2008). This is particularly true for soldiers who have experienced combat. A study by Yale University found that male veterans who had been in combat were more than four times as likely as other men to have engaged in domestic violence (Lutz 2008). Some attribute this to the difficulty some soldiers seem to have separating their training as soldiers with their life off of the battlefield. Liz Kelly (2000: 59) has gathered evidence of this trend around the world. She argues:

> Evidence from women in Croatia echoes the experience of women in Northern Ireland, that during armed conflict domestic violence involves many more incidents with weapons; the battlefield and home are not separate as ideology suggests they are. Nor are these effects limited to those living in the "combat zone": Canadian shelter (refuge) workers noted that during the Gulf War women told stories of their husbands dressing in army uniforms before beating them, frequently after watching the TV news.

This finding is consistent with feminist critiques of a perceived public–private divide. Society does not break down into the public sphere for men and the private sphere for women. Norms for society impact all areas of that society. If militarism legitimates violence to address a perceived threat, then it is easier for violence to be legitimated in general. In fact, some feminist scholars see the trend of increased domestic violence as linked to the process of engaging in violence in general. In the military, violence is considered to be a legitimate and necessary means to achieve one's goals. Catharine Lutz (2008: 224) claims "[t]aking a life already requires that soldiers violate the most basic precept of human society. In a military increasingly forced or even willing to bend international codes of conduct in prosecuting wars, soldiers may absorb an attitude that they are above the law at home as well."

Reports of the high levels of domestic abuse in military couples have encouraged many to examine the response of military institutions to incidents of domestic abuse involving soldiers. Some claim there appears to be little institutional incentive to rid the service of members who engage in domestic abuse (Lutz 2008). It is costly to train new soldiers if abusive ones are dismissed. A wide-ranging 2003 investigation by the *Denver Post* into domestic abuse and rape in the US military found that domestic abuse, particularly spouse abuse, is frequently reported but infrequently acted on. In 2000, 12,068 cases of spouse abuse were reported and only 26 led to courts-martial. The report found that military leaders consistently choose administrative punishments over criminal prosecution for soldiers accused of domestic abuse (Herdy and Moffeit 2003). More recent reports by *The New York Times* paint a similar picture of inactivity on behalf of the military to punish soldiers who engage in domestic abuse, particularly as the wars in Afghanistan and Iraq progressed (Alvarez 2008; Alvarez and Sontag 2008). Wartime pressures on military families and on the military itself have complicated the Pentagon's efforts to deal with domestic abuse during wartime (Alvarez and Sontag 2008). In fact, in some cases service members who have been charged with and even convicted of domestic violence crimes have been deployed to additional tours of duty.

In addition to domestic abuse, there has been a great deal of attention paid to sexual misconduct in the military in recent years. This "misconduct" takes the form of sexual harassment and sexual assault, and has impacted both soldiers and civilians. Sexual assault in the military is typically regarded as a separate phenomenon to wartime rape. Many feminist scholars see them both as issues that relate to larger patterns of militarized masculinity; however the later phenomenon mainly refers to the violation of an enemy's women. In the US military, a 2010 report by the Department of Defense stated there were 3,230 reports of sexual assault filed in the previous fiscal year (Bumiller 2010). This figure does not include sexual harassment charges. A 2003 study of US female veterans concluded that there were several characteristics of the traditional military environment that appear to have an impact on risk of rape. The study found that "work environments that allow inappropriate sexual conduct, however subtle, can significantly increase women's risk of rape, suggesting a continuum of violence, with rape the most severe form of coercion" (Sadler et al. 2003: 271). When the military leadership behaves in ways that suggest that sexual harassment is not a serious issue, including things like making sexually demeaning comments or gestures, this encourages a sexualized environment where numbers of rapes seem to increase, and victims are less likely to report the incident. It has been documented that the hierarchical and patriarchal structure of the military makes reporting sexual assault difficult. Additionally, the act of reporting assault can lead to an individual being ridiculed, reprimanded, and even being placed at greater risk for additional trauma (Broadbent 2011; Dowell 2008). Women who have reported sexual assault have reported receiving "poor medical treatment, lack of counseling, incomplete criminal investigations, and threats of punishment for reporting the assaults" (Dowell 2008: 220).

It is important to understand the relationship between sexual abuse and mental health among civilians and military personnel alike. Post-traumatic stress disorder (PTSD) is an anxiety disorder that can occur after experiencing or witnessing a traumatic event. PTSD that stems from military service has been widely discussed in the US in recent years in response to the huge numbers of soldiers that have been deployed to Afghanistan and Iraq. It is an important consequence of militarization that negatively affects both men and women. In the United States, the government has attempted to simplify access to health care and benefits for soldiers suffering from PTSD. While most regard this move as laudable for helping provide services for those in need, some organizations argue these types of moves do not necessarily confront some of the most gendered sources of PTSD. Several scholars and veterans organizations have argued that general regulations on PTSD do not necessarily address PTSD that stems from sexual harassment and abuse in the military (Whitworth 2008). This problem is compounded due to the fact that many of the models of the impact of military deployment on PTSD are based on the experiences of male service members (Street et al. 2009).

Sexual misconduct, domestic abuse, military prostitution, and wartime rape all relate to women's bodies. These are all complex issues that involve a range of processes, structures and actors. Across each of them, however, is a link to the process of militarization. When military solutions are regarded as appropriate, military institutions receive significant support from the state. As seen in the case of military prostitution, this support from the state has even meant the assurance that male soldiers would be given access to women's bodies because of their perceived sexual needs. As seen in the discussion of domestic abuse and sexual misconduct in the military, some states have been unwilling/unable to severely punish those who engage in security violations at a personal level. Viewing militarization through gender lenses requires examining these kinds of issues and asking why they persist.

Gender in Militarized Institutions

Since the military is the central institution associated with militarization, it is essential that we understand its role in society, but also women's various roles within it. Women participate in fewer numbers than men in all militaries around the world. There is a great deal of debate about what the "appropriate" role for women in the military is and about what the presence of women in the military mean for the institution. Some argue that the phenomenon of women joining the military, along with openly gay individuals, is an avenue for the alteration of a masculine institution and may be a demonstration that this change is already underway. At the same time, other optimistic individuals argue that because the military is regarded as an important institution for displaying loyalty to one's state, it offers an opportunity for new citizens to prove their patriotism. For example, many Japanese-American women signed up for the military during the Second World War to prove their loyalty and further their education in the US (Eisenstein 2008: 31).

Others argue that women who join the military are liable to become indoctrinated in the dominant existing military masculinity. Several scholars claim that viewing women's military service as connected to women's liberation masks the consequences of militarization for society (Eisenstein 2008; Enloe 2000; Peterson and Runyan 2010). While several states around the world have pointed to the presence of women among their ranks as evidence that they represent an important move towards equality in society, the mere presence (sometimes a very small number) of women does not necessarily mean an institution is democratic or strives for gender emancipation (Eisenstein 2007; Peterson and Runyan 2010). Recall that both men and women are actively involved in supporting patriarchy and inequality, most often without recognizing that they are doing so. Adding women to an institution that depends on and furthers militarized masculinities without challenging those masculinities will likely do nothing to fundamentally change the institutions themselves. Beyond this, there remain differences in the ways male and female soldiers fit into the institutions. There is an extensive literature that outlines the ways women who serve in militaries find themselves under pressure to remain "feminine" (Steans 2006). Additionally, in many militaries women are distinguished by their inability to serve in combat roles which allows for a separation of roles of male and female service members.

The debate about whether or not women's presence in militaries around the world will fundamentally change the institutions assumes that women will be added to militaries in increasing numbers. This is not an uncontroversial idea, particularly when the debates includes whether or not women should serve in combat roles. Throughout history there have been arguments made that the military is a man's place. These arguments take different forms. One is that men are physically stronger than women, so therefore more able to undertake the tasks associated with combat. Marcia Kovitz (2003: 2) explains:

> The arguments of supporters and opponents of women's military service center on two ostensibly distinct yet fundamentally related issues: women's right to serve and their capacity to serve, both are often reduced to what is seen as the last male bastion, combat. Regarding their capacity, the points of contention concern claims of women's innate physiological inferiority to men in everything from strength (especially in the upper body), stature, speed, and metabolism, to the incapacitating effects of menstruation and childbirth.

The claim that women are physically unfit to serve often ignore arguments about technological developments in the military over the last few years and their impact on the status of women in combat. Despite technology problematizing the exclusion of women in combat due to a need for "brute strength," it is still gendered. Higate (2003: 208) argues "technological developments themselves will continue to be masculinized, and women's role within them considered somewhat peripheral." Even though the excuse of women's lack of combat effectiveness is somewhat neutralized through technology, they are likely to remain on the margins of military institutions because of the hegemonic masculinity that permeates them.

There have been very vocal claims that women do not belong in combat roles at all. Many are familiar with the often-cited 1995 quote by then US Speaker of the House Newt Gingrich that "females have biological problems staying in a ditch for 30 days because they get infections" (Seelye 1995). This quote is interesting for a variety of reasons, including the apparent hesitance for Gingrich to openly use the term menstruation, his assumption that modern conflict frequently requires extended stays in ditches, and lastly, the assumption that a menstruating soldier would be unable to perform her duties under his hypothetical scenario. Along somewhat similar lines, Kingsley Browne (2007) claims women's inclusion in the military is a liability for the institution. In a controversial book titled *Co-ed Combat: The New Evidence that Women Shouldn't Fight the Nation's Wars*, Browne (2007: 291) argues:

> Inclusion of women creates a segment of the military that is physically weaker, more prone to injury (both physical and psychological), less physically aggressive, able to withstand less pain, less willing to take physical risks, less motivated to kill, less likely to be available to deploy when ordered to, more expensive to recruit, and less likely to remain in the service even for the length of their initial contracts. Women are placed in units with men who do not trust them with their lives and who do not bond with them the way that they do with other men.

In several places throughout the book, Browne (2007: 11) claims "military effectiveness must be the touchstone of military manpower policy." His central argument in the book is that integration of women into combat positions undermines military effectiveness to the point that national security suffers with women's inclusion.

The debate about women's acceptability as combat soldiers has larger ramifications for military institutions. The issue of women's exclusion from combat roles has larger implications for women's place in military establishments in general. If women are excluded from combat roles, it will likely hinder their ability to compete for promotion with their male counterparts who have combat experience. In the US military, many top positions require service in combat capacity as a prerequisite (Goldstein 2001). If women are barred from combat, they can only hope to rise to a select number of positions in the military. There has been strong resistance to giving up the male-only combat rule in the United Kingdom and the United States in particular. Not all states share this position. Since the late 1980s, several states, including Canada, Israel, and New Zealand,

and now Australia, have lifted restrictions on women serving in front lines capacities (Siegel 2011).

There is not a singular female experience or role in militaries or militarized societies. Women play a variety of roles in militarized societies. In some cases, they serve in combat or other military positions. For this reason, it is important to recognize women's agency when discussing the place of women in militaries around the world. There have been several studies in recent years that stress women are perfectly capable of choosing to act in ways that conform to notions of military masculinity. Many feminists are particularly skeptical of notions of gender that expressly associate women with peace/gentleness and men with war/aggression. These dichotomies are overly deterministic and they serve to bolster the argument of those who wish to keep women out of full membership in military service and policymaking. At the same time, it is important to understand whether or not women who serve in militaries are treated differently than their male cohorts. Examples from Israel and the US illustrate that this is often the case.

The Israeli military has had compulsory conscription, for both men and women, since the early days of the state's inception in 1948. Despite this status of mandatory military service for women, there are important differences in the experiences of men and women regarding military service. Firstly, men and women tend to do different types of jobs as part of their military service. Women typically serve in traditional feminine jobs like secretarial and administrative positions. Orna Sasson-Levy (2003: 445) explains women's typical military roles as social workers, nurses, and teachers "reflect the feminine professions in the Israeli labor market and are based on the perception of women as caretakers. The military's gender division of labor places women in auxiliary roles behind the lines, while reserving for men (not *all* men, but *only* men) the high-status combat roles at the front." Secondly, unlike men, women are often exempt from service. A 2003 guide to military service put out by the Israeli state explains that men and women have different standards for exemption. For men it says "Exemptions from the army for men are extremely rare. Each case is investigated very carefully." On the other hand, for women it says "Women may be exempted from military service for reasons of religious conscience, marriage, pregnancy or motherhood." This can be seen as evidence that in Israeli society, as in most societies, women are seen first and foremost as mothers and daughters while men are the true providers of security.

Women have served in the US military for over half a century. Women began serving in significant numbers during the Second World War. At the war's peak, women made up about 3 percent of US forces. After the war was over, the number of women in the US military dropped drastically, but never to zero. During the early 1970s, women were integrated into the US military in large numbers, coinciding with the end of conscription after the Vietnam War and the switch to an all-volunteer army. The US deployed women soldiers to a combat zone for the first time during the Gulf War of the early 1990s. In this conflict nearly 40,000 US women participated, which was 7 percent of the US forces deployed. As of 2010, women make up around 14.5 percent of the active duty personnel in the United States military. The largest number of women serve in the Army, followed closely by the Air Force then Navy. By far the smallest number of women serve in the Marine Corps (Department of Defense 2010a). Across all branches of the military, women of color are heavily represented.

In the US, women are still prohibited from serving in direct combat roles (combat arms specialties in the infantry and armor units); however they often serve in roles that bring them in contact with direct violent confrontations. This can include serving as military police, medics or combat logistics specialists. Over one hundred women have died during the conflict in Iraq and around thirty have died in Afghanistan. Sixty percent of those deaths are classified by the military as due to "hostile acts" (Nordland 2011). The debate about women's role in the military was recently energized by debates over the stories of Pfc Jessica Lynch and Pfc Lynndie England, two US soldiers who made headlines because of their participation in the US "war on terror." The stories of these two women prompted questions in the US over the role of women in the military as well as larger questions about the nature and agency of women in general. Pfc. Jessica Lynch, an Army supply clerk in the 507th Maintenance Company, made headlines when she was captured and held as a prisoner of war in Iraq. Iraqi forces captured Lynch on March 23, 2003 near Nassiriya when her convoy got lost in the desert. The attack on the convoy left 11 soldiers dead and 9 wounded. Lynch was badly injured in the attack. She was rescued on April 1, 2003 when US commandos staged a raid on the hospital where she was being held. The story of Lynch's capture and rescue began as a tale of a female Rambo going down fighting but quickly evolved into an account of a young, petite blonde being saved by courageous soldiers from mistreatment at the hands of Iraqis. The first accounts of Lynch's ordeal described her firing on her attackers as chaos erupted around her. The *Washington Post* ran an article under the headline "She Was Fighting to the Death." Reporters soon learned that this image of the attack was not accurate, and she had actually been sitting in the Humvee praying during the attack after her gun jammed. After this realization, many commentators recast Lynch as a victim – both of a dangerous war and of Pentagon propaganda. Lynch has overwhelmingly been depicted as a young, pretty woman who was used by the Pentagon's narrative creation machine. Most of the articles and documentaries that came out about her rescue paint her as a small-town girl who joined the Army to help pay for college, and not as a feminist statement. They stress that her dreams for her life are modest and stereotypically feminine – to settle down and become a housewife and kindergarten teacher (Takacs 2005).

There have been a host of analyses of Lynch's story that view it as part of society's tendency to fit women into familiar categories. In the first place, Lynch was portrayed as a real-life G.I. Jane who symbolized the progressive nature of the US military and the just nature of the Iraq war. After the facts came out that disputed this depiction, she was described as a "woman in peril" who experienced victimization at the hands of Iraqis and the US military, but who still needed to be saved by male soldiers (Lobasz 2008). Stacy Takacs (2005: 301) argues the "[d]ocumentaries about the rescue fetishized Lynch's femininity and vulnerability in order to remasculinize a coed military and militarize the identities of civilian men and women." She and others see this story as evidence of narratives that further the process of militarization in society and reinforce the military masculinity that typically accompanies it. Furthermore, many question why Lynch in particular was the subject of so much attention. If she was a male soldier would her story be so well known today? Also, if she was not a pretty white woman would she have gotten the same level of attention? The fact that there were two women of color involved in the same incident as Lynch, but who received relatively little coverage, is evidence to some of the primacy of white femininity as a story told in our society. Specialist Shoshana Johnson, an African American woman who was taken hostage, and Pfc. Lori Ann Piestewa, a Native American woman who was killed are rarely discussed in the same way, or with the same frequency, as Lynch.

The case of Pfc. Jessica Lynch, along with general examinations of female soldiers in the US and Israel, helps illustrate the fact that female soldiers are often treated differently in military institutions. This differential treatment is sometimes very overt, like banning women from combat roles, and sometime concealed, like the pressure some female soldiers have expressed feeling to remain feminine. Feminist scholars and activists differ on how they view this treatment of female soldiers. On the one hand, some argue women should be free to perform the same duties and achieve the same status as male soldiers. This position claims treating women differently creates resentment from both male and female service members and ensures that women will not truly gain the same footing as men in these institutions. On the other hand, some argue women should not be encouraged to enter into an institution that is deeply gendered and would be extremely difficult to change. As will be discussed in Chapter 3, some feminists view a peaceful world without the dominance of military institutions as the only real path to security.

Militarization in Non-state Institutions

It is also important to consider the gendered nature of militarization in non-state institutions. Militarized institutions like insurgent groups or terrorist organizations are important sites of gendered identities and norms. The militarized masculinities at play in non-state groups that engage in violent conflict are similar to those seen in state militaries. These include masculinities that encourage displays of strength and toughness. These organizations are also dominated by males in terms of their members and those that serve in leadership roles (Parashar 2009). At the same time, these organizations typically involve women playing a variety of roles in their campaigns. In many instances, the contributions of women is downplayed or not acknowledged. For example, Swati Parashar (2011) argues that women in the Kashmir conflict have largely been excluded from religious and nationalist discourses. Women have played important roles in the various phases of the conflict in Kashmir, including acting as political activists who courier equipment and other items, providing food and shelter to militants, and intelligence gathering and reconnaissance functions. They have even formed exclusively women's groups to participate in the struggle, yet these contributions are rarely discussed. Parashar (2011: 302) finds that:

> Women's militant activities rarely find a discussion in the
> mainstream discourses of militancy in Kashmir. The discomfort
> at any kind of suggestion that women did/do participate in the
> militancy is so rampant that anytime a Kashmiri woman is caught
> by the security agencies as an overground operative of any of
> the militant groups, the local media clamors to establish her
> innocence and unearths her tragic personal saga. The matter may
> be *sub judice* but the verdict of innocence is passed through the
> local media.

This tendency to ignore the participation of women in violent movements corresponds with the connections between militarization and masculinities. Men are regarded as fulfilling a form of masculinity when they join militarized groups, but women are often either ignored or explained away. This tendency to treat violent women as an exception in need of explanation will be further discussed in Chapter 4 with the debate about women's participation in terrorist and/or militant organizations.

Additionally, organizations like drug cartels can be and have been heavily militarized. In fact, in the case of drug trafficking to the US, a militarized policy response has been the norm for decades. In 1986 President Ronald Reagan formally elevated drug trafficking to the status of a state security threat through a security directive (Andreas

2003). This "War on Drugs" has two militarized sides, the various state-run militarized institutions and the drug cartels. This is an interesting example of a militarized discourse being used purposely to discuss an issue that was not previously conceptualized as a state security threat. Beyond simply using militarized language to think about drugs, states in the Americas increasingly launched a militarized response to the issue by deploying militaries to the front lines of the perceived "drug war" (Andreas 2003).

Like state militaries, terrorist organizations, and insurgency groups, drug cartels are closely associated with men and masculinity. Al Pacino's gun-wielding and tough-talking character Tony Montana became a popular symbol of drug dealers in both the general public and among Latin American drug dealers themselves who are reported to imitate Montana's tough style (Campbell 2008). This desire to appear tough and powerful through the drug trade is not limited to males, however. Some young women have been enthusiastic to engage in drug trafficking because it is regarded as a role in which they can be powerful and celebritized for that power in ways similar to men in their communities (Edberg 2004). Women's femininities varies in much the same ways their roles in drug trafficking vary. Howard Campbell (2008) analyzes four main levels of female participants in the drug trade on the US-Mexico border: female drug lords, middle-level women, low-level mules, and women whose involvement is minimal and is largely the result of their connections with men in their lives. Some of these women have adopted macho postures and sought out the opportunity to display some of the characteristics often reserved for men in their societies, including engaging in dangerous adventures. This image of *macha* "queenpins" is not the only, or even the most common, role for women in this militarized environment. Much of the variation in the experience of women in drug trafficking coincides with class, with lower-class women often engaging in criminal drug-related activity out of economic desperation. The differing roles of women in drug trafficking offers an interesting example of the connections between militarization, gender norms, and marginalization. A militarized environment results in fairly rigid expectations about masculinity and femininity, with military masculinities becoming closely associated with power structures and hierarchies. A subset of women in drug trafficking communities have attempted to adopt potent forms of masculinity for their own ends. At the same time, other women have been drawn into this world because of economic marginalization or victimization. These various experiences should once again remind us that there is no singular experience of women. A challenge many feminists undertake is to consider how militarization can be rethought with emancipation as a driving goal.

Militarization as Obstacle to Emancipation?

One of the goals of each chapter is to highlight the emancipatory potential that gender lenses offers when we use them to examine key themes and topics in security studies. At its most basic level, the idea of emancipation informing this book would suggest that militarization and militarism are likely incompatible with the emancipation of both men and women. Militarism increases the chances of war by legitimizing military solutions to problems. Booth (1991) expressly states that war and the threat of war are direct constraints to emancipation. People are not free to choose their path in life if war and conflict result in loss of life, livelihood, or physical harm. Militarism also closes off debate by immediately raising a single set of policy choices to the top of the list, sometimes at the expense of examining alternative policy choices that could actually foster emancipation (Cohn 1993). At the same time, there are gendered implications of militarization's tendency to close off debate. The issue of gender is not typically a visible one for many of the world's policymakers. This means that gender often gets brought in to the process of policymaking through debate and discussion. If military solutions are presumed to be the best ones for addressing the problems of a state without reserving time and space for debate about this assumption, then what are the chances that the security needs of women and men at a personal level will be incorporated into policymaking? Gender relations and inequalities are typically regarded as "natural" or something that can be taken for granted. What happens if policymaking occurs without taking the time to reflect on the gendered impacts of military solutions? Additionally, women's voices will be less likely to be involved in this kind of policymaking because they are represented in fewer numbers than men in most military institutions.

Militarism and militarization are both oriented more toward the security and stability of states rather than the individuals inside them. The idea of the protection racket highlights the fact that militarized institutions use discourses that suggest protection is a primary aim; however, the strategies associated with militarized institutions often result in insecurity at an individual level. The examples of wartime rape, violence, and abuse highlight the sources of insecurity at an individual level that can stem from militarization. While women experience these forms of insecurity in greater numbers than men, these are phenomena that also touch the lives of men and boys in some cases directly and in some cases indirectly. Rape, violence, and abuse constrain choice and result in insecurity at an individual level and, in some cases, the level of the community. In fact, genocidal rape is designed to produce insecurity within a defined group. Emancipation would come in the form of removing the sources of insecurity associated with these phenomena. It involves freeing individuals, both men and women, from the abuse and fear that accompany these processes. Related to this, military prostitution can be the result of a lack of other choices, so therefore emancipation would result in freeing up individuals to make other choices with their bodies if they so prefer.

In addition to these impacts on people's bodies, militarization can often dehumanize a perceived enemy through the processes of othering. It can justify state spending into the defense sector at the expense of other sectors that could contribute to human well being. Military spending has been reduced in some regions, like Europe, over the past few years, but continues to represent a huge share of economies in other regions, including Asia (SIPRI 2011). Additionally, despite recent commitments to introduce a "leaner" military, the US continues to spend a huge amount on defense each year. None of these processes fits comfortably with the idea of removing constraints, but rather introduces constraints of their own. The clearest path to emancipation, then, may lie in challenging militarization and militarism. Both of these forces have important consequences for society, many of which are gendered and represent an obstacle for certain individuals to thrive.

3

Gender in Peacekeeping and Peacebuilding

The homepage for the Women's International League for Peace and Freedom (WILPF), a peace organization that was established in the early 1900s, features two images side by side. The first is a soldier crouched down aiming a gun. The second image features a group of young girls sitting on the ground in what looks like a classroom setting. The caption for the images reads "Which is the better investment?" This question hints at the organization's argument that militarization and conflict are damaging to society. WILPF, along with other organizations that are active at the international level, claim peace is a legitimate path to security. Along these lines, there has been a great deal of scholarly work on peace in the international community. This means that security studies not only includes a narrow focus on war and but also includes the study of how to avoid conflict and what happens in the aftermath of conflict. The potential use of military force to maintain peace between two potential foes, or *peacekeeping*, has become relatively prevalent in the international community since the Second World War. The United Nations (UN) in particular has become a key player in peacekeeping actions in the international community during this time. In recent years there has been recognition that peacekeeping operations have unique gender dimensions. For example, in 2000 the UN Security Council adopted Resolution 1325, which called for gender mainstreaming into peacekeeping operations, and for understanding the impacts of armed conflict on women and girls. This act, followed by other initiatives and resolutions, raised the issue of how peacekeeping actors need to take gender into account.

Additionally, there has been a shift from simply focusing on conflict prevention and management, typically associated with peacekeeping, towards an emphasis on aiding states in the process of recovering from war. This second approach has come to be known as *peacebuilding*. Gender has entered discussions of peacebuilding through considerations of the fact that women often find themselves among socially and economically vulnerable segments of the population, so it is understood that peacebuilding efforts and humanitarian relief efforts that address their welfare is a necessary phase of post-conflict reconstruction. This chapter explores the role of women in peacekeeping and peacebuilding efforts, as well as gendered elements to the overall conceptualization of these important security topics. The chapter ends with a brief look at women's involvement in peace organizations throughout the international community.

Peacekeeping

Peacekeeping in general terms is an attempt to stop conflict by the deployment of outside actors, typically members of the militaries of states. Peacekeeping missions can take several forms – individual states can act unilaterally in a peacekeeping mission, groups of states can organize a peacekeeping mission, or the UN can organize a peacekeeping mission. There are a variety of reasons why individual states may want to get involved in peacekeeping operations: for example, concerned regional neighbors may wish to intervene in a conflict occurring close to home. At the same time, former colonial powers may still have close ties and a vested interest in creating stability in a former colony. Finally, states may see peacekeeping as an opportunity to maintain and deploy a military that has no conflict or domestic tasks as a way to justify military budgets. Most states prefer to act as part of a multilateral peacekeeping operation, often under the UN (Bellamy et al. 2009). This is seen as preferable to unilateral action by states who wish to benefit from the perceived legitimacy of action that can be said to be global in nature. Therefore, the UN has become a central actor in peacekeeping from the latter half of the twentieth century to the present. Despite the fact that the UN Charter does not explicitly mention peacekeeping, the organization has become closely associated with peacekeeping throughout the international community. The UN's peacekeeping efforts have been recognized twice by the Nobel committee. Lester B. Pearson, one of the early architects of peacekeeping, and the UN's Blue Berets and Blue Helmets, won Nobel Peace Prizes in 1957 and 1988 respectively.

The first UN peacekeeping force was deployed in 1956 to the Sinai during the Suez Crisis. Early UN peacekeeping missions mainly involved establishing a buffer position between two conflicting groups that had given their consent to the establishment of a peacekeeping operation. There were thirteen such missions between 1956 and 1978. This element of getting the consent of involved parties, along with impartiality and the minimum use of force became the three guiding principles of UN peacekeeping over time (Bellamy et al. 2009). Subsequent generations of UN peacekeeping missions expanded their role to include military and police functions, the creation of state institutions, monitoring elections, monitoring human rights, and the delivery of humanitarian aid (Whitworth 2004). This expansion of activities during the course of peacekeeping has raised questions within the international community about the appropriate role of peacekeeping missions. Should peacekeeping be limited to stopping immediate hostilities, or should it include a transformation of a state to be less conflict-prone?

Most of the broader peacekeeping missions have taken place in the post-Cold War context. When the Cold War ended in the early 1990s, there were several revisions to the way actors in the international community thought about security. Peacekeeping in the post-Cold War period offered the UN an opportunity to reassert itself as an active, essential international actor. Additionally, several states have viewed peacekeeping missions as a chance to utilize their militaries in the absence of immediate domestic or international conflicts. For some this meant justifying having a military at all. For example, Japan and Germany have been pointed to as states that have used peacekeeping missions as a way to revive the international image of their state and military (Whitworth 2004). These states were seen as aggressors by many in the aftermath of the Second World War and thus a peacekeeping function allowed them to demonstrate that their militaries were forces that could encourage peace rather than wage war.

There are other states that view peacekeeping as a vital part of the identity of their military. Canada has at times closely identified its military with the role of peacekeeping. Lester Pearson, the man awarded a Nobel Prize for his role in promoting the idea of peace-keeping, was Canada's Secretary of State for External Affairs and later Canada's 14th Prime Minister. Since 2008 Canada has celebrated National Peacekeepers' Day on August 9 to celebrate those who have served or are currently serving in peacekeeping operations. The country even features a female peacekeeper on their 10 dollar banknotes. She wears a combat uniform and a blue beret. There are also doves, a commonly used symbol of peace, and the phrase "In the service of peace." This banknote, issued in 2005, is one in the "Canadian Journey" series which celebrates Canada's "culture, history, and achievements" (Bank of Canada 2012).

Although Canada, Germany, and Japan have been discussed as having a specific motivation for engaging in peacekeeping or iden-tification as peacekeepers, they are not the states that contribute the greatest numbers to global peacekeeping forces. As of November 2011 the countries with the greatest contribution of police, military experts, and troops to UN peacekeeping operations were Bangladesh, Ethiopia, India, Nigeria, and Pakistan. Each of these five states contributed at least five thousand individuals to UN missions. Bangladesh had the highest total contributions with 10,496 fol-lowed closely by Pakistan with 9,374 (UN Peacekeeping 2011a). It is notable that these countries, along with most of the other countries that contribute a large number of troops for these kinds of missions are Southern states. There have been fewer Northern states that have contributed heavily to peacekeeping missions in recent years com-pared to Southern states. At the same time, most of these missions have been deployed to Southern states.

Gendering Peacekeeping

Since peace and peacekeeping have increasingly become topics of scholarship within security studies and concerns for the UN and the greater international community, it is important to consider these issues through gender lenses. This requires asking questions like who benefits most from peacekeeping? How does peacekeeping impact notions of masculinity and femininity? What happens when those sent in to keep the peace are a source of insecurity for local populations?

A Peacekeeping Masculinity?

While there are several sets of actors that can engage in peacekeeping, it is overwhelmingly members of state militaries that carry out peacekeeping missions. States contribute troops and other military personnel to UN missions, as the UN has no troops of its own. As of November 2011, the majority of people engaging in UN peacekeeping missions are troops. Of the 98,647 individuals deployed as part of UN peacekeeping operations 83% were troops, around 2% were military experts and around 15% were police (UN Peacekeeping 2011a). Each of the categories represent militarized environments that are typically associated with masculinity.

Beyond state actors, peacekeeping, and humanitarian missions have increasingly been undertaken by private security companies (PSCs), often alongside state militaries. Some PSCs have viewed engaging in peacekeeping as a way to help legitimate their company and overcome some of the remaining stigma of being associated with the "mercenary" label (Leander 2005; Spearin 2008). What is potentially problematic for feminist scholars is the fact that most PSCs are made up of large numbers of former military personnel who have experienced similar training to soldiers and have been socialized into the same militarized institutions infused with military masculinities.

The high prevalence of militarized personnel in peacekeeping operations raises a logical question – what is the consequence of soldiers engaging in peacekeeping missions? As was discussed in the previous chapter, militaries around the world tend to produce military masculinities that are remarkably similar. Characteristics associated with most military masculinities include aggressiveness and stoicism. These characteristics are purported to be necessary for an effective warrior, but what about for an effective peacekeeper? Whitworth (2004: 3) explains that "[l]ying at the very core of peace-keeping is a contradiction: on the one hand, it depends on the individuals (mostly men) who have been constructed as soldiers, and on the other hand, it demands that they deny many of the traits they have come to understand being a soldier entails." If military personnel have been trained in ways that encourage or legitimate the use of violence, what does this mean when they are restricted in the use of violence during peacekeeping operations? As was mentioned above, the minimum use of force has been one of the trinity of peacekeeping principles within UN operations. These contradictions are interesting to consider for how they impact the identity of those tasked to keep the peace in the international community.

At first glance, a peacekeeping masculinity might appear to be more benign than many of the military masculinities discussed previously. This does not have to be the case, however. Some scholarship suggests that, like many military masculinities, peacekeeping masculinity relies on the construction of an other in binary terms. Those that need peacekeepers are primitive, irrational, aggressive, and in need of protection and the peacekeepers themselves are civilized, rational, peaceful, and humanitarian. The effect of this is a patronizing discourse that legitimizes intervention (Duncanson 2009). Consider labels like "Responsibility to Protect" (discussed in Chapter 5) or "Saving Strangers" which have been used to describe peacekeeping operations and humanitarian intervention (Wheeler 2000). In an analysis of peacekeeping masculinity that accompanied the British military during peacekeeping in the Balkans during the 1990s, Claire Duncanson (2009: 72) claims several British soldiers "construct their masculinity in relation to many different groups of other men, including for example politicians, journalists and [nongovernmental organization (NGO)] workers, but the most common 'Other' for their constructions of the 'Self' is the Balkan soldier." As discussed in Chapter 2, the process of othering has significant ties to gender. It is often the case that whichever group is perceived as the other is understood to fail on some test of masculinity. In the context of peacekeeping, this failure of masculinity may be the failure to protect their territory without outside help.

An additional problematic element of the othering that has gone along with peacekeeping masculinity is this gendered discourse of protection. Peacekeeping is often envisioned as masculine soldiers protecting vulnerable women and children. The traditional roles of men as protector and women as protected are assumed to be natural (Willett 2010). This masks the complexity of issues like women who are active participants in the conflict that peacekeepers are there to halt and peacekeepers who behave in ways that lessen the security of local populations. It is a continuation of the protection racket in which women are portrayed as vulnerable and promised protection. In this discourse men are the protectors and heroes. This myth is challenged by stories of sexual exploitation and abuse that has accompanied peacekeeping missions in recent years.

Sex and Peacekeeping

There has been a great deal of attention of late to the on-the-ground behavior of peacekeepers. The media has released a number of stories of peacekeepers having inappropriate relationships, including relationships involving sexual exploitation and abuse, with members of local populations. The UN defines sexual exploitation as "any actual or attempted abuse of a position of vulnerability, differential power, or trust, for sexual purposes, including, but not limited to, profiting monetarily, socially or politically from the sexual exploitation of another." In more extreme cases, they define sexual abuse as "the actual or threatened physical intrusion of a sexual nature, whether by force or under unequal or coercive conditions" (UN Conduct and Discipline Unit 2010). The UN has adopted a zero tolerance policy on sexual exploitation and abuse, however there have been widely reported cases of violations to this policy in recent years.

A part of the issue might stem from the "peacekeeping economies" that spring up around peacekeeping operations. Kathleen Jennings (2010: 231) explains:

> The term "peacekeeping economy" refers to the industries and services (e.g. hotels, bars, restaurants, transport) that come into being when a peacekeeping operation arrives in an area. It caters primarily to international actors, provides some jobs for locals, and depends on the custom and cash associated with an international presence. A peacekeeping economy thereby

encompasses the skilled, semi-skilled or unskilled formal sector jobs available to local staff in UN or NGO offices (secretarial, translation, cleaning, cooking, driving, guarding); informal work (such as housecleaning, laundering, running errands) for international staff; and "voluntary" or "forced" participation in the sex industry, whether independent or mediated through a third party (pimp, madam, trafficker). The "peacekeeping economy" thus refers to the economic multiplier effect of peacekeeping operations via direct or indirect resource flows into the local economy, as well as to the construction or reconstruction of housing stock and other infrastructure, including "entertainment infrastructure."

These peacekeeping economies can have both positive and negative impacts for local populations. For example, there have been studies and reports to the UN on the contribution that peacekeeping economies make to building infrastructure and jump-starting economies post-conflict (Carnahan et al. 2007). At the same time, there can be important gender differences in how people experience the peacekeeping economy. There is evidence to suggest that women engage in much of the unskilled and lower-paid work while men are more often in positions of ownership and control (Jennings 2010).

One element often included in these peacekeeping economies is a prostitution network. These prostitution networks are often portrayed and discussed by peacekeepers as a typical (and possibly expected) part of their missions. The (most frequently) women and girls are understood as willing to have sex with soldiers and humanitarian workers. There does not appear to be much awareness of the unequal power relationship at play with these interactions. In various missions in Africa women have been discussed in discourses that reflect a stereotyped hypersexualized African woman who may prey on the biological urges of soldiers (Higate and Henry 2004). In the past there has often been a tendency to treat the sexual relationships between peacekeepers and locals as evidence that "boys will be boys" (Simić 2010). Evidence of this includes the fact that condoms were distributed by the UN as a part of peacekeeping missions (Higate and Henry 2004). This is despite the fact that sexual relations during peacekeeping operations are formally discouraged and sexual exploitation and abuse expressly forbidden.

This depiction of prostitution as unproblematic masks the power relationships involved in these kinds of interactions, as well as the potential that these may be predatory economies in which women and girls may feel compelled to engage in prostitution in order to make a living. There are certainly many cases when prostitutes have a high degree of agency, however this must not overshadow those instances where they do not. War-torn economies can often leave women and girls with limited economic opportunities, and thus prostitution is seen as a viable option (Mazurana 2005). The income disparity between peacekeepers (and support staff) and local populations can sometimes result in local suppliers of food and accommodation raising their prices to levels that are out of the reach of local people (Higate and Henry 2004). This may result in increased numbers of women and girls turning to prostitution.

The case of peacekeeping in Cambodia offers an interesting picture of the role of prostitution in post-conflict areas. The United Nations Transitional Authority in Cambodia (UNTAC) was deployed between November 1991 and September 1993. This remains one of the largest missions deployed by the UN, with 22,000 military and civilian personnel involved. One unintended side-effect of UNTAC's presence in Cambodia was an increase in inflation due to an artificial economic boom. One result of this economic situation was a rise in prostitution in the country (Bellamy et al. 2009). Prostitution in Cambodia grew rapidly during the course of the mission. The Cambodian Women's Development Association estimated the number of prostitutes in Cambodia grew from about 6,000 in 1992 to more than 25,000 at the height of the mission (Whitworth 2004). As these numbers suggest, prostitution was not a new phenomenon in Cambodia; however the increase in the number of women engaging in prostitution over a short time-span is notable. Additionally, reports suggest prostitution also spread from urban areas into rural areas as well. An important consequence of the increase and spread of prostitution appears to be a dramatic rise in cases of HIV and AIDS in the country. The World Health Organization (WHO) reported "75 percent of people giving blood in Phnom Penh were infected with HIV (though some observers consider this an inflated estimate) and another report indicated that 20 percent of soldiers in one French battalion tested positive when they finished their six-month tour of duty. Most observers noted that while UNTAC was not responsible for bringing HIV and AIDS to Cambodia, it did contribute to its spread" (Whitworth 2004: 68). A rise in sexually transmitted diseases as well as the phenomenon of "peace babies" or children born to local women who had a sexual relationship with a peacekeeper are important consequences of peacekeeping that the UN has investigated but that need continued examination (Higate and Henry 2004).

The interaction between peacekeepers and the local population has also gotten scholarly and media attention because of widely publicized cases of peacekeepers sexually exploiting or abusing local individuals. One of the most damaging cases was the discovery that UN soldiers exchanged food and money for sex in the Democratic Republic of the Congo (Kanetake 2010). There have been a variety of allegations of sexual misconduct committed by UN peacekeepers dating from the 1990s in the Balkans, Cambodia and East Timor, in West Africa in 2002 and in Sudan in 2007. These allegations served to tarnish the reputation of UN peacekeeping around the world, and the UN responded by authorizing various inquiries into peacekeeping practices. In 2000 the United Nations High Commissioner for Refugees and Save the Children UK reported on sexual misconduct in Sierra Leone, Guinea, and Liberia. These reports motivated the UN to launch a series of investigations and specifically include harsh language on sexual misconduct in peacekeeping codes of conduct (Simić 2010). The UN's zero tolerance policy on sexual misconduct, however, is difficult to implement because of the limited disciplinary power the UN has over peacekeepers. Punishment for sexual misconduct is ultimately the responsibility of contingent-contributing states and not all have demonstrated a willingness to prosecute individuals accused of exploitation or abuse. For example, in 2007 the UN expelled more than 100 Sri Lankan peacekeepers from a mission in Haiti for sexual abuse and exploitation, sometimes involving minors (US Department of State 2008). This was the largest single withdrawal of soldiers from a UN peacekeeping mission. Despite the decision by the UN to expel the forces, it is not known whether any of the soldiers have been prosecuted by the Sri Lankan government.

The difficulty in punishing those responsible for committing sexual misconduct is worsened because sexual misconduct is typically cast as an off-duty act by a peacekeeper and therefore not a direct UN responsibility. According to some, the UN sends mixed messages about sexual misconduct committed by its peacekeepers. "On the one hand, it expresses grave concern about the exploitation of the vulnerable and vows to take more stringent measures against it; while, on the other hand, it is eager to cool public fever against the misconduct, on the grounds that it was the 'behaviour of a relative few.' This illustrates the UN's sensitivity to its public reputation and its desire to divert public attention from the stain on the record of UN peacekeepers' success and dedication" (Kanetake 2010: 209). Attention to issues of sexual exploitation and abuse has cast a spotlight on gender and the UN in a significant way.

Security Council Resolutions 1325 and 1820

Over time, there have been various calls for international actors to consider the connections between women and war. In particular there have been calls for the UN, as a major actor in the realm of peacekeeping, to consider gender within peacekeeping missions. In response to these calls the UN Security Council passed Resolution 1325 in October of 2000. Resolution 1325 is a short document that mentions various aspects of the connections between women and war. Some of the items contained in the resolution include: a concern that "civilians, particularly women and children" are negatively affected by armed conflict, a call to implement international human rights law that protects the rights of women during and after conflict, a call to "mainstream a gender perspective into peacekeeping operations," a call for specialized training of peacekeeping personnel in the rights and needs of women during conflict, and a recognition of the need to consolidate data on the impact of armed conflict on women and girls (UN Security Council 2000).

One interesting passage of the resolution states "an understanding of the impact of armed conflict on women and girls, [and] effective institutional arrangements to guarantee their protection and full participation in the peace process can significantly contribute to the maintenance and promotion of international peace and security." In this passage, we see there is recognition that understanding how gender impacts conflict resolution and peacemaking can have larger ramifications for international peace and security. This is one of the clearest statements made within the UN that taking gender into account and recognizing the unique security needs of different members of the population is of global importance.

While many regard the resolution as an enormously positive step, there is criticism of the way in which gender is discussed in Resolution 1325 (Willett 2010). The language of the resolution overwhelmingly talks about the needs and rights of women (and children) during and after conflict without necessarily mentioning the needs, rights, and roles of men during conflict. One exception calls on those involved in planning post-conflict activities to "consider the different needs of female and male ex-combatants and to take into account the needs of their dependants." Using a feminist curiosity, we can ask why this seemingly limited gender perspective was used in this document. The resolution calls on actors involved in peacekeeping to "adopt a gender perspective," but it is not made clear how broad this gender perspective should be. Many of the specific elements called for in the resolution include adding women to the peacekeeping process at various levels. However, simply adding in women without addressing deeper gender issues can be counterproductive (Shepherd 2008).

The Security Council took up additional issues of "women, peace and security" in 2008. Resolution 1820 principally calls on the international community to take steps to prevent sexual violence, particularly against women and children, during wartime. The resolution links sexual violence to human rights abuses and increased difficulties in resolving conflict. The resolution:

> Stresses that sexual violence, when used or commissioned as a tactic of war in order to deliberately target civilians or as a part of a widespread or systematic attack against civilian populations, can significantly exacerbate situations of armed conflict and may impede the restoration of international peace and security,

affirms in this regard that effective steps to prevent and respond
to such acts of sexual violence can significantly contribute to the
maintenance of international peace and security . . . (UN Security
Council 2008)

One section of the resolution specifically mentions the steps that
parties to armed conflict can take to eliminate sexual violence. It
mentions stressing military disciplinary measures, training troops
on the prohibition of sexual violence, and "debunking myths that
fuel sexual violence." This language suggests that those responsible
for drafting the resolution are trying to target the sexual violence
perpetrated by the military community – both during conflict and in
post-conflict settings by peacekeeping forces.

Both Resolution 1325 and Resolution 1820 encourage the international community in general and UN peacekeeping bodies in
particular to consider the unique needs and sources of insecurity
that women face in conflict and post-conflict situations. Both tend
to advocate for adding women to various roles, including planning
peacekeeping missions, negotiating conflict resolution mechanisms,
and serving in field-based UN operations. Both resolutions also cast
women along with children as particularly vulnerable populations
during and after conflict (Shepherd 2008). These resolutions are often
regarded as necessary steps toward getting gender on the agenda of
the peacekeeping community; however both are viewed as lacking
in important ways. Some of these drawbacks will be discussed below.

Mainstreaming Gender in Peacekeeping

With the tenth anniversary of Resolution 1325 in 2010, there were a
series of reports and articles assessing the impact of the resolution on
the peacekeeping process. Many of these reports specifically address
whether the resolution has been successful at promoting gender
incorporation within the UN. The UN has adopted two strategies to
achieve gender equality – gender balance and gender mainstreaming.
Gender balance refers to the degree to which women and men participate within the full range of activities associated with the United

Nations. Full gender balance is the ultimate goal of the UN for all professional posts. Since women have historically been represented in fewer numbers within the UN, the strategy of gender balance involves documenting women's existing participation as well as examining the obstacles to women's participation and efforts made by different actors to increase their participation (Mazurana et al. 2005).

While it is not uncommon to hear about gender balance within the UN, it is more typical to hear the phrase gender mainstreaming. The strategy of gender mainstreaming was adopted in the Platform for Action from the Fourth UN World Conference on Women in Beijing in 1995. Since then, several UN branches have included a specific goal of gender mainstreaming in various documents and reports. The UN (2002: v) has defined gender mainstreaming as:

> the process of assessing the implications for women and men of any planned action, including legislation, policies or programmes in all areas and at all levels. It is a strategy for making women's as well as men's concerns and experiences an integral dimension of design, implementation, monitoring and evaluation of policies and programmes in all political, economic and societal spheres so that women and men benefit equally and inequality is not perpetuated. The ultimate goal is to achieve gender equality.

This very clearly states that gender equality is the ultimate goal, and gender mainstreaming is conceptualized as a strategy to achieve that goal. The term "mainstreaming" is intended to stress that a simple count of men and women in UN branches is not enough to ensure that the particular needs and perspectives of both men and women are being incorporated into UN policymaking.

This raises the question, has gender been mainstreamed in peacekeeping? Most assessments conclude that there has been a mixed record on gender mainstreaming at the UN. On one hand various departments, like the Department of Peacekeeping Operations (DPKO) and Department of Disarmament Affairs (DDA), have issued research papers or briefing notes on the ways in which gender should be taken into account within their areas of operation (Whitworth 2004). These reports seek to underscore the fact that conflict is a gendered activity, and that postconflict recovery necessitates the full participation of both women and men. They also seek to incorporate gender issues into all levels and types of policy analysis (Raven-Roberts 2005).

On the other hand, there remains a great deal of confusion over what gender mainstreaming is and how to accomplish it. Although the task of gender mainstreaming has been set for over a decade, there is a sense that most UN branches remain unclear what the process should entail. Nadine Puechguirbal (2010: 183), former Senior Gender Adviser for the UN peacekeeping mission in Haiti (MINUSTAH), has argued:

> In most missions, top and senior management are not gender
> aware and do not give enough support to the Senior Gender
> Advisor, beyond paying the usual lip service. There is still a
> lack of understanding of what gender entails as well as a lack of
> political will to take gender seriously. Senior managers still don't
> understand the cost of ignoring gender because they are unable
> to "think outside the box" and change the way of conducting
> peacekeeping operations.

This quote exhibits a frustration apparent in much that has been written on gender mainstreaming in the UN.

There are additional difficulties because of the nature of the UN itself. The UN is a vastly complex institution in which it is sometimes difficult to coordinate efforts. The UN has been criticized as lacking an effective system of management and evaluation to adequately standardize principles of programming, monitor programs, and hold staff accountable for adhering to practices and goals (Raven-Roberts 2005). This makes coordinating efforts at gender mainstreaming difficult and makes monitoring those efforts also difficult. Further complicating the picture is the fact that the UN also subcontracts elements of peacekeeping out of other bodies, like NGOs. It becomes difficult to coordinate gender mainstreaming outside of the UN and it is difficult to monitor implementation. At the same time, some speculate on the level of commitment to agendas like gender mainstreaming that actually exists across the UN. Whitworth (2004: 120) argues the UN context "is also one in which diplomatic protocol, departmental turf wars, and the protection of (some) member states' reputations take precedence over issues such as gender." These factors mean there are some important obstacles to gender mainstreaming within the UN. Despite this, gender mainstreaming remains an important goal.

Painting Women as Peaceful Mothers and Victims

Several voices have claimed that one major obstacle to effective gender mainstreaming in peacekeeping is the way women are portrayed in discussions of war and conflict. It is often the case that women are depicted as victims, mothers, or inherently peaceful. It is important to note that these are constructed discourses that feminist scholars often find problematic. For example, there are important implications to the portrayal of women as vulnerable in the language of Resolution 1325. There are several instances where women and children are lumped into a single category. Women are rarely portrayed as having agency, much less as active participants in conflict. Shepherd (2008: 131) explains that gender equality is conceptualized within UNSC Resolution 1325 as "the advancement of women, paying scant attention to the situations in which women are active in the oppression of other women and men are similarly disadvantaged. Furthermore, 'gender equality' assumes difference, thereby obscuring the discursive mechanisms through which the difference is reproduced." In many policy reports women are portrayed as a homogeneous group that is uniformly vulnerable in times of conflict. It is true that many women are vulnerable and victims of insecurity during conflict, however it is counterproductive to assume all women experience conflict identically. Case studies on Sierra Leone (Gizelis 2009; MacKenzie 2010) illustrate the complex roles women play in conflicts. For example, in the civil war in Sierra Leone women were actively involved in war activities and planning, were the victims of rape, slavery, and displacement, and were active participants in peace movements. Despite the diversity of women's roles, in post-conflict discourses women were overwhelmingly discussed as victims. The result of this is that when the country was attempting to move from conflict to post-conflict, women who had been combatants were largely left out of the peacemaking process. Women and girls were not viewed as "real" soldiers but described as sex slaves, abductees, camp followers, or domestic workers (MacKenzie 2010). This shows that discourses on women's vulnerability have concrete impacts for peacekeeping and peacemaking. Because women were not seen as combatants, they were typically excluded from the peacemaking process. On the other hand, peace negotiators turn to those associated with conflict, including the leaders of local militias and warlords, to discuss the terms of peace and future security. If women are seen as victims then they are excluded from the "real" business of conflict resolution. They can also be passed over for positions within the post-conflict government. Susan Willett (2010: 147) explains that during the process of conflict resolution "resources are prioritized for disarmament, demobilization, reintegration and security sector reform. These are targeted at militarized men."

Another potentially negative element in the portrayal of women is as mothers and as inherently peaceful. Women are often defined as mothers and associated with children, regardless of whether or not the individuals in question actually have children (Puechguirbal 2010). Supposedly "natural" characteristics of maternalism and peacefulness are associated with women. A glimpse at women's participation in the conflict in Northern Ireland demonstrates that there are serious implications associated with this kind of portrayal. In conflict-resolution discussions women were typically seen as peaceful. Because of this, the women who were invited to take part in the discussions were largely women associated with peace activism. Female combatants were largely excluded from the negotiation table. Sandra McEvoy (2010: 144) explains the "assumed link between femininity and peacefulness creates a selection effect for the sort of women who are allowed to participate in peace processes. Women included in peace processes are often those women who play roles traditionally associated with femininity, advocating for and brokering peace agreements rather than invested in the conflict." One of these roles traditionally associated with femininity is motherhood.

UN peacekeeping missions need to be aware of the unique needs of both men and women and do so in a way that avoids painting women as victims without agency. Uncritical associations of women as victims and men as perpetrators of violence during conflicts are negative for both groups. Again, this tendency of putting labels on people is not what gender mainstreaming should be about. Instead, gender mainstreaming should be about problematizing the relationships between masculinized protectors and the feminized protected. It means challenging the influence of military knowledge over non-military knowledge, and assessing the various roles both men and women play during conflict.

Adding Women to Peacekeeping Operations

Security Council Resolution 1325 specifically mentions increasing the number of women involved in peace processes from UN offices to members of operations on the ground. In particular, the resolution includes calls for the Secretary-General to appoint more women as special representatives and envoys. Up to 2009, there were only seven women who held the position of special representative to the Secretary-General (SRSG). Data from November 2011 illustrates that about 4% of personnel associated with UN peacekeeping missions were women. Women made up around 4% of the military experts, 3% of troops, and 10% of police associated with peacekeeping missions. These numbers have slowly been increasing in the years since this data was available in 2005 (UN Peacekeeping 2010). Additionally, the missions with the largest total number of female troops deployed are the African Union/United Nations Hybrid Operation in Darfur (UNAMID), and the United Nations Interim Force in Lebanon (UNIFIL) with 463 female troops each (UN Peacekeeping 2011b).

There are two main arguments made for increasing the number of women in the peacekeeping process. First, it is thought that having women involved in peacekeeping allows a greater participation from society and therefore the opportunity to build a more lasting peace (Gizelis 2009). If a greater number of people in a post-conflict country feel a connection to the peacekeeping process, then there will be greater social capital peacekeepers can draw on. Second, having women actively involved at all levels of peacekeeping may help change the nature of the mission in positive ways. These positive changes range from a greater likelihood that victims of rape and other forms of sexual abuse will have people that they feel comfortable talking to, to the likelihood that male peacekeepers will keep more strictly to the established codes of conduct for peacekeepers.

The second reason specifically addresses including more women as peacekeepers on the ground. It appears to be premised on essentialist notions of women as inherently more peaceful and nurturing than men. The UN has argued "[w]omen's presence improves access and support for local women; it makes male peacekeepers more reflective and responsible; and it broadens the repertoire of skills and styles available within the mission, often with the effect of reducing conflict and confrontation" (quoted in Simić 2010: 189–190). Female peacekeepers are assumed to be more cooperative than men and it is understood that their presence makes both the male peacekeepers and civilians refrain from bad behavior. This almost seems as if the role of female peacekeepers is to police their male counterparts and civilians who would be more aggressive in their absence. Women are thought to have a "civilizing" effect on the post-conflict environment. What this ignores is the fact that the women being recruited into peacekeeping may be female soldiers who have been trained within an institution dominated by militarized masculinity.

Actively attempting to recruit women into peacekeeping operations goes against the trend of recruiting current and ex-military personnel into humanitarian and peacekeeping work, in which women appear in fewer numbers than men (Duncanson 2009). A military background may influence the way peacekeeping is conceived and carried out, with traditional security threats privileged over alternative notions of insecurity, like personal or human insecurity. Some argue individuals with military backgrounds may even regard attempts to incorporate gender into peacekeeping as trivial and a waste of time (Raven-Roberts 2005). This speaks to whether attempts to simply add more women to the existing peacekeeping model fulfill gender mainstreaming. If women are being recruited simply because they are assumed to be more peaceful and nurturing than men, then this does not coincide with gender mainstreaming. It is a positive step for women to be included in peacekeeping operations in greater numbers simply to address the large gender imbalance that currently exists in this area, however it should not necessarily be taken to mean that gender mainstreaming has been achieved.

A 2010 study carried out by the UN Department of Peacekeeping Operations (DPKO) and the Department of Field Support (DFS) argues that more needs to be done to include women at various levels of peacekeeping. In particular, the study addresses the limited participation of women in peace negotiations, national security institutions and governance initiatives. It calls on UN peacekeeping missions to work with local women, national authorities and member states during the course of peacekeeping operations to increase the participation of women in these areas. The study also found that effective inclusion of women in post-conflict governance is often hindered by discrimination (UN Department of Peacekeeping Operations 2010). These findings suggest that even if there are greater numbers of women acting as peacekeepers, it does not mean women will necessarily have a strong voice in their post-conflict society. Peacekeepers eventually leave, while local women are left to cope with the post-conflict realities. In particular, the fact that women are often left out of peace negotiations supports the claims of many that targeting those who have engaged in fighting for participation in peace negotiations can lead to negative long-term repercussions. While there does appear to be a commitment to gender mainstreaming from the UN, it is clear that there is more work to be done before this goal is reached.

Evidence suggests that working toward gender equality is important both as a general goal for social justice, as well as a goal that impacts international peace and security. A 2009 study on gender and UN peacekeeping operations suggests that in countries where women have high life expectancy, UN peacekeeping missions have a higher chance of success. The study uses the admittedly limited variable of life expectancy ratios, but the findings suggest an interesting point. "An empirical analysis of post-conflict cases with a high risk of conflict recurrence shows that UN peacekeeping operations have been significantly more effective in societies in which women have relatively higher status. By contrast, UN peacekeeping operations in countries where women have comparatively lower social status are much less likely to succeed" (Gizelis 2009: 505). This means states that have made progress towards gender equality have a better chance of effective peacekeeping. This finding would suggest that working towards gender equality is an important goal for a multitude of reasons.

The Potential for Marginalization?

Another important problem with current UN approaches is that they tend to conflate "gender," "women," and often "victim," which masks the complexities involved in the various processes of conflict and post-conflict. There is also a concern that existing strategies of gender mainstreaming may actually result in marginalization rather than mainstreaming. Because the UN is such a central body for peacekeeping, it is necessary to engage with it, however the challenge is to do this without being marginalized or co-opted. Voices that want to incorporate gender into peacekeeping must often adopt the language of the UN, including their conceptualizations of peace and security. They must also be aware of the hierarchies and culture of the UN (Whitworth 2004). These voices face a difficult balancing act of packaging their message in such a way that it can be incorporated into existing structures and continually challenging those structures as gendered.

Gender mainstreaming is largely the task of gender units and advisers within the UN. The tasks of the gender units and advisers include monitoring the gender balance of missions, providing gender awareness training, liaising with local women's groups, and disseminating relevant UN material and reports. Gender awareness training is provided to mission staff as well as local personnel, including politicians, police, military and other civilians tied to peacekeeping operations. It is hoped that this training will allow for gender mainstreaming to take place at all levels of peacekeeping operations.

Making gender a separate category in UN peacekeeping with separate offices can result in marginalizing the work being done. In the first place, there is often little room made in peacekeeping budgets for gender mainstreaming programs. Additionally, gender is often relegated to a small section of reports on missions. This can result in gender only being mentioned in that one small section rather than being incorporated throughout UN documents (Puechguirbal 2010). Related to this is the fact that gender units may be expected to interact with particular elements of a post-conflict society. Whitworth (2004: 131) explains "a separate gender unit tends to result in local women's NGOs liaising with the unit, while other local political actors – the majority of whom will likely be men – deal with UN officials in mainline departments and offices, the majority of whom are also men and who often enjoy more direct access to the chief of mission." A separate gender unit may end up dealing exclusively with women's organizations. This is a valuable task to be sure, but it does not necessarily advance gender mainstreaming of UN peacekeeping as a whole.

One of the main obstacles to widespread, effective gender mainstreaming in peacekeeping is the tendency in post-conflict contexts for gender issues to be put on the back burner. When fighting stops, the priority has been to tend to the "real issues" in society like addressing the political and economic structures. This ignores the fact that gender has a direct impact on political and economic issues in society and these should be understood from the ground up as new institutions are being created. Issues like concerns about physical security, access to decisionmaking, land-rights issues, and health and reproductive care are all vitally important issues for a post-conflict society to debate and act on (Willett 2010). Instead, the attitude during the peacekeeping period is often that gender issues can be handled later. This represents a missed opportunity to act on important issues that have lasting impacts on how a society functions.

Peacebuilding

The international community has also placed an emphasis on aiding states in recovering from war. This approach has come to be known as "peacebuilding." Various peace initiatives, like peace committees and truth and reconciliation commissions, have been used to pacify societies in the post-conflict period. There have particularly been calls to target local organizations and interests in peace initiatives as an attempt to make the process more bottom-up than simply top-down (Andrieu 2010; Chopra 2009). Heidi Hudson (2010: 259) claims that there are several elements of peacebuilding, including "security, justice and reconciliation, social and economic well being, and governance and participation." As this list illustrates, there are multiple facets to peacebuilding. It is a process geared toward healing the grievances that instigated conflict and preventing those grievances from reappearing in society. Peacebuilding can also include coming up with specific policy options for how a state will be organized in the post-conflict phase.

Many recent peacebuilding efforts have stressed the benefits of promoting liberal ideals like democracy and capitalist economies (Andrieu 2010). In 2002, George W. Bush claimed "[w]e seek a just peace where repression, resentment and poverty are replaced with the hope of democracy, development, free markets and free trade" (quoted in Pugh et al. 2008: 2). It is argued that building these types of institutions in post-conflict societies has the greatest chance of achieving a lasting peace. The concept of peacebuilding has become regularly used by scholars and international actors like the UN. In 2005 the Security Council and the General Assembly created the Peacebuilding Commission (PBC). The commission was inaugurated in July 2006 with a mandate to help countries who have recently experienced conflict and are in a transition to peace. According to their website, the PBC:

> [P]lays a unique role in (1) bringing together all of the relevant actors, including international donors, the international financial institutions, national governments, troop contributing countries; (2) marshalling resources and (3) advising on and proposing integrated strategies for post-conflict peacebuilding and recovery and where appropriate, highlighting any gaps that threaten to undermine peace. (UN Peacebuilding Commission 2011)

The countries currently on the agenda for the PBC are exclusively African states, including Burundi, Sierra Leone, Guinea-Bissau, Central African Republic and Liberia. The commission seeks to address several of the facets understood to promote peace. For example, in Burundi the commission is trying to achieve good governance, strengthen the rule of law, instigate community recovery, and address issues of land ownership. As peacebuilding efforts like these continue within the international community, it is important to understand how they are gendered.

Gender and Peacebuilding

The challenge of looking at peacebuilding with a feminist curiosity means trying to understand the gendered nature of the peacebuilding process. Women often enter discussions of peacebuilding through considerations of the fact that large numbers of them are often represented among the marginalized segments of a population, so it is understood that peacebuilding efforts and humanitarian relief efforts that address their welfare is a necessary phase of post-conflict reconstruction. This fits in with the justice, social and economic well being, and participation elements of the peacebuilding process. The UN has specifically recognized the need to mainstream gender in the peacebuilding process. In January 2011, Ambassador Peter Wittig, the head of the PBC, discussed the issue of promoting justice in peacebuilding efforts by saying "From power-sharing and rotation, active participation of women in decisionmaking processes, to fair distribution of wealth and economic opportunities, societies emerging from conflict struggle to rebuild themselves on the basis of new rules of the game" (UN News Service 2011). This represents a perspective in which the post-conflict setting offers an opportunity to increase the participation of marginalized groups, including women, in societies where their participation was limited before.

Rwanda is often described as an example where gender mainstreaming was relatively successful in the post-conflict phase. In 1994, the transitional government acknowledged the particular gendered experience of the conflict, including the staggeringly high number of rapes during the genocide. The government also openly recognized the need for women's participation in peacebuilding and governance for those processes to be successful. The Rwandan Constitution includes a commitment to gender equality, and reserves at least 30 percent of posts in decisionmaking positions for women. Since 1994

Rwanda has consistently achieved high levels of gender balance in their parliament (Hudson 2010). While there have been some areas of the peacebuilding process in which gender mainstreaming has not been as successful in Rwanda, overall there were great strides made in facilitating the participation of women in areas like the legislature and the judiciary.

Despite the positive example of Rwanda and others, gender concerns have not always been a central element of peacebuilding. Even in other parts of Africa, gender has not been significantly incorporated in the peacebuilding process. In that region, the African Union (AU) has played a role in peacebuilding alongside the UN. The AU's Post-Conflict Reconstruction Policy Framework stresses the need for humanitarian and development issues to be at the heart of peacebuilding efforts. Women have been labeled a "special needs group" who need particular attention in the post-conflict phase (NEPAD 2005). Despite this, the Policy Framework does not pursue gender mainstreaming or offer specific recommendations on how to increase the participation of women. When African states use the Policy Framework to inform policy, there is no guidance on how to mainstream gender into the peacebuilding process (Hudson 2010). Mainstreaming gender in the peacebuilding process is vitally important because it involves shaping the institutions of society that are meant to be lasting. The very heart of the peacebuilding process is changing society in ways that encourage peace and security. If that goal is conceptualized broadly to include encouraging security on the ground for marginalized groups, then achieving justice and working towards the increased participation of women in governance is a necessary step.

Women's organizations have been actively involved in attempting to give women a voice in the peacebuilding process. While this is important and impressive, it also could result in marginalization of gender concerns, as was discussed above. It is possible that gender mainstreaming will be overlooked in the implementation of peacebuilding reforms. This could be because it is considered to be a secondary concern to the "real business" of achieving a lasting peace. Alternatively it could be overlooked because those involved in peacebuilding are not exactly sure what gender mainstreaming is or how it should be achieved. There have been several influential voices in the international community calling for recognition of the connections between justice and peace, and hopefully these voices guide the peacebuilding process in the future.

Thinking About Peace

Some actors in the international community have come to the conclusion that the only way to really ensure security is to avoid conflict altogether. Peace organizations around the world attempt to offer nonviolent solutions to conflicts. Beyond this, many peace movements consider issues of social justice and ways to build a non-militaristic society. For example, between 1945 and 1975 the Women's International League for Peace and Freedom (WILPF), an organization that dates back to 1915, took up the issue of decolonization, which it regarded as closely tied to peace. Catia Confortini (2011: 354) explains:

> Self-determination was seen as indissolubly connected to peace, through the understanding that peace and freedom were inseparable from each other. WILPF's thinking in this regard revolved around the core beliefs that peace was conditional on the achievement of equality between races (as well as between men and women); that peace was also conditional on the achievement of freedom; and that freedom meant the realization of both self-determination and human rights.

WILPF's inclusion of freedom, equality, and self-determination in their conceptualization of peace illustrates that peace does not simply suggest the absence of war. Peace is routinely conceptualized as a broad and multifaceted idea with numerous links to security.

Women have long been actively involved in peace movements around the world. It is important to acknowledge the difference between peacefulness and passivity. For many early female peace activists in the nineteenth century, peace movements were largely the only public sphere where their presence was tolerated. During this timeframe, peace was considered to be an appropriate subject (and one of the only subjects) for women to voice an opinion on. Early examples of women's peace activism include the Olive Leaf Circles, a British peace organization that brought together three thousand women to discuss peace in the 1850s (Steans 2006). Currently, organizations like CODEPINK, Women in Black, WILPF and Women's Network against Militarism all intentionally connect gender and peace activism.

One of the motivations for women's peace activism is the realization that wars and conflicts do not have clearly defined lines. The consequences of war are not limited to a battlefield but are instead felt by a number of people in a variety of ways. Today, there are increasing numbers of women who negatively experience violent conflict as soldiers and civilians. In this context, many women's peace organizations attempt to spread the idea that security can be achieved only when peace is achieved. Sanam Anderlini (2007: 5) explains that women's peace activism "is both highly localized in nature and increasingly a global movement with its own characteristics, linked to the UN and the system of international conferences and networks that have emerged since the early 1990s. As wars (particularly civil wars) destroy the social taboos and mores that protected women, so women themselves are taking a stand and saying enough is enough."

CODEPINK is one example of a women's peace organization that takes a stand against war as a means of conflict resolution. The group was founded in 2002 in an attempt to stop the United States government from entering into war in Iraq. The group's name is a play on the color-coded terror alert system in the United States. According to their mission, CODEPINK (2011) is:

> a women-initiated grassroots peace and social justice movement working to end the wars in Iraq and Afghanistan, stop new wars, and redirect our resources into healthcare, education, green jobs and other life-affirming activities. CODEPINK rejects foreign policies based on domination and aggression, and instead calls for policies based on diplomacy, compassion and a commitment to international law. With an emphasis on joy and humor, CODEPINK women and men seek to activate, amplify and inspire a community of peacemakers through creative campaigns and a commitment to non-violence.

The organization stages highly visible campaigns like attending the 2004 Republican National Convention and shouting "Out of Iraq Now" during President Bush's acceptance speech, and organizing protests during which members carry baby dolls wrapped in blankets dripped with red paint to represent children who die during the war in Iraq.

The decision of CODEPINK to draw on images of femininity and maternity, including wearing pink during protests and events, raises questions about gender, peace and security. Like CODEPINK, several peace organizations have drawn on maternalist imagery during their campaigns for peace. This includes drawing on feminine characteristics such as caregiving and connectedness and in some instances portraying women as different from men (Tickner 2001). This trend traces back to early women's peace organizations that, like suffragettes, used the idea of biological determinism as an argument in favor of women having a say in matters of peace (Steans 2006). This is met with caution by some within the feminist community. There have been frequent discussions among feminists about whether associating women with peace and depicting them as mothers can actually backfire and reinforce assumptions that women have no place in discussions of war and security. The essentialist picture of women as pacific mother appears to some as a reason for women's omission from security discussions as well as the negotiation table after conflicts.

Emancipatory Potential of Peace?

The move within security studies from a focus on war and conflict to the inclusion of peace, peacekeeping, and peacemaking is an interesting one to consider through gender lenses. Peacekeeping has been a central concern of the international community for at least sixty years. As the international community, led by the efforts of UN peacekeeping, has continued its involvement in stopping conflict and war, there has been recognition that peacekeeping has unique gender dimensions. These gender dimensions range from the cultivation of a peacekeeping masculinity to unique experience of peacekeeping and peacebuilding for both men and women. Security Council Resolutions 1325 and 1820 are high-profile examples of the international community recognizing the unique security needs of women both during conflict and in the transition to peace. These resolutions also acknowledge the unique contributions women can make in a society's transition to peace.

There have been various calls to increase the participation of women in peacekeeping and peacebuilding from a variety of voices in the international community. The participation of women is thought to result in a number of changes, including encouraging less aggressive behavior of male peacekeepers, increasing the legitimacy and approachability of peacekeeping missions, and addressing inequalities in society through the peacebuilding process. At present, peacekeeping tends to be heavily male-dominated as well as military-dominated. Actors like the UN have expressed a commitment to gender balance in peacekeeping and peacebuilding, but there have been some important obstacles to achieving this goal.

These increases in the participation of women in multiple roles are part of a larger process of achieving gender equality in the areas of conflict and peace. The primary tool for achieving gender equality, gender mainstreaming, has had a mixed record in this area. As long as gender mainstreaming is misunderstood or marginalized, the goal of gender equality will likely fall short. Additionally, as long as women are portrayed as victims without agency the peacekeeping and peacebuilding phases will not truly reflect the complexities of gender on the ground. While it is true that some women have experienced horrible abuses during conflict and, in some instances, during peacekeeping, it is unhelpful to cast all women in the same light. It is just as counterproductive as if we assume that all men are perpetrators of abuse. If the transition from conflict to peace is really to be seen as an opportunity to improve conditions within a society for groups that are marginalized, then understanding that marginalization and finding ways to showcase and expand on women's agency in peacekeeping and peacebuilding is essential.

These goals are also consistent with larger goals of emancipation. Peacekeeping at its most basic level is about stopping violent conflict. This is an important facet of removing sources of insecurity;

however, peacekeeping missions can introduce other sources of insecurity for populations. If peacekeeping economies cause economic hardships for locals, or if peacekeepers violate the standards of behavior set up by organizations like the UN and exploit or abuse local populations, then this contributes to further insecurity rather than emancipation. This is not to suggest that peacekeeping should be regarded negatively, or that misconduct by peacekeeping forces will always happen, but rather to highlight the need for peacekeeping mandates and policies to be drafted with a holistic view of security. Likewise, peacebuilding policies offer a potential space for emancipation. Peacebuilding involves identifying and addressing those issues and processes that caused conflict to occur as well as identifying ways to encourage peace and security in the future. This phase represents a unique opportunity to make emancipation a driving goal. Organizations who play an active role in peacebuilding processes, like various branches of the UN, could make removing assorted sources of insecurity a central component of these processes for the betterment of both women and men.

4

A Gendered Understanding of Terrorism

January 2012 opened with terrorist attacks in Pakistan and Iraq. In both cases Shiite Muslims were targeted while travelling or worshiping. A *New York Times* report of the January 15 attack in Khanpur, Pakistan explains "[b]y early evening 17 people had been confirmed killed and 25 injured, with the toll expected to rise. Television pictures from the scene showed black-clad women mourning over a corpse in the street while men angrily remonstrated before the cameras, beating their chests" (Walsh 2012). This description paints a picture of experiences of terrorism that are gendered – women mourn while men get angry. These gendered depictions are common in media reports following terrorist attacks, and it is necessary to examine them through gender lenses. Along with the relatively recent shift of security scholars paying increasing attention to peacekeeping and peacebuilding, there has also been a tendency for scholars to focus on terrorism. Although terrorism is an extremely old phenomenon, high-profile terrorist attacks of the past decade, including the 9/11 attacks of 2001 in New York and Washington DC, the Madrid train bombings in March 2004, the London transit bombings in the summer of 2005, the November 2008 attacks in Mumbai, and the attacks in Norway in the summer of 2011 have raised the profile of terrorism for both academics and policymakers.

Terrorists are often portrayed as angry, radical, young men, but is this necessarily the case? Why might we assume this to be the case? Most of the recent high-profile terrorist attacks are presumed to have been carried out by men. The weeks after 9/11 saw the faces of the terrorists splashed across most major newspapers. Just because these faces were all male, should we take it as given that all terrorists are men? Just because the faces were not white, should we assume that terrorism is something undertaken by "others?" Examining international terrorism through gender lenses requires asking questions like why are there pervasive assumptions made about the gender and race of terrorists? Does the presence of female terrorists require different frames for understanding the motivations and intentions of terrorists as actors in the international community? This chapter examines the complexity involved in defining terrorism, the various ways that the study and practice of terrorism are gendered, our particular interpretations of female terrorists, and the process of othering that accompanies discourses of terrorism. Additionally, the chapter explores the resurgence of masculinity that accompanied the US-led "Global War on Terror" in the aftermath of the 9/11 attacks, and some of the consequences of these counterterrorism policies for the international community.

What is Terrorism?

Scholars began to study terrorism as a distinct subject in the late 1960s and early 1970s. Before this time, scholars studied political violence as a part of war or insurgency (Jackson et al. 2011). Early terrorism scholarship has been characterized as lacking many of the resources that the field has today. These resources include funding and established researchers (Silke 2009). The nature of terrorism scholarship has witnessed important shifts in the past decade, as the field as a whole has experienced a huge influx of attention. Academic conferences, book series, and journals have seen an explosion of submissions and publication of terrorism research. 14,006 terrorism-related articles were published between 1971 and 2002. Of these articles, over half (54%) were published in 2001 and 2002 (Ranstorp 2009). Another, albeit crude, measure of the increase in scholarly attention to terrorism is the increase in panels and papers on terrorism presented at the annual International Studies Association (ISA) conventions in recent years. These annual meetings are a chance for scholars who work on international research to come together and discuss their latest projects. At the 2000 meeting, there was one panel on terrorism featuring three papers dealing with the topic. By 2003, there were nine panels and fifty-four papers featuring terrorist, terrorism or counterterrorism in their titles. These panels ranged from topics like "Terrorism in the 21st century" to "Terrorism and the Environment." The 2010 convention saw thirty-one panels and one hundred and sixty-five papers with those words in their titles. While it is true that some of this increase is likely due to the growth of the organization as a whole, this trend demonstrates that there are more and more scholars who are either directly conducting research on terrorism or at least framing their work in the language of terrorism.

Academics have engaged in spirited debates about how terrorism should be defined, and how terrorism as a phenomenon should be understood and studied. Critical terrorism studies (CTS) is a field of academic work that challenges some of the foundational assumptions of traditional terrorism discourses. This approach is closely associated with the work of Jeroen Gunning, Richard Jackson, and Marie Breen Smyth, among others. Jackson et al. (2011) describe CTS as an academic approach that incorporates a wide variety of voices, many of which are found outside of the mainstream, and critically examines many of the guiding assumptions about and conceptualizations of terrorism. At its root, CTS treats terrorism as a socially constructed idea, meaning that "deciding whether a particular act of violence constitutes an 'act of terrorism' relies on judgments about the context, circumstances and intent of the violence, rather than any objective characteristic inherent to it" (Jackson et al. 2011: 35).

It is extremely difficult to offer a single definition of terrorism. While it is beyond the task of this chapter to give a full survey of the various definitions of terrorism, I will include a few as examples. Terrorism is defined differently by individual states, and even among agencies within a single state. The US Department of Defense and Federal Bureau of Investigation (FBI) work under different definitions of terrorism (Sjoberg et al. 2011). The US Department of Defense states that terrorism is "the calculated use of violence or threat of violence to inculcate fear; intended to coerce or to intimidate governments or societies in the pursuit of goals that are generally political, religious, or ideological" (Theohary and Rollins 2011). Australia has worked under a definition of terrorism "as certain types of serious harm to people, property, public health or safety, or an electronic system, where it is intended to coerce a government or an international organisation, or to intimidate the public, in order to advance a political, religious or ideological cause" (Saul 2007: 3).

Robert Pape (2005: 345), a well-known terrorism scholar, defines terrorism as involving "the use of violence by an organization other than a national government to cause intimidation or fear among a target audience." Similarly, Audrey Cronin (2003: 33) claims "the shorthand (and admittedly imperfect) definition of terrorism is the threat or use of seemingly random violence against innocents for political ends by a nonstate actor." These definitions suggest several things. First, they both suggest that only nonstate actors are terrorists. There is some debate among scholars whether states can be viewed as terrorist actors. For example, the above-mentioned US Department of Defense and Australian government definitions of terrorism do not specify that only nonstate actors are terrorists. CTS scholars frequently point out that state actions can at times exhibit characteristics associated with terrorism discourses (Jackson et al. 2011).

The term "state-sponsored terrorism" has been used by many terrorism scholars as a way to identify state involvement in terrorist activities. State-sponsored terrorism involves states backing the activities of terrorist organizations, often to destabilize other states. Many scholars have studied the tendency of Iran and Syria to support terrorist organizations under this heading of state-sponsored terrorism. This scholarship notes a fairly recent shift from state-sponsored terrorism, which dominated between the 1970s and 1990s, to transnational terrorism or international terrorism involving cross-border network structures (Brandt and Sandler 2010; Heupel 2007).

A second component of most definitions of terrorism is that terrorist acts intentionally use violence in order to cause fear. The very term "terrorism" gets at this quality. Terrorist acts are designed to terrorize a population. One way to spread fear is to attack civilians. This tactic is intended to make a population feel particularly vulnerable because you never know if you could be involved in an attack. Consider the list of terrorist acts at the beginning of the chapter – the 9/11 attacks of 2001 in New York and Washington DC, the Madrid train bombings in March 2004, the London transit bombings in the summer of 2005, the November 2008 attacks in Mumbai, and the 2011 Norway attack. The targets in each of these attacks were civilian population centers, with the exception of the Pentagon building. They targeted people traveling on airplanes or trains or just generally going about their daily routines.

Finally, this strategy of spreading fear is in pursuit of a goal or set of goals. This is a component of most definitions of terrorism. Terrorist organizations use violence in order to achieve a particular objective. The US Department of Defense's definition includes political, religious, or ideological goals. These goals do not necessarily have to be clear-cut, but there is some sense of a successful outcome. Some scholars claim that terrorist organizations often target civilians, particularly in democracies, so that those civilians will put pressure on their government to change their behavior in ways that are consistent with the demands of the terrorists (Pape 2005). For example, if you are a civilian in country A and you are experiencing terrorist attacks (or you fear a terrorist attack) presumably because of your government's support for country B, then you may petition the government to stop supporting country B. Scholars and policymakers spend quite a bit of time trying to determine the exact goals of terrorist organizations (Abrahms 2006).

These characteristics of terrorism tend to be discussed frequently within mainstream terrorism scholarship. Critical approaches to terrorism problematize these characteristics. In fact, the act of defining something as terrorism, or a terrorist act, can be a political act. In much the same way that defining something a "security issue" implies certain actions should be taken and certain actors should take the lead, identifying something as an act of terrorism has important implications for policymaking. The way terrorism is defined suggests the range of actors involved and the types of activities that will "count" as terrorist actions. Some scholars suggest that states use discourses of terrorism in order to discredit sections of society and justify certain policies (Grewal 2003; Gunning 2007; McDonald 2009). Particularly since 9/11, there has been an increased tendency to use the frame of terrorism to talk about certain organizations in the international community. Then-President Vladimir Putin of Russia was quick to side with US President Bush on the "Global War on Terror" in the months after 9/11. Putin's government has been accused of linking the Chechen fight for independence with international terrorists connected with Al-Qaeda without convincing evidence to support the claim (Nivat 2008). Additionally, some scholars have claimed most violent acts committed in the context of the Palestinian/Israeli struggle "whether against military or civilian targets, tends to be labeled 'terrorism' by Israel and its supporters" (Holt 2010: 368). Uses of violence that are labeled "terrorism" tend to be understood differently than other uses of violence. They are widely discredited and often depicted in essentialist terms.

There is some debate among scholars about the use of the terms terrorist and terrorism. Some scholars prefer to use terms like militancy (Parashar 2011) or resistance movements (Holt 2010) over terrorism or terrorist organizations. Organizations that are included on terrorist watch lists and feature in scholarly works on terrorism do not identify themselves in those terms (Sylvester and Parashar 2009). They are more likely to view themselves, and be viewed by their supporters, as fighters with a legitimate right to use violence towards their goals. Thus, the common question of whether a group should be labeled as terrorists or "freedom fighters" (Sluka 2009: 142). This distinction is raised frequently in discussions about organizations who use violence in struggles for independence or self-determination.

Counterterrorism

Terrorism scholarship and policymaking involves not only an examination of movements and organizations that use violence, but also an examination of potential policies to halt terrorism. At its most basic level, counterterrorism refers to strategies to stop or reduce terrorist attacks. Some states have distinguished between counterterrorism (which is related to offensive strategies) and antiterrorism (which is related to defensive strategies). The international community is marked by a long history of states adopting counterterrorism measures; however a spate of new counterterrorism legislation was issued after 9/11 by states as diverse as Australia, Canada, India, Jamaica, South Africa, Tanzania, the United Kingdom, and the US, among others (Jackson et al. 2011). Despite the similarity in timing, these states have adopted a range of counterterrorism strategies, some of which are extremely different in scope and method. Jackson et al. (2011: 231) argue "[r]esponses to terrorism can be usefully considered under four broad approaches: the use of force; intelligence and policing; homeland security; and conciliation and dialogue." They go on to argue that conciliation and dialogue approaches were widely used in the pre-9/11 era, while force-based approaches became more widely used in the days after the attacks. Despite these general trends, there remains a great deal of diversity among the strategies that individual states adopt (Katzenstein 2003; Rees and Aldrich 2005; Wolfendale 2006).

Critical approaches to terrorism evaluate counterterrorism strategies for how they impact security at multiple levels. Since violent counterterrorism measures can negatively impact security at an individual level, critical terrorism scholars have argued that these policies need just as much evaluation as the phenomenon of terrorism itself (Toros and Gunning 2009). A society that is characterized by militarism is very likely to adopt militarized responses to terrorism. These militarized responses have a range of potential impacts for society beyond their original goal of having an influence on the likelihood of terrorist attacks. A militarized understanding of terrorism results in terrorists being viewed as engaging in warfare rather than criminal activities. The United States' militarized response to 9/11 will be discussed below, and serves as a clear example of militarization guiding policymaking. Richard Jackson (2009: 74) explains:

> [T]he global counterterrorism campaign known as the "war on terror" is based on a particular series of defining narratives. The most important narrative at the heart of the war on terror is the notion that the attacks of 11 September 2001 amounted to an "act of war." This narrative in turn, logically implies that a war-based counterterrorism strategy is both necessary to counter the threat and legal under international law. Consequently, a great many terrorism studies texts take it as axiomatic or common sense that the war on terror, and force-based counterterrorism in general, is both legitimate and efficacious. In this way, the notion that responding to terrorism requires force and counter-violence, and

sometimes even war and torture, has come to assume a form of
widely accepted "knowledge."

This suggests that terrorism and counterterrorism discourses fundamentally guide the policymaking process as well as security studies.
Post-9/11 counterterrorism policies in the US, UK and Australia were
guided by discourses of terrorism that portrayed terrorist threats as
undermining "our way of life" and "civilization" (Wolfendale 2006).
These discourses led to counterterrorism policies that clashed with
civil rights, and in some cases human rights and human security.
A feminist curiosity enables us to evaluate the role and impact of
gender in these guiding discourses.

Terrorism as Gendered Phenomenon

An important piece of the examination of terrorism through gender
lenses is to dispute the assumption that terrorists are men. This is
part of a larger feminist task of challenging the understanding of
women as peaceful and men as violent. Jean Bethke Elshtain's (1987:
4) foundational discussion of beautiful souls and just warriors was an
important step in this process. Women are understood to be peaceful, beautiful souls, while men are cast as violent – either eagerly
or reluctantly. She argued "these tropes on the social identities of
men and women, past and present, do not denote what men and
women *really* are in time of war, but function instead to re-create and
secure women's location as noncombatants and men's as warriors."
This dichotomy between beautiful souls and just warriors serves to
make men's violence ordinary or expected and women's violence
unthinkable. While there are a variety of understandings of gender
across societies, this supposition that women are peaceful tends to
be prevalent across many of them. Once these tropes become com-
monplace in society, the thinking becomes: of course men would
serve in militaries and terrorist organizations, they are the violent
ones. An extension of this thinking is that when women are violent,
there needs to be an explanation furnished for this behavior. It is not
viewed as natural.

This assumption that women's violence needs explanation stems from the idea that by engaging in violence, women are violating their nature as a beautiful soul. Laura Sjoberg and Caron Gentry (2007) have argued that across different ideas about what women *ought* to be, there tends to be a standard for women to be nonviolent. When women then break this standard, they are typically understood to be "bad" women. This is in contrast to violent men, who might be seen as bad individuals or bad citizens, but not as bad *men*. In other words, the violent act does not challenge most dominant ideas of masculinity. Sjoberg and Gentry (2007: 9) explain:

> [W]omen who commit acts of violence in defiance of national or international law are not seen as criminals, warriors or terrorists, but as *women criminals, women warriors,* or *women terrorists*. The operative element of this characterization is that these narratives include a group that is "suicide bombers" or "war criminals" or "perpetrators of genocide" and a separate group that is women who would otherwise be members of those groups but for their femininity. Because women who commit these violences have acted outside of a prescribed gender role, they have to be separated from the main/malestream discourse of their particular behavior.

Violent women in many cases are perceived as separate from the rest of their sex; people who require explanation and understanding because of the severity of the breach of "acceptable" behavior.

These struggles of portraying and understanding violent women are particularly acute when discussing terrorism. Females involved in terrorism go against nearly every accepted version of femininity. These actions are often explained away in an attempt to get back to societal understandings of masculinity and femininity. The need to explain women's association with terrorism illustrates how the phenomenon of terrorism is gendered. Terrorism is a complex process, but one in which "gender relations happen among members of terrorist organizations, between terrorist organizations and their target audiences, between terrorist organizations and states, and between states" (Sjoberg et al. 2011: 7). There has been recent growth in feminist scholarship on terrorism alongside other mainstream and critical approaches to terrorism research (Sylvester 2010). This section draws on this feminist scholarship in order to question many of the key assumptions about terrorism and the strategies used to address terrorism. Much of this scholarship challenges us to rethink the ways we understand the very concept of terrorism. For example, many feminist security scholars are critical of the tendency to draw a stark line between states and nonstate actors in terrorism scholarship. They view it as indicative of a larger trend in viewing states as protectors of "vulnerable" citizens without critically examining this role. Sjoberg (2009: 71) claims "the state's security is often won at the price of the security of its marginalized citizens. If that is true, the dichotomy between terrorists and counterterrorists is artificially stark." This critique also extends to the types of violence that are typically examined in both terrorism scholarship and policymaking. These areas are typically concerned with killings and bombings that are perceived as gender-neutral, but what about the use of wartime rape? Should this be included in definitions of terrorism? One of the motivations for wartime rape is spreading intimidation and fear in a rival population. This speaks to the second major component of most definitions of terrorism – the intentional use of violence in order to cause fear. Additionally, what happens when we challenge the gender-neutrality of terrorist attacks? There is evidence to suggest that many suicide bombings claim a higher number of female victims because of their location and timing (Sjoberg 2009). These are the kinds of issues that are raised when we examine international terrorism through gender lenses.

Discourses of terrorism are deeply gendered in ways that echo the gendered nature of processes of militarization as well as peacekeeping. Men are seen as those who take action, and women are the passive members of society, typically in need of protection. Christine Sylvester and Swati Parashar (2009: 181) argue:

> Again, the fate of terror women can seem to be in hands other
> than their own. We know of state veiling and unveiling of women.
> We hear daily of honor killing of women to preserve the good
> name of their families. We heard Laura Bush, wife of George
> W. Bush, speak out early in the post-September 11 lead-up to
> war about the importance of liberating Afghan women from the

> Taliban government. Women are taken hostage by insurgent
> groups in Columbia, the Philippines, Iraq, and elsewhere, and
> sometimes are rescued by state forces . . . Today, women can be
> fought over, humiliated, or protected by states and terrorists alike.

Women often get tangled up in the protection racket of states. They
are portrayed as actors without agency or fragile entities that need a
strong state to protect them. It is important to note at the outset that
there is not a single set of experiences that women have related to
terrorism. Women have been the victims of terrorist attacks, their
treatment and situation has been used to justify actions against terrorist networks, they participate in counterterrorism missions, and
they participate in terrorist plots. Despite this variety of roles, women
are often assumed to be passive victims or conflicted supporters of
terrorism.

It is important to understand the ramifications of depicting women
as passive and men as active. It impacts scholarly understanding of
terrorism, but also the counterterrorism policies of states and international actors. Beyond this, it is also essential to understand how
terrorist organizations are gendered. One of the most obvious topics
to explore in this section is the experiences of women in and around
terrorist groups. Women have a long history of being affiliated with
terrorist organization, from their involvement with the Russian nihil-
ist organization Narodnaya Vola in the late nineteenth century to
their participation in Al-Qaeda today (Gentry and Sjoberg 2011). It
is also necessary to understand how terrorist organizations are gendered even when women are not visible. Women play different roles
in and around terrorism, some supportive and some opposing, and
each of these roles is shaped by gender expectations and norms.

Women and/in Terrorist Groups

Terrorist organizations routinely have women associated with them,
however, like most militarized institutions, they have often been
institutions dominated by masculinity. Men typically make up the
leadership of these groups, and the discourses used by them (as well

as those used to describe them) are masculine (Ferber and Kimmel 2008). For example, over time the Palestinian struggle has become both more militarized and more masculine. Maria Holt (2010: 373) explains that the first Palestinian uprising, or *intifada*, which took place between 1987 and 1993, was marked by the participation of large segments of society, including large number of women who joined street protests and participated in neighborhood committees. This has changed somewhat in the second intifada which "was characterised by armed struggle, which tended to take place on the margins of communities, and by much greater violence, which permeated all areas of life. As a result, opportunities for women became increasingly limited and many women report feeling excluded from the public and political sphere." This report suggests that as the movement became militarized, women's place in it changed.

Terrorist organizations can be infused with masculinity in both their discourses and actions. For example, there are reports that Mohammed Atta, the most well-known 9/11 attacker, specified in his last will and testament that he did not want women to attend his funeral, nor did he want a pregnant woman or a person who is "not clean" to visit his grave (Sylvester and Parashar 2009: 182). There are also reports that Atta and others visited strip clubs and had lap dances shortly before boarding the planes on September 11 (Brison 2002). These actions must be examined through gender lenses in order to reveal how they fit in to larger associations of masculinity and femininity in society. The behavior of these men is interesting because it speaks to standards of acceptable behavior that are gendered.

Many scholars have noted terrorist organizations using and reinforcing gender norms (Berkowitz 2005; Ferber and Kimmel 2008; Qazi 2011). Again, while it is important to avoid essentialization, there have been patterns of the presence and absence of women in terrorist groups. Women who join militant groups can find themselves in similar positions within these organizations. Farhana Qazi (2011: 29–30) explains that because of their gender "women are often viewed as more alluring, attractive, and agile by violent male-dominated groups. The perception that women can strap on a bomb and perpetrate successful terrorist attacks compels Muslim men to reconsider 'hiring' women even when conservative members argue against a woman's involvement." On January 27 2002, 28-year-old Wafa Idris became the first woman known for suicide terrorism for the Palestinian cause. Idris killed herself and an elderly man and wounded 150 people in a Jerusalem shopping street after detonating a bomb. There has been speculation about whether she intended to kill herself or just to plant the bomb; however, in the aftermath of the attack she has widely become recognized as the first known woman to engage in suicide terrorism in the Middle East (Schweitzer 2008). Earlier that same day, Yassir Arafat addressed a group reported to include more than one thousand women at his compound in Ramallah. He called these women "my army of roses that will crush Israeli tanks" (Berkowitz 2005). He encouraged the women to join the armed resistance against Israeli occupation. Calling militant women roses is a telling statement about perceptions of masculinity and femininity. It is unlikely that a group of militant men would be referred to as flowers. The depiction of women, even militant women, as flowers contrasts with the idea of their crushing tanks. Their femininity in some ways is retained, even when they are being called on to engage in behavior that violates most standards of femininity.

The international community has repeatedly reacted to women engaging in suicide terrorism with shock. In fact, in response to an attack featuring a female terrorist in March 2002 George W. Bush said, "When an 18-year-old Palestinian girl is induced to blow herself up and in the process kills a 17-year-old Israeli girl, the future is dying" (quoted in Ness 2005: 353). This quote suggests that what is found shocking is the fact that it involves two girls rather than suicide terrorism in general. It is reported that former Iraqi President Saddam Hussein looked at the first attack by a Palestinian female suicide bomber as a way for the West to be shaken. He said it may make them ask "What is this injustice suffered by the Arabs in general and the Palestinians in particular that could prompt women to carry out fedayeen operations? Moreover, this operation will impact on men, all men, in the Arab homeland. The fact that women have turned themselves into rifles will evoke men's sense of shame before their own women, before God, and before themselves" (quoted in Hasso 2005: 37). Again, the response was to anticipate a strong reaction to the attacks and to view them as an important shift in the conflict itself. Additionally, Hussein's comments serve as a rebuke to men for not living up to their manliness and requiring women to do their jobs in the fighting. This tendency to use female suicide bombers as a way to shame men into supporting or participating in a violent struggle continues in Iraq today (Stone and Pattillo 2011). These perceptions trace back to societal assumptions about gender, and should be included in how we understand terrorism and terrorist organizations.

Many organizations associated with terrorism have incorporated ideas of appropriate masculinities and femininities into their ideologies. In some cases these are relatively constraining ideas, and in other cases groups have expressed a commitment to women's rights. "Some revolutionary movements use 'women' as symbols of liberation and modernization, encouraging them to dress as they wish, to aspire to professional positions, and even to participate in the military" (Sylvester and Parashar 2009: 184). In particular, the Liberation Tigers of Tamil Eelam (LTTE), a movement for a separate Tamil homeland in Sri Lanka, listed women's emancipation as an aspect of the revolution. Beyond the Tamil Tigers, the Revolutionary Armed Forces of Colombia (FARC), and the Shining Path of Peru have expressed commitment to gender equality as a part of their revolutionary goals (Gentry and Sjoberg 2011).

Female Terrorists

The phenomenon of female terrorists who play an active role in attacks has received a great deal of attention by both scholars and the media. While terrorism touches the lives of many women either directly or indirectly, some women play a very active role in terrorist organizations. While women's engagement in terrorist activities is still lower than men's participation, there has been an increase in the number of terrorist organizations that are employing female terrorists. The Syrian Socialist National Party (SSNP) was the first organization to deploy a female suicide terrorist. This organization was a secular pro-Syrian Lebanese organization that was active in the 1980s in anti-Israeli campaigns. The LTTE was the next major group to employ women as bombers. The woman who detonated an explosive which killed Indian Prime Minister Rajiv Gandhi in 1991 was reportedly dispatched by the LTTE (Bloom 2005). The third group to employ women, the Kurdistan Worker's Party (PKK), was also using female suicide bombers in a campaign for a sovereign homeland. The PKK was formed in the mid-1970s to secure a sovereign homeland for the Kurdish population of southeastern Turkey. Similarly, in 2000 Chechen separatists became the fourth major group to adopt female suicide terrorism. Chechen terrorists have used women in several high-profile cases of attacks on Russian military and civilian targets. Women have most recently been used as suicide bombers by organizations from the Palestinian territories and Iraq (O'Rourke 2009).

Since 2000, there have been well over one hundred terrorist campaigns that have featured women. Female terrorists have been active in Afghanistan, India, Iraq, Israel, Lebanon, Pakistan, Russia, Somalia, Sri Lanka, Turkey, and Uzbekistan (O'Rourke 2009). One result of conceptualizing terrorism as beyond the natural realm of women is that female terrorists may have an easier time carrying out attacks. Because women are often considered to be beautiful souls who would not dream of engaging in violence, they are less likely to arouse suspicion. This may mean they are not stopped at checkpoints and may be less likely to be stopped by police forces. In fact, in January 2004 Hamas claimed it used a female bomber to carry out an attack "because of growing Israeli security 'obstacles' facing its male bombers" (MEED 2004: 3). Similarly, in 2005 a group of Iraqi insurgents dressed up as women and attacked a police checkpoint in the town of Buhriz. The attack resulted in the death of six police officers and the injury of a further ten (Wong 2005). Additionally, since there are cultural norms about searching the bodies of women, female terrorists may have an easier time concealing weapons or explosives. This is particularly true in many countries in North Africa and the Middle East (Qazi 2011). This concealment is even easier if women are active in societies where wearing loose, full-body coverings is common. This can allow them to carry explosives attached to their bodies. At the same time, it is difficult for security forces to actively search women for explosive devices because of cultural norms and because of a shortage of female soldiers or police officers in countries that anticipate terrorist attacks, like Iraq (Stone and Pattillo 2011). These examples show that organizations have taken advantage of the fact that society sees women as nonthreatening and treats them differently from men. Similarly, female bombers in Chechnya, Palestinian/Israel, Kurdish regions, and Sri Lanka have feigned pregnancy in order to conceal additional explosives on their bodies (Zedalis 2008; O'Rourke 2009). Given the discourses of maternalism that often accompany understandings of femininity, this is an interesting example of using the accepted idea of women as mothers to make them more effective killers (Gentry 2009).

Heightened shock value is another tactical advantage terrorist organizations have anticipated receiving from using female terrorists, particularly those involved in suicide terrorism. Because most societies view women as peaceful, it becomes seen as shocking when they are not. This is magnified when the terrorist attack involves suicide terrorism. Suicide terrorism can be defined as "a motivated violent attack, perpetrated by a self-aware individual or individuals actively and willingly killing themselves along with their chosen targets" (Haddad 2009). As demonstrated in the quotes by George W. Bush and Saddam Hussein, suicide bombings carried out by women are depicted as particularly noteworthy. Some organizations have tried to capitalize on these perceptions within society (Cunningham 2003).

Several feminist scholars have studied where female terrorists seem to be most prevalent. While female terrorists typically make up a small percentage of most terrorist organizations and carry out a small percentage of overall terrorist attacks worldwide, there are some types of organizations that seem more willing to employ or accept female terrorists. The first organizations to employ women as suicide bombers were secular organizations. This is consistent with a larger trend of women tending to be more active in secular over religious terrorist organizations. Indeed, nearly 85 percent of attacks conducted by women have been carried out on behalf of secular organizations (O'Rourke 2009). In the 1960s and 1970s women were active in violent left-wing organizations across several countries. Even into the 1980s and 1990s, women participated almost exclusively in secular organizations. It is important to point out that even though there was some participation of women in these secular organizations, they still often played support roles and rarely held leadership positions within the organizations (Cunningham 2008; Ness 2005).

Most scholars attribute this lack of female involvement in religious terrorism to the powerful significance that religious extremism places on females remaining in traditional roles (Ness 2005). This may imply that woman are not actively sought out or recruited by many religious terrorist organizations, and also that women may not actively seek involvement even if they are supportive of the organization's goals and tactics. While it is true women have not played an active role in most religious terrorist organizations, there is evidence that this might be changing. In 2004, a religious Palestinian organization, Hamas, claimed responsibility for an attack carried out by a female terrorist. Some argue the shift can be attributed to the tactical advantages of deploying women as bombers. As was discussed previously, religious organizations have seen that female bombers are less likely to be thoroughly searched and are often able to go unnoticed to target sites. The attacks carried out by women are also given a greater degree of discussion within society. Likely for these reasons, religious organizations like Hamas, Palestinian Islamic Jihad (PIJ), and Al-Qaeda in Iraq have all deployed female bombers in recent years. Despite this increase, there are debates about how female terrorists are viewed within Islamic organizations. Farhana Qazi (2011: 32) explains:

> The debate among male terrorists about the *mujahidaat* (literally, female fighters) is part of an ongoing discourse among members of al-Qaeda and other terrorist or insurgent groups. Leading clerics and some Muslim scholars offer varying legal opinions, or fatwas, on the permissibility of female suicide bombers, but most agree that women have served in important supporting roles, and indeed there is ample evidence within classical Islamic scholarship that this is the case. For example, early Muslim women in seventh-century Arabia nursed the wounded, protected their homes when men left to fight in the early battles, and in a few well-documented cases, trained and fought valiantly alongside men to ensure the faith's survival.

This illustrates that incorporating women into fighting roles is not something regarded as unproblematic by members of religious militant organizations. Instead, it is something that requires discussion and justification. Hamas, PIJ, and Al-Qaeda in Iraq has kept the proportion of female attackers low, at around 3 percent, and have even required that female bombers be chaperoned to their destination by male organization members. This may be an intentional strategy to prevent the alienation of male supporters who may find the idea of female terrorists problematic (O'Rourke 2009).

Representations of Female Terrorists

The ways society understands violent women is important for reflecting on issues of gender more broadly. There has been a clear tendency to depict female terrorists as exceptions to the rule of peaceful women in the global media, and in some instances, within academic scholarship. There is a fascination with female terrorists by the media that goes above and beyond the typical media response to violent incidents. Even if the number of casualties from an attack carried out by a woman is small, it tends to generate a large amount of news attention. Not only do violent women receive more media coverage, but they also receive different kinds of media coverage. A consistent trend in the coverage of female terrorists is speculation about the motivations of the women who engage in terrorism (Friedman 2008; O'Rourke 2009; Sjoberg et al. 2011). It appears that women's violence requires explanation in ways that men's violence does not. Male terrorists can be understood to be engaging in activities that do not fundamentally challenge gender norms in most societies. Violence tends to be carried out more frequently by men than by women. Because of this, women who engage in violence are regarded as shocking and in some sense unintelligible. It is important to understand media representations of violent women because they give us clues about the dominant discourses surrounding gender as well as terrorism. The media is an important vehicle for the transmission of ideas of what is acceptable, appropriate, and possible in society. The way they represent female terrorists offers a glimpse of the ways that women's violence is understood.

Early examples of the depiction of female terrorists in Spain and West Germany in the 1970s relate to some of the above points. Patricia Melzer (2009) explores the representation of female members of the left-wing militant group Red Army Faction (Rote Armee Fraktion or RAF) in the West German press following a high-profile, violent incident involving the group. At the height of the group's activities, more than 50 percent of its members were women. Melzer finds that the media largely dismissed the women as "terrorist girls" and demonized them as "wild furies." The media portrayals overwhelmingly present these violent women as aberrations of femininity. These women are not-quite-women because they engage in behavior that is typically reserved for standards of masculinity. They violate an image of women as passive and non-violent. It is particularly striking that women from the RAF were portrayed this way when there were so many women who were actively involved in the organization. In fact, some argue that two women in particular, Ulrike Meinhof and Gudrun Ensslin, provided some of the most significant leadership of the group through rallying members and providing the ideology that fundamentally shaped the organization (Gentry and Sjoberg 2011).

During a comparable timeframe of the 1970s, female members of the Basque separatist organization ETA were represented in the Basque and Spanish media as the girlfriends of male members who were lulled into the organization against their will or even against their knowledge. In fact, many female ETA activists were absolved or given lighter prison sentences than their male counterparts by judges who were presented with the defense that the women were just following orders or were coerced into participation by a male member. This portrayal shifted in the late 1970s and 1980s to something similar to the representation of West German women's engagement with political violence as evidence of "bad" women. The Spanish press began quoting police sources who called female ETA militants "dangerous elements." In many reports women's armed activism is directly linked to perceived sexual deviance – either promiscuity or lesbianism (Hamilton 2007). These descriptions demonstrate the above-mentioned discussion that violent women are seen as requiring some kind of explanation.

Some may point out that the above examples are from the 1970s and 1980s, and ideas about gender have changed in much of the world since that time. So, are violent females portrayed differently now? In many ways, female terrorists continue to be framed as either violations of femininity or as fragile women who have been manipulated into engaging in violence. Studies of more recent media coverage of female terrorism suggest that there is a range of motivations that are typically suggested for why women would involve themselves in terrorism. These include several that have already been mentioned, including the influence of men, and the desperation that comes from being unable to fulfill society's expectations of being married and having children. Two other motivations often mentioned are revenge, typically revenge for the death of a close male family member, and liberation. Liberation or political commitment is rarely offered as an exclusive reason for why women engage in terrorism. There is almost always the suggestion that rather than being solely motivated by the goals of the organization, female terrorists have some deep personal reason for engaging in violence (Friedman 2008). Some studies actually find there is little difference in the motivations of men and women to engage in terrorism (O'Rourke 2009). If this is accurate, then it is important to understand why there is an assertion to the contrary. As has been repeated time and again throughout this book, examining issues in security studies through gender lenses results in rethinking what are taken to be "natural" assumptions. Currently, there appears to be an assumption that men and women are such different creatures (i.e. one is prone to violence and the other peace) that if they are both engaging in terrorism there must be a different explanation for both.

Another fascinating trend is for the physical traits of female terrorists to be discussed in much greater frequency than their male counterparts (Emmanuel 2002; Friedman 2008; Nacos 2008). Reports about female terrorists are often accompanied by descriptions of their hair, bodies, clothing, etc. This can be seen in media reports of Idoia López Riaño, a Basque fighter who has been accused of 23 assassinations and who's widely used nickname is "the Tigress." Reports throughout the 1990s routinely include descriptions of her appearance ("tall," "green eyes," "magnificent beauty," "spectacular physique," "slave to her body and her hair") (Hamilton 2007). Media reports of male terrorists rarely include these kinds of personal descriptions. Why is this the case? Why should the media think that we would be more curious about what female terrorists look like and dress like than male terrorists? Is it simply because there are fewer of them? Is it because they are the ones violating society's expectations of them? Is it to reaffirm their femininity in the face of this breach of gender norms? Is it to determine whether their physical appearance would make it less likely that they would be desirable as a marriage partner, thus offering some explanation for their motivation? These are questions that come about when we use a feminist curiosity to explore the subject of terrorism.

Terrorism and "Othering"

Terrorism discourses in the media, scholarly community, and policymaking community are marked by the idea of exceptionality and othering. This othering links to perceptions of race, ethnicity, and gender. Terrorists are viewed as exceptional actors, despite the fact that they are not the only actors in societies that use violence. They are viewed as something outside, an other to be explained. In the current era, when a terrorist attack occurs in a state in the global North, the first response by the media is to look outside the state for the culprit(s). This was clearly visible in the aftermath of the attack in Norway in the summer of 2011. On July 22, Norway experienced a deadly attack in and around Oslo which resulted in the deaths of 77 people. When news of the attack first hit the international community there was immediate suspicion that a militant Islamic organization must be responsible. There was speculation about motives, including Norway's involvement with NATO in Afghanistan. The story soon turned away from assigning blame to militant Muslims and instead blaming a native Norwegian who is said to be a fundamentalist right-wing anti-Muslim. Anders Behring Breivik is thought to have carried out the attack on his own, and has been charged under terrorism laws in Norway. Before the attacks, Breivik prepared a 1,518-page manifesto in which he rages against

Islam, multiculturalism, and feminism. He claimed that feminism "is bent on 'transforming a patriarchy into a matriarchy' and 'intends to deny the intrinsic worth of native Christian European heterosexual males.' But more than that, it has succeeded. The 'feminization of European culture' has been underway since the 1830s, and by now, men have been reduced to an 'emasculate[d] . . . touchy-feely subspecies'" (Jones 2011). This demonstrates multiple gendered dynamics at play within a single case. Society assumes that terrorists will be men, but non-white men. In the case of Norway, the attacker was a man, but without the identity or ideology that has dominated post-9/11 assumptions about terrorist motivations. He was motivated by his perceptions about what was acceptable or appropriate for Norway, including ideas about race, ethnicity, and gender. Sociologists have noted the prevalence of this perspective among groups who feel threatened by a perceived other. A terrorist reaction to this perspective is not a new occurrence. Abby Ferber and Michael Kimmel (2008: 875) note several entwined themes that run through their research on terrorist organizations: "the experience of humiliation; the attempt to recover something that is believed to have been lost; and the attempt to reassert masculinity."

Militant groups engage in othering the society that they fight against, while at the same time society engages in othering those same groups. This process of othering has been observed in several cases of terrorist groups, including groups who use violence in the course of the Chechen conflict. This conflict is often characterized as being fought between the Russian state and "desperate" Chechen groups. This desperation is tied to ideas of hysteria and irrationality, both of which are associated with femininity. Caron Gentry and Kathryn Whitworth (2011: 145) explain that:

> In Chechnya, women's involvement in the conflict is used as a reference point by the media to indicate just how desperate the society-in-conflict is. This gender dynamic is then blamed upon radical Islamic forces, solidifying the neo-Orientalist gaze. This intersection of gender and race undermines and obfuscates the legitimacy and credibility of the Chechen cause, without differentiating between legitimate cause and/or actors and illegitimate methods of violence.

Even though Chechen militants are typically Muslim, many studies find that they are motivated by nationalist rather than religious goals or alternatively nationalist goals coupled with religious justification (Ness 2008; Speckhard and Akhmedova 2008). Associating Chechen actors with terrorism, and Islamic terrorism in particular, closes off debate about why these individuals are choosing to engage in violence.

The Chechen case also exhibits othering through the depiction of female Chechen terrorists as "black widows" or zombies. Women have become a central feature of the Chechen resistance movement against Russia. Chechen factions have used women as suicide bombers with deadly results. Suicide bombing was not used during the first phase of the conflict between 1993/1994 and 1996, but was employed in the second phase of the conflict and became associated with women rather quickly. June 7, 2000 marked the first attack carried out by women. Khava Barayeva and Luisa Magomadova drove a truck packed with explosives into a Russian Special Forces headquarters in Chechnya. Since this attack, there have been many others carried out either exclusively by women, or along with men. Two of these were large mass hostage-taking events – the takeover of the Moscow Dubrovka Theater in 2002, and the Beslan school in North Ossetia in 2004. Additionally, women have taken part in some of the deadliest strikes, including the coordinated bombings of two passenger flights in August 2004 that caused 90 deaths, and twin attacks on the Moscow subway in March 2010 that killed around 40 people (Pape et al. 2010). In fact, the average number of casualties per attack by Chechen women is 20.9, while it is 13.3 for men (O'Rourke 2009).

Chechen female suicide bombers have become known as "black widows," a name evoking the image of either a deadly insect or a classic femme fatale. These black widows are said to be women who are driven to terrorism after the death of a husband or other close male relative at the hands of Russian forces or in the course of the independence struggle. This idea of losing a family member in some way relates to a revenge motive, but also is frequently linked to being a woman on her own in a society where that status will be regarded as problematic. In reality, some of the female suicide bombers have lost relatives during the conflict, but others have not. The Russian government has adopted the term black widows for the female suicide bombers; a term which essentially denies these women political agency and locates their motivations in the private realm rather than the public one. Rather than understand the female terrorists as being motivated by political goals, they are seen as grief-stricken, which possibly clouds their judgment, or that they have become desperate without a husband or father to depend on. In fact, when a terrorist attack features a woman it has become routine to look for evidence of the death of a loved one. In a report about an attack in July 2003 in which a woman blew herself up at the entrance to a Moscow music festival a *New York Times* reporter wrote that "little seems to explain" why the woman would do such a thing. He went on to report that the woman in question, Zulikhan Elikhadzhiyeva, had "no dead father, husband, brother or son to motivate her" (Friedman 2008: 847). Many individuals, both male and female, who join terrorist organizations have lost loved ones in the course of a conflict, but this likely speaks more to the dangers of living through a conflict than a gender-differentiated explanation of terrorist motivations (Zedalis 2008).

The Russian government has also been quick to explain the phenomenon of female suicide bombers by claiming Chechens sell their women into terrorism, or else women are drugged or forced into terrorism. Despite the fact that there is little evidence to substantiate these claims, they persist in discussions of Chechen terrorism (Sjoberg 2009). An adviser to the Russian president has claimed "Chechens are turning these girls into zombies using psychotropic drugs. I have heard that they rape them and record the rapes on video" (Friedman 2008: 847). Several reports on female terrorists in Chechnya use the term *zombirovaniye* or "turned into zombies" to describe the process of women being brainwashed into terrorism. The idea of zombification implies that these women are changed from something natural, perhaps a nonviolent, nurturing woman, to something unnatural and horrifying like a zombie or a violent woman that kills innocent civilians, including children. Like the term black widow, the idea of zombification is a simplification that suggests that "good" women are transformed into "bad" women which explains why they would engage in an activity that violates the standards of acceptable behavior, and particularly acceptable female behavior. Beyond this, most studies find that it is false. Andrzej Zaucha has written about the phenomenon of Chechen female terrorists, and argues that the Russian government is being strategic when they portray Chechen women as zombie killers. He claims that "[o]fficially, according to the Russian authorities, things are not so bad in Chechnya, so they don't want anyone to believe these women would have their own grounds for committing these crimes – they want us to think they have been forced or brainwashed" (quoted in Groskop 2004: 33). The tendency to portray Chechen women as black widows or zombies reflects a process of othering. Female terrorists are regarded as unnatural entities, which forestalls conversations about whether they are individuals with legitimate grievances against the state. This process of othering is widespread in media representations of terrorism, as well as some academic scholarship, and counterterrorism policies. The US "Global War on Terror" was a counterterrorism strategy that featured othering at its outset. It is an important case to examine because of the scope and scale of the policies that went along with it and the ramifications it had for a variety of actors across the international community.

US "Global War on Terror" Through Gender Lenses

Although terrorism has been a tactic used throughout history, the international community has focused on it as a growing phenomenon in the last few decades. A turning point for how terrorism is understood in the US came with the attacks on 9/11. Although the US had experienced terrorist attacks before 2001, 9/11 represented a new scale of the phenomenon felt in the country. The experience of 9/11, to have a strike on US soil that caused the death of thousands of civilians, has been understood by various scholars as presenting a challenge to the United States' sense of self. It revealed vulnerability and was perceived as necessitating a shift in conceptualizing an "enemy." An enemy could be inside the borders of the state rather than outside the state. The counterterrorism response by the US government, under the administration of George W. Bush, to the attacks in New York and Washington DC was to launch a "Global War on Terror." This endeavor has resulted in direct military confrontation/occupation of first Afghanistan, then Iraq by US military forces. It has also resulted in the detention of individuals suspected of terrorism at US detention facilities like Guantanamo Bay in Cuba, which in 2002 was designated as the central prison for suspects considered "unlawful enemy combatants." This section uses gender lenses to explore the ideas behind the US "Global War on Terror" as well as activities that have taken place under its heading.

What does it mean to fight a "Global War on Terror"? Terror is perceived to be that which makes us vulnerable to the strategy of terrorism. If a population were to not feel fear or terror in the aftermath of an attack, then terrorism as a tactic would not be effective. Is that what the US government had in mind when they launched the "Global War on Terror"? The government of the United Kingdom felt more comfortable with the label the "war against terrorism" in their discussions of support for US policies after 9/11. Since US policies under the "Global War on Terror" centered on finding states and organizations that harbor, aid, and comprise terrorists, this might have been a more appropriate label. Does the fact that the US government chose to identify "terror" rather than "terrorism" as the target of the endeavor suggest anything? Some have argued it is actually telling that the Bush administration named the emotion of terror as the thing under attack rather than the tactic of terrorism in general. If you are convinced that language is powerful and choices of language have meaning, as many feminist scholars do, then this choice might suggest that the Bush administration's policy choices were guided by a reaction to the feeling of vulnerability as much as a reaction to the event of 9/11.

One result of the "Global War on Terror" has been a form of resurgence in the respect for military masculinity. As discussed in Chapter 2, military masculinity has long been a highly valued version of masculinity across societies. The post-9/11 period saw a revival of the notion of hypervalorized male military protection and rescue (Peterson and Runyan 2010). In fact, the "Global War on Terror" has "been presented as a hyper-masculine war where virile and aggressive men, fighting for the honor of their nations, and freedom, lead the forces on either side" (Parashar 2010: 169). Most of the images and voices represented in the days after 9/11 were overwhelmingly masculine. This goes beyond the fact that most were male (something that regularly occurs in the political realm) and suggests that their message reflected a particular form of masculinity (Shepherd 2006). President Bush led the way with sound-bites such as "[e]ither you are with us, or you are with the terrorists," which he declared on September 20, 2001. This statement was directed at states in the international system, however it symbolizes an "us versus them" war that was portrayed as being about "good versus evil." The result of these simplistic dichotomies is to shut down debate and mask the complexities involved in any conflict.

Many of the analyses of US actions after 9/11 contrast orientalism on one hand and occidentialism on the other (Nayak 2006; Nusair 2008; Tickner 2002). These studies use the concepts popularized by Edward Said (1978) and others to reveal how this "us versus them" conflict was created on both sides. The Middle East is situated in the exotic "orient," which is seen as fundamentally different from "us." The orient is depicted as mysterious as well as "dark, impure and dangerous" (Nayak 2006: 43). People from the region came to be seen with suspicion. Meghana Nayak (2006: 46) argues that "Orientalism enables the simplistic division of the world into the Orient, or the hotbed of terrorism, ignorance, poverty, oppression, racism and misogyny, and the US-led West, or the savior, beacon of light and teacher of democracy and equality *par excellence*." The dominant narratives after 9/11 painted the Middle East as a largely homogenous region which suffered from these flaws. This may have helped with the process of shifting the focus of the "Global War on Terror" from Afghanistan to Iraq despite the multitude of differences in the circumstances of the two states. One facet of this process involved raising attention to the status of women. Focus was placed on the treatment of women in Afghanistan in particular and the Middle East in general as evidence of "their" backwardness and "our" progress, with very little said about the gender inequalities that still pervade the West.

On the other hand, voices within Al-Qaeda and beyond also depicted an ideal-type enemy. The US, as an extreme version of the

West in general, was the occident. The traits associated with the occident were "materialism, liberalism, capitalism, individualism, humanism, rationalism, socialism, decadence, and moral laxity" (Buruma and Margalit 2002). Feminism can also be added to this list. In a 1998 interview with al-Jazeera, Osama bin Laden equated women's participation in traditionally male spheres with weakness. He claimed:

> Our brothers who fought in Somalia saw wonders about the weakness, feebleness, and cowardliness of the US soldier . . . We believe that we are men, Muslim men who must have the honour of defending [Mecca]. We do not want American women soldiers defending [it] . . . The rulers in that region have been deprived of their manhood. And they think that the people are women. By God, Muslim women refuse to be defended by these American and Jewish prostitutes. (Quoted in Judt 2001)

For both sides, the treatment of women and women's place in society was associated with confirming their identity (we have the "right" outlook on women) and solidifying the evils of the other. Women and gender relations were superficially the subject of debate without actually spurring reflection at a deep level. The appropriate or possible role of women was largely being discussed by men in a heavily masculinized environment. For both sides, women were still overwhelmingly seen as "beautiful souls" that they were fighting for – either women who are at risk from being exposed to the decadent, immoral values of the West or women who are at risk from the violent, backward actions of the Orient.

This process of othering and the possible ramifications of it became the subject of debate when the story broke of US forces engaging in the torture of individuals captured in the course of the wars in Afghanistan and Iraq. Several of the most outrageous of these stories centered on prisoner abuse in Iraq. Abu Ghraib, a penal compound west of Baghdad, gained worldwide media attention in 2004 when photos were released that showed American soldiers mistreating Iraqi prisoners. These photos showed naked prisoners stacked like human pyramids, prisoners on all fours being led on a dog leash, prisoners being made to simulate sex acts. Most media outlets in the US and elsewhere reported on the story with a sense of shock that this could take place. Other voices expressed less shock at the account. If the narrative used to justify a war centers on depicting an enemy as violent, dangerous, backwards individuals who are somehow less human, is it shocking when people involved in the conflict then treat "enemies" as animals? The military and the Bush administration explained the event as the poor behavior of a few "bad apples" within the bunch. They argued that it was not symptomatic of a larger trend of oppressing Afghan and Iraqi citizens, but rather an isolated incident. In general, this is not an isolated incident. This story of dehumanizing an enemy is not unique to the wars associated with the "Global War on Terror," but rather is a tradition with a long history in warfare. As discussed in Chapter 2, it becomes easier to witness and engage in the horrors of war if you can separate yourself from what is going on around you.

When the photos of prisoner abuse were released, the public was no longer separated from what was going on in the wars. The prisoners in the released photos were men. Most of the prisoners being held at Abu Ghraib were men, but there were some forty-two women among the population. Reports into prisoner abuse at Abu Ghraib, such as the widely cited Taguba Report which was the result of an inquiry into the scandal, highlight sexual abuse of female detainees along with the torture and abuse of male detainees. This abuse of female prisoners has not been the subject of much inquiry. In response to questions raised about the sexual abuse of female prisoners, a spokesman for the Multi-National Force in Iraq said there had been no allegations of rape made by any female detainees (Masters 2009). This suggests that the subject will not be investigated as long as the women involved are silent. Should we be surprised that they are silent? The stigma of sexual abuse makes their silence a safer option. When an investigation *was* launched in 2004 into the alleged rape of two women by four US soldiers on guard duty at a Baghdad shopping district the investigation was eventually closed for "lack of evidence." In documents about the investigation, soldiers interviewed claimed that they thought the women were prostitutes (Goldenberg 2005). This looks like an attempt to shift the narrative from abuse at the hands of a powerful actor to evidence of engaging in a sexual exchange with knowing parties. Now the blame can be placed on the women rather than the soldiers. It is a similar situation to sections of the Taguba Report which outline the existence of photographic evidence of male MP guards "having sex" with female prisoners (Harding 2004). Although not impossible, it seems unlikely that an equal relationship could have been forged between guard and prisoner which would make a sexual relationship completely consensual (Masters 2009).

Although these reports of sexual abuse of female detainees is an important occurrence within the "Global War on Terror," it did not get many headlines. Instead the headlines focused on the abuse and torture of male prisoners. Many of the photos released from Abu Ghraib showed detainees being dehumanized and humiliated in specific ways. Male prisoners were forced to strip naked, wear women's underwear, and simulate sex acts in front of each other and in front of female soldiers. Many scholars have argued that these represent not only an attempt to humiliate the detainees, but to humiliate them through feminizing them. "Feminization is a process of imposing allegedly feminine characteristics on a person – man or woman – or a group or a kind of activity. Often the goal of feminizing someone (or something) is to lower his (or its) status. Feminization provokes anxiety when particular forms of masculinity are culturally, academically, politically, or economically privileged" (Enloe 2007: 95). In this case, US soldiers used feminization to shame the enemy and to reinforce ideas of dominance (Nusair 2008; Richter-Montpetit 2007; Sjoberg 2007).

Additionally, many feminist scholars have paid particular attention to the fact that the media and society in general reacted differently to the participation of male and female soldiers in the torture and abuse. Three of the soldiers linked to torture were women – Megan Ambuhl, Lynndie England, and Sabrina Harman. Another woman, General Janis Karpinski, was the brigadier general in charge of the prisons in Iraq. General Karpinski is the only officer to have been relieved of her command and given a written reprimand over the charges. If the media reacted with shock that US soldiers were engaging in the dehumanization and humiliation of Iraqi prisoners, it reacted with even more distress that female soldiers were involved.

This reaction echoed the shock expressed when women engage in suicide terrorism – surely *women* weren't involved in that. In the case of the events at Abu Ghraib, there is photographic evidence that women *were* involved. There are pictures of Sabrina Harman, one of her smiling next to a pyramid of naked, hooded Iraqi prisoners and a second of her smiling over the corpse of a prisoner. There are also the two extremely well-known pictures of Lynndie England, one with a prisoner on a leash and another of her pointing at a prisoner's genitals while giving the "thumbs-up" sign (Sjoberg 2007). These pictures show that female soldiers were involved at least enough to know about the abuse and pose for pictures while it was taking place.

In many ways Lynndie England became the face of the Abu Ghraib scandal. Her name became intricately linked to the idea of prisoner abuse in Iraq. England was not the only person linked to the event, nor was she the only woman involved. Why has her name and story become so well known? Why is her name gotten more attention than Charles Graner, an Army reservist accused of leading the prisoner abuse and who was sentenced to 10 years in prison for his involvement? Cynthia Enloe (2007: 100) explains that:

> Women, by contrast, were conventionally expected by most
> editors and news watchers to appear in wartime as mothers
> and wives of soldiers, occasionally as military nurses and truck
> mechanics, and most often as victims of wartime violence.
> Women were not – according to the conventional presumption
> – supposed to be the wielders of violence and certainly not
> the perpetrators of torture. When those deeply gendered
> presumptions were turned upside down, many people felt a sense
> of shock.

England became the ultimate "bad apple" – a bad soldier whose behavior is even worse because it violates standards for acceptable behavior during wartime while simultaneously violating standards for acceptable female behavior. England violated these standards in multiple ways, by engaging in prisoner abuse, by getting pregnant before marriage, and even by not looking very feminine (Lobasz 2008).

It is revealing to contrast the portrayal of Lynndie England to those of Jessica Lynch (Just 2006; Lobasz 2008). Both were young women from small towns in West Virginia who wanted to join the military to see the world and make money to go to college. That is largely where the similarities end in terms of how the women are understood. As discussed in Chapter 2, Lynch became seen as what a female soldier ought to be – pretty, feminine, brave. On the other hand, England was portrayed as exhibiting many of the presumed reasons that women should not be soldiers – they will engage in sexual relationships with male soldiers (creating distractions and problems), and they will be unable to make tough calls under pressure.

Since the stories of Lynch and England, there have not been many widely recognizable women identified with the "Global War on Terror." When President Barack Obama was elected in 2008 there was a shift in US policy away from the idea of a war on terror, but a continuation of the conflicts in Iraq and Afghanistan albeit with some significant revisions. For one thing, there have been less of the heavily masculinized language and sentiments coming out of the Obama administration as compared to his predecessor. Additionally, there have been significant reductions in the scale of the operations in both Iraq and Afghanistan. The American military formally ended its mission in Iraq in December 2011, and President Obama has declared a significant reduction of troops involved in the conflict in Afghanistan. The US is expected to hand over security functions to the Afghan government by 2014 if not before. There are a number of points typically offered to explain these policies. First, this might be evidence that the US government is responding to a new economic reality and fierce domestic debates about government spending. Second, the US public may be frustrated with the long timeframe of the conflicts.

One of the recent events to capture the media's attention was the operation on May 2, 2011 launched by the US into Pakistan that resulted in the death of Osama bin Laden. Several elements of this event provide fodder for our feminist curiosity. Firstly, the individuals directly involved in the operation were overwhelmingly male. From the male members of elite "Seal Team 6" who carried out the mission, to the male target who became known as "public enemy #1," to the male President who kept a watchful eye over the operation, the event serves as a reminder of how much militarized counterterrorism remains the domain of men. In a photo released just after the raid which accompanied the story in most major newspapers, we saw President Obama sitting at a table in the White House Situation Room surrounded by men as he watched the operation unfold. There are only two women who make an appearance in the picture – Hiliary Clinton, the Secretary of State, and Audrey Tomason, a member of the National Security Council. The photo made even more headlines a few days later when news came out that it had been published in a Yiddish-language weekly in New York, *Di Tzeitung,* after being digitally altered to remove the two women in the frame. The publication later apologized for removing the images of the women and explained that they have a policy against showing the images of women in their publication (Mackey 2011). While this might strike some as a rather small event, feminist scholars may read it as a literal attempt to erase the presence of women in public life. When reality is altered in such a way that makes women's presence and voice invisible, no matter what the scale, it is important.

We also saw the role of women blurred in the account of the raid as the facts of the story came out in the days following it. The first story released by the Obama administration on the day of the raid claimed that Osama bin Laden had been killed after a firefight with Navy Seal commandos in which he used his wife as a human shield. Indeed, some headlines the day after the raid focused on his use of his spouse as a human shield. The next day, the administration claimed that bin Laden was not in fact armed and his wife had not been a shield. She had rushed toward the commandos and was shot in the leg (Bumiller 2011). Why the conflicting stories? Some of the confusion likely stems from the rapid flow of information and the difficulties in sorting fact from misperception in the wake of an event that everyone is rushing to cover, but why this particular misperception? Is anyone served by a narrative in which Osama bin Laden is painted as a coward who not only hides behind someone in the face of danger – but hides behind a *woman*? Was this an example of using gender norms, and a perceived failure to live up to them, to belittle an enemy? It is difficult to be certain, but it would not be very different from the feminization and othering that typically accompanies depicting an enemy.

"The Global War on Terror" is an illustrative example of both how gender is infused in strategies of othering that accompanies understandings of terrorism and the range of impacts that stem from militarized responses to terrorism. These counterterrorism policies have been evaluated by critical scholars for how they impact security broadly defined (McDonald 2009). This means going beyond a narrow understanding of counterterrorism as a set of policies designed to enhance the security of the state, to a view of counterterrorism that sees it as a set of policies designed to remove one source of insecurity, but that may result in a threat to the security of individuals. Counterterrorism can pose a security threat in a number of ways, including infringing on civil liberties and legal protections, and even injury or death during a militarized conflict. Jessica Wolfendale (2006) points to post-9/11 state policies as well as the past activities of military dictatorships in South America as evidence for the claim that the threat of terrorism has been used numerous times to justify a variety of policies, including undermining the right to privacy and the right to legal counsel as well as justifying the use of torture and secret trials. She goes on to argue that "[c]ounterterrorism legislation and practices therefore threaten not only actual terrorism suspects (who might be considered legitimate targets of these practices) and innocent people wrongly suspected of terrorism but the stability and democratic nature of states. If past practices are anything to go by, these counterterrorism measures threaten the lives and security of individuals and states to a greater degree than the threat posed by terrorism" (Wolfendale 2006: 764).

Counterterrorism policies can also be gendered. An example of this is the report that West German GSG 9 anti-terrorism force was ordered to "shoot the women first" (Jackson et al. 2011). This phrase became the title of a book about female terrorists by Eileen MacDonald and "grew out of the idea that women are supposed to be that much more ruthless and aggressive than men" (Gentry and Sjoberg 2011: 74). How we understand violent women dictates the policies that will be created to deal with them. If violent women are understood to be such an aberration that they become even more dangerous and aggressive than men, then we will get policies like "shoot the women first." For these reasons, it is essential that we think critically about terrorism and counterterrorism in ways that reflect the gendered nature of the phenomena.

Emancipation and Terrorism

Terrorism has a long history in the international community. It is a complex phenomenon that must be examined critically. Some actors view terrorism as an unforgivable offense that violates every standard of good behavior for society. Others remind us that movements or groups who are painted as terrorists regard themselves as legitimate combatants in a struggle for self-determination or some other goal. Our task now is to understand terrorism and terrorist organizations in all of their complexity. We do ourselves a great disservice if we use incorrect assumptions and misperceptions to understand terrorism. Overcoming this requires engaging in reflexive scholarship about why actors may choose to use the term terrorists to refer to an enemy, or the varied impacts of counterterrorism policies. This reflexive scholarship has not always been the norm in terrorism studies. Andrew Silke (2009: 46) asserts that "terrorism research is increasingly driven by a need to provide a short-term, immediate assessment of current groups and threats. Efforts to establish more contextualized and stable guiding principles have been almost entirely side-lined." Examining terrorism through gender lenses aid in reflecting critically on terrorism within the international community.

Gender lenses reveal that multiple actors in and around terrorism use gendered discourses and engage in gendered behavior. States evoke discourses of protection to justify counterterrorism policies that can often result in insecurity. Organizations identified as terrorist groups are typically dominated by masculinity, even when they have significant numbers of women as supporters and participants. The media depicts female terrorists as violations of the beautiful soul category whose behavior requires explanation above and beyond what is required for male terrorists. Each of these examples trace back to standards of masculinity and femininity that guide not only general assumptions about acceptable behavior, but more specifically have guided the way terrorism is understood by the states who try to fight it and the groups who are associated with it.

In this chapter I have argued that terrorism and counterterrorism are concepts with multiple ties to security, but how does this relate to strategies of emancipation? Thinking about the connections between terrorism and emancipation is complicated. Some of this complexity stems from the challenge of understanding multiple perspectives on terrorist organizations. Some of the complexity comes from the challenge of understanding the motivations involved in associating with organizations labeled "terrorist." Several scholars have directly confronted the links between emancipation and terrorism, and reached various conclusions about it (Herring 2008; McDonald 2009; Sylvester and Parashar 2009). Thinking about emancipation within critical terrorism studies, Matt McDonald (2009: 121) argues that "a commitment to opening up dialogic space for a wider range of voices to be heard is central to redressing the structures of inequality and deprivation that both constitute forms of violence and provide conditions in which the specific use of force is more likely to occur." Likewise, Jackson et al. (2011: 77) claim "for critical scholars committed to emancipation, an increased awareness of the role played by gender in the roots or causes of political violence can point to more effective alternatives to violence and to ways of ending or mitigating its damaging effects."

Some of the debate in this area is centered on whether women see militant groups as a path to emancipation. Interviews with women in Lebanon and the West Bank gathered by Maria Holt (2010: 369) suggest that some women "believe that religiously inspired activism has given them confidence to face the enemy." These women view Israeli policies as occupation and an obstacle to their emancipation. Others are skeptical about the possibility of terrorism resulting in gender emancipation. Qazi (2011: 43) argues that women's participation in many earlier national liberation movements has not significantly improved the status of women in those societies. She points to women's contributions to armed movements in Algeria and Palestine and the lack of gender emancipation in these societies as examples of a continuation of power relations and gender hierarchies. She claims that "there are no conflicts today that have elevated the status of the Muslim woman, nor are there any that address the societal and religious norms that solidify the role of the Muslim woman. While her participation in suicide attacks serves the overall group or social movement, her individual contribution is seldom recognized." These examples demonstrate that thinking about emancipation is complex, and requires reflexivity. It also requires actively listening to those who experience insecurity and whose emancipation we are concerned with.

Along these lines, Sylvester and Parashar (2009) caution that analysts of gender and terrorism should aim for an emancipatory security agenda only through careful attention to the myriad voices involved in the stories of terrorism. "[E]mancipation has a built-in appeal to those denied opportunities to reach beyond inherited identity into new areas of self-definition, and as a process of removing constraints and conditions associated with counterterrorism operations with names like 'Enduring Freedom' and 'Iraqi Freedom'" (Sylvester and Parashar 2009: 190). At its most basic level, freeing people from obstacles to their choices could mean freeing people to engage in more terrorism if that is what they choose to do. Terrorism is a strategy used for the achievement of a specific set of goals. Rather than being passive victims of terrorist plots, gender lenses reveal that both men and women freely choose to partake in militancy because they view it as a means to achieve a goal. While many IR scholars may have normative issues with this idea of emancipation, it reflects the challenging conversations that must take place if terrorism scholarship and policymaking is truly reflexive. We must understand why people choose to engage in acts marked as terrorism and potentially ask whether there are other avenues for the achievement of their goals that do not involve violence and insecurity of others. Thinking about emancipation and terrorism requires listening to all actors, identifying multiple sites of insecurity, and working toward removing them.

5

Human Security and Gender

East Africa experienced a severe food crisis in 2011. Reports by the UK government as well as Oxfam and Save the Children claim the famine may have killed up to 100,000 people and otherwise negatively impacted up to thirteen million people, most of them children and women (Hillier and Dempsey 2012; Slim 2012). Stories like these make headlines in international news sources, but are they security issues? For most of the history of security studies, the dominant idea of security was that of state security/national security. This version of security is concerned with the security and stability of the state, and seeks to identify threats to that stability. The famine described above would only be considered a state security issue to the extent that it threatened the stability and existence of the state itself. The dominance of state security discourses began to be challenged over time, particularly in the years after the end of the Cold War. In this time period, scholars and policymakers paid increasing attention to the large number of civil wars the international community was experiencing, and the multitude of negative consequences of those civil conflicts. These negative consequences impacted state actors to be sure, but they were also felt at levels below the state and included huge levels of displacement, ethnic cleansing, genocide, and mass rape to name a few (MacFarlane and Khong 2006). Coupled with this was an increased recognition that wars and conflict do not only impact soldiers, but have devastating impacts on civilian communities. In fact, civilians are intentionally targeted in nearly a third of conflicts where belligerents have the capacity to commit atrocities against them (Sjoberg and Peet 2011). Beyond examining the range of negative effects of war and conflict, scholars cast their attention to events and issues that threaten the ability of humans to live, including famine and poverty. These examples of insecurity, in addition to others, began to be recognized as threats to *human security*.

Human security is a concept which represents an avenue of expansion (both broadening and deepening) for security scholarship. It is a concept that has garnered significant attention from both academics and policymakers. There have been institutes, conferences, book series and journals all centered around the concept of human security. For example, the *Journal of Human Security* focuses on issues as diverse as population, economics, diplomacy, ethnic conflict, terrorism, religious extremism, and human rights. This chapter explores topics associated with human security through gender lenses, and asks how our understanding of human security as a security narrative changes when we include gender. Some scholars have welcomed notions of human security as a way of avoiding state-centered ideas of security. However, many feminists have cautioned that human security must still consistently take into account gender and gender-based inequalities. Through an examination of issues like human trafficking and global health, this chapter will introduce readers to the connections between expanded security ideas that relate to security for people, and gender.

What is Human Security?

Establishing a single characterization of human security is easier said than done. Like terrorism, human security is a concept with a multitude of definitions. The United Nations Development Programme (UNDP) is credited with establishing one of the early approaches to human security. The organization took a lead role in encouraging the international community to rethink the insecurity that is daily experienced across the globe. The UNDP's 1994 Human Development Report, entitled *New Dimensions of Human Security*, represented this shift in thinking about security, at least among some within the UN. The report set the stage for defining human security. It claimed that:

> The concept of security has for too long been interpreted
> narrowly: as security of territory from external aggression, or
> as protection of national interests in foreign policy or as global
> security from the threat of a nuclear holocaust. It has been related
> more to nation-states than to people . . . Forgotten were the

legitimate concerns of ordinary people who sought security in
their daily lives. For many of them, security symbolized protection
from the threat of disease, hunger, unemployment, crime, social
conflict, political repression and environmental hazards. With
the dark shadows of the cold war receding, one can now see that
many conflicts are within nations rather than between nations
. . . In the final analysis, human security is a child who did not
die, a disease that did not spread, a job that was not cut, an ethnic
tension that did not explode in violence, a dissident who was not
silenced. Human security is not a concern with weapons – it is a
concern with human life and dignity. (UNDP 1994: 22)

We see from this quote that the creators of the report saw the concept
of human security as a way to bring in the concerns of people on the
ground. It was conceptualized as being both people-centered and
universal. The report also went on to identify two main components
of human security – freedom from fear and freedom from want.
There are seven elements of human security identified in the report
– economic security, food security, health security, environmental
security, personal security, community security and political security.

In addition to the 1994 Human Development Report, the
Commission on Human Security (CHS) greatly contributed to highlighting the idea of human security within global policymaking
circles. Launched after the 2000 Millennium Summit, the CHS was
headed by Sadako Ogata and Amartya Sen and was tasked with conducting research on human security and issuing their findings in a
final report. Sen, an Indian economist and Nobel laureate, is regarded
as one of the chief thinkers about human security within the UN
system. The final report to come out of the Commission in 2003 was
titled *Human Security Now* and reflected the ongoing debates about
what human security is and how it can be incorporated into policymaking. The report outlined the strategies of protection and empowerment as necessary to work towards human security (Commission
on Human Security 2003: 10).

> *Protection* strategies, set up by states, international agencies,
> NGOs and the private sector, shield people from menaces.
> *Empowerment* strategies enable people to develop their resilience
> to difficult conditions. Both are required in nearly all situations

of human insecurity, though their form and balance will vary tremendously.

The inclusion of empowerment and the idea of human security being about the "freedom to take action on one's own behalf" suggest that the CHS was also trying for something of a bottom-up approach to human security rather than a perspective that views states or other powerful entities as the providers of human security exclusively. Protection is regarded as the first key or step to achieving human security, but after protection is achieved then individuals can be empowered to act on their own behalf. The report claims that "[p]eople empowered can demand respect for their dignity when it is violated. They can create new opportunities for work and address many problems locally. And they can mobilize for the security of others" (Commission on Human Security 2003: 11). This empowerment is to be achieved by providing education and information, building public spaces that encourage tolerance and discussion, and encouraging local leadership. Many of the elements tied to empowerment sound like liberal elements of society, including support for democratic elections and freedoms like a free press and the freedom to organize. The report also identifies multiple actors as important to the search for human security. It claims that states are no longer the sole actors on security issues. NGOs, international and regional organizations are listed as also playing important roles in the provision of human security.

As well as its influence within branches of the UN, several states in the international community have specifically adopted the language of human security into their policymaking. The states most commonly associated with human security are Canada, Norway, and Japan. These states conceptualized human security slightly differently; however, each attempted to incorporate human security into both domestic and international policymaking. Canada in particular is often regarded as having played a leading role in incorporating elements of human security into policy. Their perspective on human security stressed the "freedom from fear" aspect of human security much more than the "freedom from want." According to a 1999 Canadian concept paper, human security is "freedom from pervasive threats to people's rights, their safety, or even their lives," and the key strategies for strengthening human security are "strengthening legal norms and building the capacity to enforce them" (DFAIT 1999). Human security policymaking in Canada is closely associated with one individual – Lloyd Axworthy, a former foreign minister. The focus on policymaking under Axworthy was the human costs of violent conflict and the safety of people who experience violent conflict (MacFarlane and Khong 2006).

In addition to these unilateral human security initiatives, Canada and Norway signed a bilateral agreement in 1998 that formed the Human Security Network, an informal network of states that advocate action against threats to human safety and well being. Membership in the network has changed over time and has included Austria, Canada, Chile, Costa Rica, Greece, Ireland, Jordan, Mali, the Netherlands, Norway, Slovenia, South Africa (as an observer), Switzerland, and Thailand. In April 2011, Switzerland made a series of presentations before the UN General Assembly in connection with their role as chair of the network. In one of these presentations, the delegate from Switzerland acknowledged that member states typically work under different definitions of human security; however, there is a recognition that there are a number of core conditions that must be met for people to live in a secure environment. These include:

> Protection from all forms of violence, including armed violence, protection from life-threatening diseases, the existence of essential economic and social prerequisites such as the existence of shelter, water, food, sanitation and a safe environment, including preparedness for natural disasters, and the protection of fundamental rights and freedoms, including the protection from arbitrary behavior of the state. (Seger 2011)

This network illustrates that several states have, at least on paper, committed to some vision of human security. There are various policy initiatives that are associated with the human security community. These include the signing of the Ottawa Convention banning anti-personnel land mines (1997), the creation of the International Criminal Court (ICC) (which began in 2002), the Kimberley Process for the monitoring of conflict diamonds (which entered into force in

2003), and support for the notion of "responsibility to protect" which will be discussed below (Owen 2008; Paris 2001).

Threats and Vulnerabilities

Both state security and human security discourses contain a concern about threats. In many instances these threats to human and state security are overlapping. This idea of a connection between human security and state security is raised by several scholars and policymakers when they claim that human insecurity is worsened by state security threats like war or terrorism (Reardon and Hans 2010). At the same time, there are also important differences between state security and human security. For one thing, the list of concerns that accompanies each concept is different. When space is made for individual-level concerns through the discourse of human security, we tend to consider things like unemployment, poverty, drugs, crime, pollution and human rights violations (Thomas 2001). Part of the process of broadening the focus through human security involves shifting from a concern with threats to a focus on both threats and vulnerabilities. As discussed in Chapter 1, threats are typically defined as entities or phenomena that undermine safety and stability. Most security scholarship and policymaking over time has been about eliminating or reducing threats to the state (Liotta 2002, 2005). Threats can also negatively impact human security. On the other hand, vulnerability is what opens the door for threats. A vulnerability exists "when humans are exposed to potentially harmful developments and lack the means to effectively prevent, limit, or cope with the damage that may occur from them" (Soroos 2010: 178). Vulnerabilities are typically less clearly identifiable than threats and are often linked to interdependence among related issues. Because they are less tangible than threats, there is frequently disagreement about the best or adequate response to them (Liotta 2002). For example, an invading army is a *threat* to both state and human security. The state's stability is at risk from such a threat and human beings are likely to experience insecurity as a result of the violent conflict that accompanies the invading army. Less direct is the case of poverty. Poverty makes one vulnerable to a host of threats, including malnutrition, poor health, and lack of liveli-hood. Each of these threats has a negative impact on human security. In order to conceptualize human security and make policy that addresses it, it is necessary to think about both the threats to human security and the vulnerabilities that spawn those threats.

Debating Human Security

Despite the enthusiasm about human security from several states and international organizations, the concept has not been embraced by everyone. States like the US, China and Russia have appeared fairly hesitant to adopt the idea of shifting security discourses to the indi-vidual (MacFarlane and Khong 2006). Within academia, the idea of human security has also had a mixed reception. Raleigh and Urdal (2007: 675) argue that there was "an interest among Western national security establishments to identify potential threats that could legiti-mize their continued existence" in a post-Cold War world. On the one hand, this is evidence that the security terrain shifted signifi-cantly in the days after the fall of the Soviet Union. On the other hand, it illustrates that the security label has been used strategically. Actors create, maintain, and use linkages to exercise influence in a particular realm (Selin and VanDeveer 2003). There is significant evidence that actors have linked a variety of issues to security discourses in order to gain attention to them. For example, several scholars have linked health issues like HIV/AIDS to security discourses to "raise interna-tional awareness and generate more resources to combat the disease" (MacLean 2008: 476). The idea is that if your issue can be included in the realm of "high politics" then you are more likely to receive atten-tion and resources. Many have argued that the development com-munity strategically used the language of security when adopting the term human security to capture attention for a cause they felt needed additional resources (King and Murray 2001).

Some security scholars regard human security with skepticism and question whether loading the idea of "security" down with new meaning is a positive move. These voices often characterize human security as a broad, unruly concept that muddies the waters of security scholarship. The sentiment is typically that there are very real, very important threats to state security that exist within the international community that take priority over insecurity at lower levels. For those with this mentality, security at lower levels can only be achieved through a strong and stable state. On the other hand, scholars have used the idea of human security to shed light on what they see as some of the important failures of state security (DeLarrinaga and Doucet 2008; Hoogensen and Rottem 2004; Owen 2008). These thinkers claim that it is often the state that is responsible for the conditions of insecurity that are experienced daily through things like militarization, economic policy, and social policy.

Outside of these debates about state versus human security, there is a great deal of criticism about the concept of human security and whether it is a useful alternative security discourse. Criticisms range from the charge that human security is too vague, to an argument that discourses of human security have done little to really challenge existing security frameworks and beyond. The critique of definitional ambiguity is often leveled at human security discourses, and it is difficult to dispute (Chandler 2008; King and Murray 2001). There is a huge array of human security definitions and some of these are quite vague. Some scholars argue that human security is a discourse that is left fuzzy by design. In his often-cited survey of human security, Roland Paris (2001: 88) claims human security "is the glue that holds together a jumbled coalition of 'middle power' states, development agencies, and NGOs – all of which seek to shift attention and resources away from conventional security issues and toward goals that have traditionally fallen under the rubric of international development." He argues that the only way this large collection of actors can work together is *because* the idea of human security is vague. Beyond this charge that actors actually have a vested interest in keeping human security vague, he and others argue that human security will continue to be difficult to use as a guide for policymaking.

Beyond a general frustration about what human security actually refers to are critiques about the impacts of human security discourses. This includes the charge that human security may look like a radically new perspective at first glance, but actually allow for security as usual. Some are concerned that it can too easily be co-opted by the state and military establishments in order to defend the further expansion and justification of military campaigns (Bellamy and McDonald 2002; Chandler and Hynek 2011; Gilmore 2011). Others argue that human security discourses place states as the dominant actors in providing security or development for people, further adding to the primacy of states in the international system (Duffield 2007). Still others claim that it allows Northern states to further their liberal policy push into other countries. The focus on the individual within human security discourses is taken by some as an example of this critique. "The link with the individual, the clear sense that the means of alleviating the security concerns of the individual entailed the 'development' of that same individual within liberal economics, and the belief that a pluralist state was best placed to achieve these ends are all utterly consistent with the broader development turn" (Christie 2010: 176–177). This unease about individualism within human security discourses, as well as larger concerns about whether human security is essentially a Northern discourse, has made some scholars and policymakers skeptical about the future of human security as a discourse. Some of this skepticism is present within the feminist security community.

Feminist Perspectives on Human Security

Once again, there is not a single feminist perspective. There is a variety of feminisms and so there is a variety of feminist perspectives on human security. That being said, one major critique of human security raised by a host of feminist scholars is the extent to which gender is currently left out of human security perspectives. For one thing, "human" is not neutral and is certainly not gender neutral. As is seen in debates about human rights, humanity has rarely been conceptualized in ways that implied equal standing for every person on the planet (Wibben 2011). The early lines of the US Declaration of Independence are generally taken as an example of a statement about the rights of humanity. These lines claim that all *men* are created equal and they are endowed with certain unalienable rights (life, liberty and the pursuit of happiness). In practice, human beings were treated very differently in the late 1700s (and sadly still are today) depending on their gender, race, and class. The most obvious breach of this sentiment is the fact that slavery was still a thriving business at the time these words were written. If people can be excluded from the category of humanity, does human security offer the universal protection and path to security that it suggests at first glance? From a feminist perspective, the "human" in human security is thoroughly gendered and so the discourse should reflect that. At odds with this endeavor is the focus on the *individual* within conceptualizations of human security. UNDP's 1994 Human Development Report claims human security is *people-centered*. "It is concerned with how people live and breathe in a society, how freely they exercise their many choices, how much access they have to market and social opportunities and whether they live in conflict or in peace" (UNDP 1994). This has been taken to mean that human security is centered on individuals rather than states. This notion is challenged by those that claim this individualism is a Northern construct that does not reflect how people actually live their lives (Christie 2010). Many sources of vulnerability and threats come from one's association with a group – gender, class, ethnic group, etc. If we focus on individuals in such a way that their larger associations are excluded from analysis, then we will likely lose sight of vulnerabilities and threats that are linked to those associations. An image that comes to mind is of looking at a satellite map on the computer. State security would be a map of the entire country. I want to look closer and so I zoom in all the way down to an individual person standing on a sidewalk. When I shift my analysis down to the individual level I may miss a great deal of context. For example, where is this person located? What is her relationship with the people around her? What vulnerabilities might this person be exposed to? A narrow focus may leave important questions out of our analysis. In much the same way, if we bring the security focus down too narrowly to solely the individual then we may lose sight of the context that allows us to understand how insecurities come about.

Because of this, gender can be used as an important tool for bringing in the concept of identity to calculations of human security (Hoogensen and Rottem 2004; Hoogensen and Stuvøy 2006). Human beings are identified as masculine or feminine by their society, regardless of whether they see themselves as fitting within these categories. This gender identification has important implications for the types of insecurities we are liable to face. This holds for being identified as either female or male. Most attention is paid to vulnerabilities stemming from being female (this is because these are widespread and systematic) but it also tells us something important about human insecurity for men. For example, while women and girls are often targeted for wartime (and peacetime) rape and other forms of sexual abuse, men and boys are also among the victims of this extreme form of insecurity. What is more, while speaking out after experiencing sexual abuse is difficult and can result in negative personal ramifications, this can be magnified for males (Carpenter 2006). For males who experience sexual abuse in societies where victimization is regarded as particularly unacceptable for men, their gender identification becomes a source of insecurity. In this way identity is important for understanding how we experience vulnerability and threats as well as for how we understand our world. Human security and human insecurity are often discussed as if they look the same for all people in all contexts and this is plainly not the case (Kent 2006).

Because of this assumption of gender neutrality within human security perspectives as well as other concerns, some feminist scholars have become frustrated by what they see as major problems with human security discourses (Wibben 2008, 2011). While human security had a great deal of potential in its early days to shift existing discourses of security away from a focus on the state, in practice a great deal of state-centric security thinking remains (Reardon 2010). Tied to this is a fear that human security may be used as justification for a larger role for the state within society. If states claim a larger role in policymaking by appealing to human security concerns and particularly if the military is put forward as an actor to address these concerns, this can result in increased militarization of society and of social concerns. As illustrated in Chapter 2, militarization has a range of gendered impacts, including a rise of militarized masculinity, disempowerment or silencing of those (men and women) who do not fit comfortably in the "beautiful soul" and "just warrior" molds, and prioritizing policies that enhance state security (including those that may actually result in human insecurity).

Is this cooptation inevitable when security discourses are used? Annick Wibben (2008: 460) argues that using security language may result in "pandering to so-called experts who make decisions based on bureaucratic or institutional requirements (and generally involving military solutions to 'security problems')." This fear is repeated by several feminists and explained by schools of thought like the Copenhagen School. Ole Wæver in particular has claimed that securitization is often accompanied by both intended and unintended consequences. While the Copenhagen School places many human security concerns outside of the realm of "international security" and does not focus heavily on gender (in fact it has been criticized for the omission), the impacts of militarization and the justification of emergency state activities that they identify are gendered (Hansen 2000). Additionally, the discourses of state security (or international security for the Copenhagen School) and human security have been used simultaneously in many states and international organizations. As such, we must take into consideration the potential for human security as a discourse to be mobilized in ways that do little to address insecurities of people on the ground.

Women's Insecurity as a Justification for Military Intervention

As voices within the international community have become increasingly outspoken on issues like human security and human rights, there have been many examples of these issues being invoked as justification for military intervention. A recent example is the international intervention in Libya. The UN Security Council, the ICC, and various states used human security language in their condemnation of Muammar al-Qadhafi and his handling of resistance to his administration during a pro-democracy movement in February 2011. The ICC, an entity whose creation is linked to networks of human security actors, issued arrest warrants for Qadhafi, one of his sons, and Libya's intelligence chief for "crimes against humanity" which were allegedly committed during the pro-democracy movement. The central concern which prompted the warrants appears to be a fear for the safety of civilians (Simons 2011). Whether or not one agrees with the Security Council's decision to intervene, it is hard to discount the role of human security concerns in this case. In particular, NATO countries appear to have been particularly concerned with having the mission understood as one of humanitarian intervention rather than a hostile act against a sovereign state. The ICC investigation may be seen as lending credibility to NATO's campaign.

This idea of using force to intervene on behalf of people whose human security is in jeopardy has become quite widespread in the international community, although it remains controversial. In a speech to the UN General Assembly in September 1999 then UN Secretary-General Kofi Annan referred to a "developing international norm in favour of intervention to protect civilians from wholesale slaughter and suffering and violence" (cited in Newman 2001: 244). Acknowledging that there may be circumstances where states should/must intervene (particularly militarily) in the affairs of another state goes against the idea of state sovereignty which has been a firm principle in the global system. Sovereignty is the recognition that a state has the right to determine policy within its borders. The ever popular International Relations story is that sovereignty has guided the behavior of states since the year 1648 and the Treaty of Westphalia. This agreement, which ended the Thirty Years War in Europe, is said to have contained an understanding between major powers that they would refrain from directly intervening in the affairs of each other. The concept of sovereignty is enshrined in Article 2.1 of the UN Charter as well as a host of other international agreements. In practice, the sovereignty of states has never been absolute; however, the international community has often kept up appearances as if it is.

Even the pretense of sovereignty as an absolute is immediately countered when humanitarian intervention is contemplated. An important component in the shift away from absolute state sovereignty is the idea of the "responsibility to protect" (R2P). The International Committee on Intervention and State Sovereignty (ICISS), an independent international body convened by the Government of Canada and made up of prominent diplomatic members of the international community, put out a report entitled *The Responsibility to Protect* in 2001. The report claimed that "[i]nternally, sovereignty signifies the capacity to make authoritative decisions with regard to the people and resources within the territory of the state. Generally, however, the authority of the state is not regarded as absolute, but constrained and regulated internally by constitutional power sharing arrangements" (ICISS 2001: 12). The report called on states to regard sovereignty as a responsibility rather than a right. This responsibility implies that states must protect the "safety and lives of citizens and [promote] their welfare" (ICISS 2001: 13). This is extended to the issue of intervention in that states can now argue that they have a responsibility to protect civilians in other states rather than a right to intervene in the sovereign affairs of another state. The Commission argued that the concepts of human security and human rights are directly tied to the responsibility to protect. The report claims that "intervention for human protection purposes, including military intervention in extreme cases, is supportable when major harm to civilians is occurring or imminently apprehended, and the state in question is unable or unwilling to end the harm, or is itself the perpetrator" (ICISS 2001: 16). The choice of the term "responsibility" is interesting in that it suggests that not only is intervention justified in some instances, but that states in the international system have an obligation to intervene in certain circumstances. In many ways, the report's definition of human security highlights the negative security implications of traditional ideas of security, including violence at the hands of state security forces. At the same time, the use of the term "protect" in R2P raises a red flag with some feminist scholars. Tied by some to the protection racket, the idea of a need for international actors to protect civilians echoes dominant narratives that are gendered and racialized "which positions the international community as the heroic, white male necessary to protect the vulnerable, inferior, feminized 'Other' – the state it must rescue" (Duncanson 2009: 68).

A very clear (and often discussed) example of using human security to justify military intervention is the US invasion of Afghanistan in 2001. In the weeks after 9/11, the American and British publics started to hear government statements and lamentations about the treatment of Afghan women under Taliban rule. On November 17, 2001 Laura Bush, the former First Lady of the US, gave a radio address highlighting the harsh treatment of Afghan women at the hands of the ruling Taliban. Around the same time, Cherie Blair, wife of then-UK Prime Minister Tony Blair, made a similar speech pleading for support of Afghan women. President Bush signed the Afghan Women and Children Relief Act (AWCRA) soon after. During the signing ceremony of the act, Bush referred to the Taliban as "a regime at war with women." With these acts, high-profile voices in the US and UK attempted to shift the discourse away from a mission in Afghanistan that is about revenge for the attacks of 9/11 to a mission in Afghanistan that is about setting women free from an oppressive, evil regime. Women's plight under the Taliban was not suddenly changed on 9/11. What appears to have changed is the willingness to focus on the plight of women in a region that the US was interested in striking militarily.

A particularly interesting piece of this story is that 2001 was not the first time forces had used women's plight as justification for intervention or control of Afghanistan. The Soviet Union used discourses of "saving" women from patriarchal social structures during their 1979 invasion of Afghanistan. At the same time, Afghanistan's mujahedin fighting forces claimed to be protecting women from the military and ideological invasions of the USSR. Next, when the Taliban were rising to power against the mujahedin, they argued that they were the best hope for "saving" women from the rapes and mistreatment at the hands of the mujahedin who had gained power during the years of conflict with the USSR (Fluri 2008; Tickner 2002). There have been numerous questions raised about the ability and/or interest that each group had in advancing the status of women; however, it remains that, just within this one country, narratives about women's human security has been drawn on by multiple, diverse groups. It seems as if women's insecurity has remained both a convenient trope for actors to draw on to gain sympathy for their cause, and it has remained a problem that no group has committed significant resources to addressing.

Many feminists have strongly critiqued the strategy of using the plight of Afghan women to justify military intervention by members of the international community (Cockburn 2010; Cole 2008; Fluri 2008; Kirk 2008; Lee 2008; Shepherd 2006; Steans 2006; Tickner

2002). In the first place, when actors have called attention to women's insecurity in these contexts they have rarely instituted policies that have been first and foremost about ensuring human security. A month after 9/11, Enloe (2002: 103) wrote:

> Anything can be militarized. Even the rights of Afghan women. In so far as Afghan women' rights – including their right to have an effective voice in the rebuilding of "post-bombing" Afghanistan – is tied to the wagon of war (that is, is militarized), those women will not have secure rights. They will have merely rights-of-convenience . . . no matter how great the temptation to hitch women's advancement to the powers-that-be's goals, it must be explored, justified and pursued in its own right. Women are not just (occasionally) convenient. They are citizens. They are fully human.

None of this is to suggest that there were not pressing human security issues in Afghanistan in 2001, or that actors in the global North were not genuinely concerned about those human security issues. Critics were rather pointing out that using human security concerns as validation for an alternative agenda does not leave the human security concerns on strong footing. What happens when those human security concerns no longer line up with the goals of those in power? Do they continue to be on the political agenda? What happens to those people whose security is challenged? Do they have to wait until their insecurity is once again convenient?

NGOs working within Afghanistan have also been critical of the strategy of using military intervention to address human insecurity. The Revolutionary Association of the Women of Afghanistan (RAWA) is an organization that works toward women's empowerment and protection. According to various reports and statements made available on their website, they argue that religious fundamentalism is the main cause of women's insecurity in Afghanistan. They go on to suggest that the US-led conflict in the country does little to address this and in fact militarization serves to promote new sources of insecurity for citizens of Afghanistan (RAWA 2009). These actors remind us that there are Afghan women working to advance human security, and have been undertaking this task long before the attention of international community was drawn to their goals after 9/11.

Rather than use human security as justification for militarization, we can rethink recent conflicts like those in Iraq and Afghanistan in ways that use human security promotion as a guiding principle. Mary Kaldor (2010) argues that prioritizing human security in Afghanistan would require civilian leadership and would mean focusing on the security of Afghans in the same way that we currently focus on the security of North Atlantic Treaty Organization (NATO) troops. It also means encouraging Afghan leadership that is trusted by the population. Questions about fraudulent elections and corruption undermine this relationship. The relationship is also undermined if the population feels that human security concerns are not actually a priority for their state.

Thinking about the promotion of human security in Afghanistan also extends to questioning whether women's security is a legitimate priority for the people in charge of determining the future of the state. Despite the statements made in support of the women of Afghanistan, the Bush administration was criticized for the fact that women were not involved in the drafting of the new constitution for Afghanistan. Others have suggested that the Bush administration could have done more to ensure that women were granted the same rights as men in the post-Taliban phase of the country (Steans 2006). Also, the fact that the Karzai government has passed repressive legislation on women demonstrates that while women's security and or rights were used as a (partial) justification for the war in Afghanistan it does not appear to be a priority in the long-term conflict (Kaldor 2010). This may be evidence for the concern that appeals to human security concerns that are merely "convenient" for powerful actors are not guarantees for effective human security policymaking.

Actors as diverse as the US, the Taliban, the Soviet Union, and the mujahedin all claimed they were protecting the women of a single state. Beyond using women's insecurity as justification for intervention or else remaining in power, influential actors point to women's vulnerability during wartime as justification for conflict in general. Sjoberg and Peet (2011) argue that wars are often justified as protecting women as a symbol of the state and nationalism. In the case of the war in Afghanistan it may be that the Bush administration found the idea of the protection of Afghan women to be a useful substitute for the idea of the protection of "beautiful souls" domestically. It was an easier case to make that Afghan women needed protection rather than American women. Initiating discussions about the insecurities of Afghan women did not prompt an evaluation of the sources of insecurity that women face daily in the US, UK, or other countries that counted themselves among the "coalition of the willing." Scholars have pointed out that while states have tapped into a global norm of human rights and human security promotion and protection, this does not always translate into policies that emancipate or empower women at home. For instance, it was just months after President Bush signed the Afghan Women and Children Relief Act that the US again refused to ratify the 1979 Convention on the Elimination of Discrimination against Women. Likewise, Australia is a country that actively participated in the "war on terror," yet the state has been criticized for what some see as its failure to effectively act on protecting women from domestic violence (Phillips 2008). These examples support the concern of those in both academic and policymaking circles who caution that human security discourses may not achieve the goals they are intended to reach. Human security narratives (including a concern about women's insecurity) can be used to justify policies and strategies that do little to advance human security. In fact, if human security narratives are directly linked to militarization and state security, then this goes directly against the original vision of human security that sought to call attention to the huge silences within state security frameworks that did not address the insecurity of people on the ground.

Gendering Human Security

All of the critiques of human security have left some wondering whether it is still a useful concept or whether we should relegate it to the "dustbins of history." Despite important criticisms, there are some within the feminist community who see the idea of human security as providing an important alternative to state security, and an alternative that could incorporate feminist goals. These voices advocate an understanding of human security that problematize both the sources of insecurity and the operations of power within society (Truong et al. 2006). One step towards meaningfully incorporating gender into discourses of human security would be to use gender identity as a way to mainstream gender in human security initiatives. "Since gender does influence what is considered a threat or violence, as well as policymaking about security, security needs to be viewed in terms of voice, identity, power and location – and to include the specific concerns of women" (Hudson 2010: 257–258). Gender identity offers a bottom-up foundational logic for understanding human security that gets around narrowing our focus to the individual in such a way that we lose sight of sources of vulnerabilities and power relationships. Gender identity, then, may be a way to make human security a more useful discourse for encouraging change in the international community.

Gender must be included in notions of human security that recognize particular challenges but also agency. We must understand that gender identity is socially constructed and malleable. We cannot lump together men or women who experience insecurity because of their gender identity and regard them as incapable. Instead we must analyze the sources of vulnerability and insecurity that develop from gender identity with the goal of resolving them. For example, both the 1994 UNDP report and the 2003 CHS report include a discussion of the protection of women and children. *Human Security Now* mentions the vulnerability of women and girls in conflict situations, including their susceptibility to gender-based violence. The report outlines these gendered insecurities but also go on to say women should have a larger role in peace negotiations and settlements, and that human security policymaking needs to do things like address gender asymmetries in livelihood. These strategies of *empowerment*, a concept that the report stresses as essential for the achievement of human security, must be formed with an eye toward the systems of disempowerment that come from gender identity.

An important issue to consider when thinking about gendering human security is which actors should be involved in promoting human security? The state has most often been connected with providing security when discourses of state security have dominated scholarship and policymaking, but what about within ideas of human security? There are differing opinions on the appropriate role for states in the provision of human security. Heidi Hudson (2005: 165) argues that "[t]he challenge lies in the way in which state security is transformed from an end to a means of promoting human security. Like it or not, the state remains the political actor with the largest capacity to mobilize resources." This suggests that, at the present time, states remain the actors with the authority that is necessary to effectively work towards human security. Because of prevalent idea of state sovereignty, states are largely responsible for making policies for their population. This is not to say that all states have the capacity or the motivation to make policies designed to promote human security, but rather that they are centrally located actors in the international community.

On the other hand, some scholars have been fairly critical about the potential for states to be seen as the dominant actors for the provision of human security. Critiques in this vein highlight the systems of patriarchy and other unequal power relationships that states exist within. Human security is unlikely if militarization and patriarchy are the guiding forces of state behavior (Reardon 2010). When states are characterized by militarism, policymaking will prioritize militarized solutions which are oriented towards securing the state. For example, some feminist scholars have explored the gendered consequences of the presence of military bases abroad. US military bases in Japan have been deemed a threat to the human security of local populations (Akibayashi and Takazato 2010; Alexander 2010). Ronni Alexander (2010: 199) argues that:

> Military coercion has become embodied through the intergenerational effects of nuclear and/or toxic contamination on Pacific peoples, their forced migration/relocation due to the contamination of their living spaces and the Amerasian and other children of mixed background living near military bases. The pollution of bodies and lands in the Pacific in the name of security in an extreme example of "inhuman security."

Human security is threatened in this case through the degradation of the natural environment as well as through the unequal power relationships between local peoples and military personnel. At times these unequal relationships have resulted in rape and other forms of abuse at the hands of soldiers (Akibayashi and Takazato 2010).

State policymaking under patriarchy props up unequal relationships and ignores security threats to marginalized populations within society (Reardon 2010). Patriarchy is so deeply ingrained within state relations that it is often invisible, which makes problematizing it difficult and necessary. Both patriarchy and militarism are characteristics of the state system which present significant obstacles to effective human security policymaking. In addition to critiques about the state system in general, other scholars are specifically critical of the discourses of human security that legitimate the intervention of powerful states into less-powerful states. Mark Duffield (2007: 122) claims "[w]hile the common definition of human security is prioritizing people rather than states, it can be more accurately understood as *effective states prioritizing the well being of populations living within ineffective ones.*" This speaks to the unequal power distribution not only within a state, but also among the states of the international community. Ideas like R2P are manifestations of this tendency.

At the same time, the idea of human security has regularly been understood to involve multiple actors – from the state, to regional organizations, to NGOs. While many feminist scholars regard this move away from state-centrism as a positive, we must also be aware that non-state organizations/institutions are also gendered. This includes the UN and various organizations that have taken a lead role in popularizing the idea of human security to date (Hudson 2005). As seen in Chapter 3, the UN continues to have some important obstacles to achieving gender balance and gender mainstreaming. Additionally, NGOs and larger social movement networks are not always progressive on gender emancipation (Vargas 2006). Gita Sen (2006: 40) explains that:

> Anti-feminist beliefs and practices are rife within many social movements, and transforming these to where the movement

becomes genuinely supportive of gender justice can be a long
drawn out and exhausting struggle. In addition, social movements
are built through processes of internal consolidation as well
as external alliance building. While a movement's own gender
practices may not be too problematic, its allies may be much
worse on gender justice. For instance, the movement to cancel
the "odious" debts of South countries often works in alliance
with the Catholic Church whose current hierarchy is vehemently
opposed to gender justice. While debt cancellation may improve
the national economic autonomy of some South countries,
making it possible for their governments to better address some
of the livelihood and basic needs of both women and men, putting
gender justice on the back burner may also have serious negative
consequences for women.

Examining human security through gender lenses necessitates
raising these kinds of issues for debate. We must be aware of potential
obstacles to the removal of gendered insecurity rather than automatically assume that a shift away from state-centrism is a step in this
direction.

Another important connection between human security and
gender is recognizing how the achievement of feminist goals corresponds with human security. For example, Bryan McDonald (2010:
27) claims that "[s]uccess in achieving food security is thus recognized
as both a component of larger efforts to provide human security and
a goal that depends on the success of efforts to improve human health
and well being through methods such as poverty alleviation, infrastructure development, education, and improvements in the status of
women." There needs to be a balanced focus on both freedom from
fear *and* freedom from want in order for these strategies of empowerment to be included within discourses on human security. There
has been a heavy focus on the freedom from fear aspect of human
security thus far. In fact, at the height of its adoption by Canada the
definition of human security was "safety for people from both violent
and non-violent threats . . . a condition or state of being characterized by freedom from pervasive threats to people's rights, their safety,
even their lives" (DFAIT 1999). Policymaking using this definition
will likely be geared more toward protection than empowerment and

can result in a continuation of security policymaking as it was before human security discourses entered the scene. The idea of empowerment should be strengthened within human security discourses, and gender identity as the foundation for a bottom-up approach is a useful starting point. According to Gunhild Hoogensen and Kirsti Stuvøy (2006: 219):

> A gender-informed approach to human security . . . allows practitioners and theorists alike to identify the ways in which insecurities develop as a result of relationships of dominance/ nondominance, how they manifest themselves according to context, in what ways problems are shared across regions (marginalization in the global north and global south, for example), and what steps are needed to address these problems, whether these be initiatives taken by those who are affected or state-based domestic and foreign policies.

This gender-informed approach to human security must illuminate the vulnerabilities that enable human insecurity to continue for both women and men across the globe. The following sections explore two human security issues, human health and human trafficking, through a gender-sensitive perspective on human vulnerability and insecurity.

Health as a Human Security Issue

It is useful to think about an issue like health through the lenses of both human security and gender. Socially conditioned ideas about gender intersect with health in numerous ways. For example, men often experience higher levels of suicide and substance abuse than women. Some trace this tendency to the pressures of living up to the culturally defined expectations of their gender (Sharpe 2010). At the same time, in cultures where girls are seen as a financial burden on families, they are less likely to receive medical treatment or they may receive treatment at a later stage in an illness when compared to boys. Additionally, women and girls experience food insecurity more acutely than men, meaning they are typically the last to receive meals in households that are food scarce (Steans 2006). These examples illustrate that while some differences in health across peoples are related to biology, many are socially conditioned.

International organizations like the World Health Organization (WHO) and policymakers have linked health to both international peace and stability (state security concerns) and human security. Health is linked to state security through a concern about issues like the health impacts of violent conflict (Iqbal 2006), and the use of bioterrorism and the impacts of pandemics (Elbe 2010). Health is associated with human security through a focus on endemic diseases like HIV/AIDS, malaria, and tuberculosis, which disproportionately impact the global South (Elbe 2010; MacLean 2008). HIV is a global health problem with a significant gender dimension. Of all the people living with HIV, slightly more than half are women and girls. This number is higher in the Caribbean and particularly in sub-Saharan Africa. Nearly 40 percent of all adult women with HIV live in sub-Saharan Africa. In this region, young women aged 15–24 years are as much as eight times more likely to be HIV positive than men in the same age group. UNAIDS (2010: 10), a widely known UN body that issues regular reports on the status of HIV infection, prevention and treatment, claims that "[p]rotecting women and girls from HIV means protecting against gender-based violence and promoting economic independence from older men." This statement relates to human security by virtue of the fact that the organization is identifying poverty as a source of vulnerability that threatens health security. Poverty is further linked through the issue of food security. It has been found that food insecurity can lead to "sexual risk-taking among women" or selling sex to get food (UNAIDS 2010: 76). In this kind of an arrangement, women and girls have less negotiating power in the relationship and so are less able to practice safe sex. This makes the transmission of HIV more likely within this community. In these cases, human security can only be achieved if underlying vulnerabilities are recognized and addressed.

Human Security Now has an entire chapter on health entitled "Better health for human security." Within this chapter there is particular mention of reproductive health. The report claims that:

> Women are often discriminated against in access to education,
> food, employment, financial resources and primary health care
> services. Addressing issues of women's status and integrating
> them into mainstream social and political systems will be
> essential for improving reproductive health and allowing women
> wider participation within society. In addition, inexpensive and
> technologically simple methods are needed to promote women's
> reproductive health. Improving the quality of reproductive health
> care and women's access to it will not only improve the security of
> billions of women around the world, but also that of their children
> and families (Commission on Human Security 2003: 100).

Reproductive health is often a controversial issue in countries. Subjects like female genital mutilation, choice surrounding unwanted pregnancies, and access to contraceptives inspire heated debate and political divisions within states (Davies 2009). In fact, it is argued that the US has not ratified the 1979 Convention on the Elimination of Discrimination against Women (CEDAW) because of the convention's inclusion of language about family planning. Groups of conservative lawmakers in the US have continually fought against ratification by linking it to ever-contentious debates about abortion (Battersby and Siracusa 2009). Despite these debates, health security is considered by many to be a fundamental component of human security. It was one of the seven elements identified in the 1994 UNDP report which popularized the concept, and continues to be raised within discussions of human security as a discourse today. Within these discussions must be a recognition that women's health insecurity stem from particular threats and vulnerabilities. Rather than treat health security as if it is gender neutral, these gendered differences need to be revealed and attended to.

These gendered differences in health security have a direct link to policy. One health issue that relates to both society (gender) and biology (sex) is pregnancy and childbirth. There are around 340,000 deaths of women from pregnancy-related causes each year. Nearly half of these occur in Africa. Many sub-Saharan countries struggle to adequately provide health services that ensure the human security of pregnant women. Uganda is a country that has recently experienced both internal and external criticism for their health record. Uganda has a significant shortage of healthcare providers and many of the country's healthcare facilities regularly run out of essential supplies and medicines. At the same time the country was experiencing these shortfalls in the health sector, the government purchased fighter jets for the defense sector. This purchase helped fuel protests by many in the country who questioned whether this state security purchase should have taken a backseat to the dire human security needs across the country. The Center for Health, Human Rights and Development, an NGO active in the country, filed a lawsuit arguing that the government violated women's right to life by failing to provide them with basic maternal care (Dugger 2011).

At the same time, there has been some policy movement towards attempting to provide health security to people with unique health needs. In recent years there have been initiatives in many African states to reduce or eliminate fees for health care for pregnant women and young children. Sierra Leone is one country where the government, aided by international donors, has eliminated fees for pregnant women, thus enabling many women to give birth in a medical facility rather than at home. After its decade-long civil war, Sierra Leone ranked at or near the bottom of most global measures of maternal and infant mortality (Bhandari 2011). It is reported that health care facilities were targeted during the conflict by the Revolutionary United Front (RUF) who saw them as symbols of government authority. This is an example of health, state security, human security and gender all coming together in one story. A state security threat contributed to worsening health levels in the country for both men and women, presenting a threat to human security. Women's reproductive health was particularly at risk. While many argue that it is still impossible to know whether reducing or eliminating fees will measurably improve health standards in these countries, there is another important component to the initiatives that relates to human security – that of feeling secure. Adam Nossiter (2011) claims "[w]omen at the clinics [in Sierra Leone] said they felt safer, having traded risky home births for at least some medical care." This feeling of security relates to strategies of empowerment within approaches to human security. A gender-sensitive human security perspective must include space for strategies of both protection and empowerment that recognize the unique insecurities men and women face because of both their gender identity and biological differences.

Human Trafficking as a Human Security Issue

Gender and human security connections can also be viewed through discussions of human trafficking. Several actors have discussed trafficking through security language in the past few years, including the North Atlantic Treaty Organization (NATO), the United Nations Office on Drugs and Crime (UNODC), the International Organization on Migration (IOM), the European Union (EU), and the Organization for Security and Cooperation in Europe (OSCE) (Friesendorf 2007; Jackson 2006). Human trafficking is an issue that is extremely difficult to understand using traditional security frameworks. Trafficking definitely has ties to state stability, including the link between trafficking and transnational organized crime and illegal migration, and the ability of states to stop trafficking or prosecute traffickers. However, feminist studies are concerned with the fate and representation of the people who are trafficked rather than how the practice of trafficking relates to state security. This concentration on humans potentially makes human security a useful framework for analyzing both how insecurities emerge and what is being done to remove these sources of insecurity.

As is the case with any criminal activity, determining the actual number of people who are trafficked across borders as well as within states is difficult. The IOM (2011) estimates that as many as 800,000 people are trafficked across state boundaries annually. Human trafficking touches nearly every region of the planet and is made possible by a complicated network of criminal activity involving forgers, money launderers, carriers, and government officials responsible for border control (Battersby and Siracusa 2009). The international community has raised the issue of human trafficking through the UN Convention against Transnational Organized Crime and its Protocol to Prevent, Suppress and Punish Trafficking in Persons, especially Women and Children. Both the Convention and its additional Protocol entered into force in late 2003. The Protocol defines trafficking in persons as "the recruitment, transportation, transfer, harbouring or receipt of persons, by means of the threat or use of force or other forms of coercion, of abduction, of fraud, of deception, of the abuse of power or of a position of vulnerability or of the giving or receiving of payments or benefits to achieve the consent of a person having control over another person, for the purpose of exploitation" (UNODC 2004: 42). It defines exploitation as including sexual exploitation, forced labor, slavery, servitude, and the removal or organs.

Human trafficking has received a large amount of attention from feminist scholars largely because of the significant percentage of women and girls trafficked each year. Additionally, a report out of the UNODC found that women make up a large number of traffickers. The report examined data gathered on the gender of offenders in 46 countries and found that women play a key role as perpetrators of human trafficking. In Europe women make up a larger share of those convicted for human trafficking offenses than for most other forms of crime (UNODC 2009).

There are a variety of factors that contribute to the high risk of women and girls for trafficking, including "gender inequality, war economies, criminal syndicates, and the destruction and destabilization of livelihoods" (Mazurana et al. 2005: 7). Examples of some of these elements are at play in stories of the trafficking of children in China. In the summer of 2011 the Chinese Ministry of Public Security reported several operations undertaken to rescue children, mostly girls, caught up in trafficking networks. Traditional ideas about the preference for male children rather than female children in China contributes to the vulnerable position many girls find themselves in. Additionally, some Chinese authorities have admitted that the penalties for trafficking are fairly lenient (LaFraniere 2011). These factors combine to make China a central source for trafficked people of both sexes.

Feminist analyses of human trafficking have seen both the state and trafficking networks as threats to security. Insecurity arises at the most basic level by virtue of the fact that trafficked persons lack freedom of movement. They are also at risk of physical, sexual, or mental abuse and poor health. Despite these severe human security risks for all of those who are trafficked, not all people involved in human trafficking receive the same attention. The sexual trafficking of white women is given much higher priority over the plight of people not trafficked for the sex trade or non-white persons (Lobasz 2010). Even global institutions like the UNODC recognize that non-sexual trafficking is underreported across the international community.

> [S]exual exploitation is by far the most commonly identified form of human trafficking (79%), followed by forced labour (18%). This may be the result of statistical bias. By and large the exploitation of women tends to be visible, in city centres, or along highways. Because it is more frequently reported, sexual exploitation has become the most documented type of trafficking, in aggregate statistics. In comparison, other forms of exploitation are under-reported: forced or bonded labour; domestic servitude and forced marriage; organ removal; and the exploitation of children in begging, the sex trade, and warfare. (UNODC 2009: 6)

While all forms of trafficking are threats to human security, it is important to recognize the difference between trafficking and migration. A narrative of victimization is used by the courts, government officials and law enforcement in many countries to describe trafficking (Harrington 2005; Hua and Nigorizawa 2010). Even when women involved in cases do not see themselves as trafficked into the sex trade, but rather as labor migrants knowingly entering the sex trade, they have been cast as victims. Treating the issue in such a way that assumes a lack of agency for all people who cross borders does not aid in empowering those whose human security is truly at risk. Unless policymakers examine the unequal power relationships or other sources of vulnerability (like poverty) that may lead people to actually be prey for sex trafficking networks, we will not address the underlying processes that support human trafficking.

Simultaneously, selectively understanding human trafficking as only involving white women who enter the sex trade silences all those people who are trafficked but do not fit this mold. This reinforces the fact that gender is intimately tied to other forms of identity for discussions of power relationships and sources of vulnerability and insecurity. "These dominant narratives rely on and reproduce troubling gender-race-nation discourses of victimization, which construct a stereotype of the 'helpless victim' that links femininity to dependency and racial 'otherness' to cultural deviancy" (Hua and Nigorizawa 2010: 402). Sexual trafficking is a fundamental threat to human security, but so are other forms of human trafficking. Focusing on sexual trafficking at the expense of other forms of trafficking is an example of selectively examining a human security issue. Part of the problem is that the public in many Northern states are exposed to the issue of trafficking almost exclusively as involving white women forced to work as prostitutes. It may be tempting for people who want to raise the profile of an issue like human trafficking to tap into a narrative that has traction for policymakers and the public but this does little to ultimately help us to understand and address the larger processes that allow human trafficking to continue and thrive.

The vulnerability of poverty has an important, direct link to human trafficking and thus human insecurity. Poverty is a pervasive motivation for people to relocate in search of additional income. For instance, seasonal urban workers may relocate to search for higher wages to either compensate for a lack of economic opportunity in their community or to supplement small agricultural earnings. These workers become vulnerable to exploitation (Battersby and Siracusa 2009). The IOM estimates that the number of international migrants worldwide increased from 150 million in 2000 to 214 million in 2011. These migrants are among the least protected groups within most states, and thus they are particularly vulnerable to human trafficking or other exploitative labor conditions (Kvammen 2011). In some instances, migrants can have a difficult time protecting their own security if they have no allies within the government of the country where they reside. If we think about how this phenomenon relates to human security it becomes clear that we need to consider vulnerability, threats, empowerment and agency in order to have a complete picture of the story. One essential facet is gender identity. It must be recognized that women play multiple roles in the human trafficking saga. Women are counted among those most at risk for trafficking, but are also actively involved in the trafficking of others. It is essential that we untangle this complex web of factors and processes so we understand how human security can be better achieved.

Both the issue of human health and human trafficking reveal important connections between gender and human security. Both issues highlight the fact that women can face particular sources of vulnerability and insecurity *because* they are women. Poverty is an important source of vulnerability that opens the door for a multitude of human security threats, including health insecurity and trafficking. Women in countries across the globe find themselves disproportionately represented among the ranks of the poor. This is a trend dubbed *the feminization of poverty* by many scholars. The concept of the feminization of poverty has been influential in the development field largely beginning in the 1990s. It is intended to call attention to the large numbers of women living in poverty as well as to call attention to the impact of macro-economic policies on women (Chant 2008). It also raises attention to the way that identity intersects with vulnerability and insecurity. Gender, along with race, ethnicity, etc., causes certain assumptions about how people fit in to power structures and other societal processes. In many societies people are made vulnerable because they are identified as women. They will have challenges receiving education in some instances, they will have a difficult time receiving sources of credit, they will find themselves left out of key economic processes. The connections between gender, vulnerability, poverty, and development should not be surprising if we consider that the most widely discussed source of human security discourses is the 1994 UNDP report. This document came out of the UN body charged with coordinating international efforts on development. The challenge remains, however, to approach human vulnerability and insecurity in ways that recognize and work to address the gendered sources of vulnerability and insecurity.

Human Security as Emancipation

Human security remains a very controversial concept within security studies and policymaking. Potential drawbacks to the concept include the fact that it may be getting so loaded down with conceptual baggage that it becomes meaningless. The idea of human security may be, and some say already has become, a giant soup that gets so big and messy that policymakers knowingly leave it on the back burner (perhaps hoping that continued stewing will condense it down to a workable policy framework). Another potential drawback is that human security may be adopted by policymakers in ways not anticipated or appreciated by those hoping for a fundamental shift in thinking about security. The tendency of states, particularly Northern states, to use human security discourses to justify military intervention runs counter to the hope of those who originally embraced human security as a way to highlight both the pressing security needs of individuals or groups, as well as the insecurities that result from activities of states. The case of humanitarian intervention in Afghanistan on behalf of women illustrated that human security justifications do not automatically lead to effective action on removing vulnerability and insecurity for people. All of these criticisms have led some to wonder whether human security continues to be a useful concept within security studies and policymaking.

Looking at human security through gender lenses means acknowledging both the positives and negatives of the concept as it is currently understood, and an engaging in analysis of whether the discourses of human security can shift in meaningful ways to more fully incorporate gender. There are significant areas of potential that remain for the idea of human security. It does still encourage a reconceptualization of security away from state security to security at different levels. Gender identity is a useful frame for guiding this reconceptualization. Acknowledging that some sources of vulnerability and insecurity stem from how people are seen within their societies – man, woman, poor, ethnic minority, etc. – can help get at some of the systematic sources of insecurity for human beings at levels below the state. This move away from state security opens space for multiple actors to play a role in the promotion of human security. This includes actors at both sub-state and supra-state levels. This may help broaden the kinds of voices being represented or heard within security debates. This broadening can hopefully allow for gender to be incorporated into security thinking and policymaking in meaningful ways – in ways that take into consideration the gendered threats and vulnerabilities that lead to insecurity. This broadening may also open up space for different notions of sovereignty if we move security out of the exclusive responsibility of states (global ideas of security). The state has a complex relationship to human security. Within the current make-up of the international community, states are uniquely positioned to act against some of the most central sources of human insecurity. At the same time, the existing structures of the international system have at best been very slow to move on removing these sources of insecurity, and at worse have exacerbated them. Human security as a broadened/deepened security discourse has the potential to encourage a reflection about how the security of people and the security of the state are related. It can offer space to raise questions about whether state security measures that run counter to the promotion or provision of human security can be justified in today's context. It allows us to wonder whether a state within which both women and men face widespread challenges to their livelihoods, prosperity, and even lives can truly be said to be secure.

As with the other topics in this book, human security has important links to conceptualizations and strategies of emancipation. Several of the constraints to emancipation that Booth (1991) originally identified as impeding emancipation, including poverty, poor education, and political oppression, have been examined as threats to human security. In this way, the concepts of both emancipation and human security relates to security of humans rather than other actors in the international community. The very definition of emancipation used throughout the book refers to empowering people to make choices. This notion of empowerment features centrally in many discussions of how human security can be achieved. The Commission on Human Security (2003) identified empowerment as those strategies that enable people to develop resilience in the face of threats and vulnerabilities. Both empowerment and emancipation relate to people being free to live according to their own definition of "the good life." Contributors to insecurity, like poverty, must be removed for people to be empowered.

Poverty alleviation and development have been incorporated into several definitions of human security as strategies of emancipation for marginalized groups, including women. In fact, the 1994 UNDP report on human security distinguishes between human security and human development, the latter of which is defined as "a process of widening the range of people's choices" (UNDP 1994: 23). This sounds very much like critical approaches to emancipation. Human security and human development were understood to work together with one another, with human security relating more to the removal of immediate threats and human development relating to overarching societal conditions. Within these discourses, development is emancipation and promoting human security is what allows this emancipation to be realized (Thomas 2001). "The 'security' in human security embodies the idea that underdevelopment is dangerous. It highlights those factors such as poverty, health crises, environmental collapse, conflict and population displacement that threaten and undermine the homeostasis of self-reliance" (Duffield 2007: 115). The challenge for feminist scholars is to critically and thoroughly evaluate the gendered nature of the obstacles to development and sources of threats and vulnerabilities. A gender-informed approach to human security is a potentially useful approach to shedding light on these issues.

6

Gender, Security, and Environment

Each year states in the international community send representatives to take part in negotiations over how to address major environmental issues. From climate change, to biodiversity, to water issues, environmental problems are considered to be important concerns for states and their citizens. During a 2011 climate change meeting in Durban, South Africa, the United Nations Environment Programme (UNEP) released a report entitled "Women at the Frontline of Climate Change: Gender Risks and Hopes" (Nellemann et al. 2011). This report highlights that people's socially assigned roles in their communities impact their livelihoods and the ways they experience environmental problems. Actors in the international system have recognized that humans and their environment are inextricably intertwined. In fact, these connections have increasingly been discussed using discourses of security. Chapter 5 illustrated how security studies experienced an important shift with the concept of human security. The idea of *environmental security* emerged within a similar timeframe, and for related reasons. In fact, one of the seven elements of human security identified in the 1994 UNDP's Human Development Report is environmental security. In its most basic form, environmental security is a concept that implies a connection between environmental degradation and security. A variety of actors, including scholars, policymakers, and the media, have increasingly made connections between these areas. Links between security and environment have ranged from concerns about potential conflict over natural resources, to alarm about the potential security impacts that natural disasters can have for human beings.

To date, there has been little systematic work done that examines the intersection between approaches to environmental security and gender. There is an extensive literature on gender and the environment alongside feminist work on security; however, this scholarship is not frequently incorporated into mainstream approaches to the connections between security and environment. This chapter will assess the terrain of the security and environment debate, and address the inclusion of gender into this debate. The chapter will address the theoretical and practical implications of ignoring the gendered aspects of security and the environment through an examination of climate change as a security issue with unique gender connections.

Security and Environment

Some of the most obvious connections between security and environment are the environmental impacts of conflict and warfare. It has long been acknowledged that violent conflict can have devastating impacts on the environment (Seager 1999). Nearly every type of violent conflict can result in direct or indirect environmental damage. Matthew Paterson (2001: 44) addresses the environmental effects of war by claiming "the environment has been an instrument and a casualty of warfare itself, as strategists have used and abused ecosystems to give themselves military advantage." For centuries, military personnel have directly targeted the environment during combat, usually at an extremely high price to surrounding ecosystems. As military technology has advanced, the potential damage to the environment has also increased. The most powerful example of this may be "nuclear winter" that scientists contend would follow extensive nuclear war (Stone 2000). At the same time, the preparations for conflict have negative environmental consequences. Several scholars have pointed out the array of environmental damage that accompanies the daily activities in and around military bases worldwide (Akibayashi and Takazato 2010; Alexander 2010).

This link between militarized parties/activities and environmental damage is just one of the ways that security and environment are understood to be connected. Beginning largely in the 1980s, scholars began raising environmental issues into the realm of high politics. As argued in Chapter 1, this was important because the arena of high politics had historically been reserved for traditional security concerns. Early connections between security and environment challenged the traditional focus of security scholarship and called for environmental issues to be taken as seriously as military security issues. Some voices clearly wanted to strategically link their issue to security discourses. This tactic involves raising environmental issues to areas that are seen as being salient. On the other hand, several actors have pointed out that there are very real connections between environmental change and central security issues like violent conflict.

There have been a variety of ways that actors conceptualize a link between environment and security. An examination of scholarly debates demonstrates that there are three different discourses used to combine security and the environment – *environmental conflict, environmental security,* and *ecological security* (Detraz 2009). While there is overlap between the three discourses, each focuses on particular elements of security and its relationship to the environment. Each discourse has its own set of narratives for discussing the connections between security and environment. These narratives determine several aspects of the overall discourse, including how broadly or narrowly key ideas and terms are conceptualized, and how the security implications of environmental degradation are understood.

Environmental Conflict

The environmental conflict discourse includes a combination of state security concerns with environmental concerns. The central concern within this discourse is the potential for actors (individuals or states) to engage in conflict over access to natural resources. These conflicts have been identified as particularly likely under conditions of resource scarcity, and are typically understood to threaten the stability of the state (Homer-Dixon 1999). There are several broad trends that are identified as increasing the likelihood of environmentally induced conflicts including population expansion and migration, environmental scarcities, globalization which brings people (and disease) into closer proximity, and increasing recognition of environmental injustice (Barnett 2001).

An example of the environmental conflict discourse is fears about a lack of water availability contributing to conflict between two parties. Recent scholarly and media attention to the possibility of "water wars" between states or between sub-state actors is a reflection of this. Even if the potential conflicting parties in question are not states, there is a tendency to relate resource conflict to state instability and overall ideas of "national interest." This discourse focuses almost exclusively on threats tied to environmental degradation or scarcity, and largely lacks a concern about human vulnerability. Rather than act as a fundamental challenge to traditional notions of state security, environmental conflict adds environmental threats to the list of items that may threaten state stability and security. Human beings play a role in contributing to environmental degradation and in engaging in resource conflict; however their security is not the central concern for this discourse.

Environmental security

The environmental security discourse is concerned with the negative impacts of environmental degradation for human beings. This discourse is much more closely linked to notions of human security than state security. The issue of resource conflict is just one of a host of issues identified as important security concerns for the environmental security discourse. In this discourse, the threat is located in negative consequences of environmental damage and those who are vulnerable are all human beings (Dalby 2002, 2009). In general, environmental security is broader than environmental conflict because of the former's concern with issues concerning all of humanity and the latter's more focused concern with those susceptible to environmental conflict.

The defining characteristic of the environmental security discourse is a fundamental concern about the negative impact of environmental degradation for human beings. This environmental degradation can come from natural processes or from human behaviors, but there is some negative aspect of the change for humans. Some of the main themes in this body of work include the environmental impact of accelerating globalization, concerns over population increases, the spread of disease, and the potentials for sustainable development.

An example of the environmental security discourse is a concern about the impact of water scarcity for people's health, livelihood, and general well being. If people lack access to safe water, then they are at greater risk of illness. Likewise, if they work in the agriculture sector then their livelihood security is threatened. There is a tendency to consider both threats and vulnerabilities within the environmental security discourse, which results in a broader conceptualization of environmental issues as well as the policies designed to address them.

Ecological Security

Finally, ecological security is a discourse that focuses on the negative impacts of human behaviors for the sustainability and security of the environment. The entity whose security is of concern in this approach is the environment itself. This means human beings are seen as an essential part of ecosystems; however, those that use an ecological security discourse do not privilege humans as the most important species. In this approach species and ecosystems are preserved for their own sake, not for their value to humans (Litfin 1999). This is noteworthy because the environmental conflict and environmental security discourses are primarily concerned with the security of human beings – either collected in states or on their own.

An example of the ecological security discourse is a concern about the negative impacts of water scarcity for an ecosystem, including plant and animal life. This discourse would likely stress the human usage of water resources as contributing to the insecurity of the surrounding ecosystem. Because it is an ecocentric (i.e. environment-centered) discourse, it is focused on policies to ensure the sustainability of the environment. This lack of particular focus on the well being of humans makes it difficult to get onto most policy agendas.

Gender and Environment

As the study of global environmental politics as progressed, there has been increased attention paid to connections between environmental damage and race, class, and gender (Newell 2005). It is often claimed that men and women have unique relationships with the environment due to socially constructed gender roles. Much of the literature that explores the connections between women and the environment outline a variety of roles women play regarding the global environment (Bretherton 2003). Some claim that women can play an important role in environmental protection, some that women are often to blame for environmental degradation because of their roles as fuel wood gatherers, etc. Additionally, some paint women as a group that is particularly vulnerable to environmental degradation because of their location on the margins of many societies. Thus, women are simultaneously cast in the roles of "agents, victims and saviours in relation to environmental change" (Awumbila and Momsen 1995: 337).

Additionally, there have been international attempts at highlighting the links between women and the environment through global conferences and NGOs. Examples of these links span back to the UN Decade for Women (1975–1985) and various conferences, particularly the Nairobi Women's Conference in 1985 and the Fourth World Conference on Women in Beijing in 1995. It was at this time that a recognition was made that issues like access to fresh water and land were essential for the empowerment of women (Galey 1986; Hendessi 1986). According to the Beijing Declaration, "eradication of poverty based on sustained economic growth, social development, environmental protection and social justice requires the involvement of women in economic and social development, equal opportunities and the full and equal participation of women and men as agents and beneficiaries of people-centered sustainable development" (UN 1995). These conferences illustrated that women are an essential element to sustainable environmental solutions, often because of their relationship to the environment in their daily lives. This message has been carried through most global environmental conferences to varying degrees.

The message is also spread by organizations like Women's Environment and Development Organization (WEDO); Gender CC – Women for Climate Justice; Global Gender and Climate Alliance (GGCA). These organizations seek to highlight the unique environmental needs and connections of women and their role in environmental decisionmaking around the world. For example, WEDO's mission is "to empower women as decisionmakers to achieve economic, social and gender justice, a healthy, peaceful planet, and human rights for all." These organizations engage in a range of activities including issuing reports on gender and environmental issues, lobbying at global environmental meetings and conferences, and pushing for gender-sensitive environmental policies at all levels of governance.

Additionally, several countries around the world have begun to recognize a direct link between women and the environment in their environmental policymaking. For example, in Bangladesh's National Water Policy, one stated objective is "To bring institutional changes that will help decentralize the management of water resources and enhance the role of women in water management" (Ministry of Water Resources 1999: 3). Additionally, the policy document says that "[i]t is recognized that women have a particular stake in water management because they are the principal providers and carriers of water, main caretaker of the family's health, and participants in many stages of pre and post harvest activities" (Ministry of Water Resources 1999: 9).

While it is difficult and dangerous to generalize about the experiences of women with regard to experiences with environmental change, there are some trends that feminist scholars have outlined. Susan Buckingham-Hatfield (2000) explains that the typical household tasks that women perform are remarkably similar across cultures, although the households themselves and the tools used to perform the tasks will vary greatly. These include tasks like caring for children and/or older relatives and maintaining the family home. These similarities lead women to generally experience environmental change differently from men, often because of this role as caregiver. Being responsible for the well being of family members means that it is often women who are most aware of environmental ills that negatively impact health (Mies and Shiva 1993). Scholars and activists also point out that around the world, women have consistently been left out of decisionmaking positions that could address these issues, and call for greater attention to the potential role for women in environmental governance.

Ecofeminism

Ecofeminism represents a widely discussed lens to view the combination of gender issues and the environment. The term ecofeminism traces back to 1974 when French feminist Françoise d'Eaubonne published the word *ecoféminisme* to refer to the movement by women necessary to save the planet. The 1970s and 1980s saw the tendency for scholars and activists to use the term "ecofeminist" to refer to their struggle to link feminism and ecology. Karen Warren (1997: 3) claims:

> According to ecological feminists ("ecofeminists"), important
> connections exist between the treatment of women, people
> of color, and the underclass on one hand and the treatment
> of nonhuman nature on the other . . . Establishing the nature
> of these connections, particularly what I call women-nature
> connections, and determining which are potentially liberating
> for both women and nonhuman nature is a major project of
> ecofeminist philosophy.

Rosemary Radford Ruether (1997) identifies two main lines of thought among ecofeminists. One line of thought sees a women–nature connection as a social ideology constructed by patriarchal culture in order to justify the ownership and domination of both women and the natural world. She claims these ecofeminists "see the separation of women from men by patterns of cultural dualism of mind–body, dominant–subordinate, thinking–feeling, and the identification of the lower half of these dualisms with both women and nature, as a victimology" (Ruether 1997: 76). These dichotomies mask who women, men, and nature really are in their wholeness and complexity. A second line of thought agrees that the patriarchal women–nature connection serves to justify the domination and abuse of both, but also believes that there exists some deep positive connection between women and nature. This approach could also view humans as embedded in ecosystems, but would reserve a particularly positive role for women in this view.

Ecofeminism, particularly the second version discussed above, has been charged with essentialism. Noel Sturgeon (1999) argues that in the academic sphere, essentialist rhetoric can lead to poor scholarship as well as ignore important differences between groups of women. Similarly, Catriona Sandilands (1999: xix) claims "most ecofeminist writing is imbricated in a cultural feminist logic of identity politics in which ontological claims to an essence – whether that essence is seen as biological or social – are understood necessarily to precede political claims." She is particularly concerned with "motherhood environmentalism" which suggests that women's concerns about the environment boil down to "natural" protective instincts about the home and family, without necessarily a strong commitment to the environment itself. Ecofeminism has thus become a term with a large amount of conceptual baggage. That being said, there is a vibrant body of scholarship on the connections between gender and the environment. Much of this scholarship focuses on the tendency for men and women to experience environmental problems differently because of their relative positions within society.

Gendering Security and Environment Connections

While scholars, policymakers and the media have increasingly been making connections between security and environment, there has been a noticeable lack of attention to the myriad ways that gender fits into these debates. For example, gender is an element that is noticeably missing in each of the above discourses on security and the environment. When gender or gender concerns are mentioned, it is typically very briefly, and only tangential to the overall discussion. Scholars associated with the Global Environmental Change and Human Security (GECHS) initiative have explicitly made a connection between gender, security, and the environment (Goldsworthy 2010; Oswald Spring 2008), but most academics associated with security and environment scholarship rarely if ever mention gender. Looking at security and environment issues through gender lenses can reveal particular gender-differentiated impacts, responses, and contributions to environmental degradation as well as call attention to the gendered assumptions in society through which these issues are typically understood. It is important to note at the outset that some feminists will object to the idea of joining the concepts of security and the environment outright. Some feminists will view the particular insecurities that militarization bring for women as reason enough to steer clear of the concept. This is similar to the arguments made by several nonfeminist authors who criticize this connection for its potential to militarize the environment and further expand the realm of issues that are seen as the purview of the state (Conca 1994; Gleditsch 1998; Levy 1995). However, I feel that presenting a counter-discourse to traditional security studies can be performed in such a way that highlights the gendered assumptions of mainstream perceptions and calls attention to the specific issues that both men and women face in the current era of environmental politics.

Evaluating security and environment discourses through gender lenses offers a unique perspective on several of the key elements of security/environment connections. As was seen in previous chapters, utilizing gender lenses requires reexamining what are often taken to be "natural" elements of debate. This is particularly important in the realm of environmental politics because the environmental issues of concern are also livelihood issues for many members of the global population. Gender lenses necessitate problematizing experiences of environmental insecurity, problematizing the proposed causes of environmental conflict and environmental insecurity, and suggesting alternative ways to address environmental insecurity. The following sections address each of these issues in turn.

Gendered Experiences of Environmental Insecurity

To begin with, bringing gender into environment and security debates forces a reassessment of the ways scholars and policymakers have conceptualized the experience of environmental insecurity. Each of the existing security and environment discourses has a tendency to treat these experiences as gender neutral. This understanding of environmental insecurity masks the important differences in the ways people experience insecurity in their daily lives. There are a range of insecurities that are linked to environmental degradation or environmental scarcity by the various security and environment discourses. Natural disasters and food security problems are two such insecurities, and each of these areas has the potential for important gendered impacts.

Natural disasters are a part of everyday life on the planet. We read about floods, mudslides, earthquakes, and hurricanes year-round in our local newspapers. These natural disasters have direct impacts on security at an individual level and can even have security implication for states. Environmental security scholars have highlighted the fact that human beings sometimes instigate large-scale environmental disasters, and can make naturally occurring ones worse. For example, water development projects on rivers have been linked to worsening floods in parts of Asia (Nishat and Faisal 2000). Flooding, like other water-related disasters, brings destruction and disease to the population that experiences it. According to UN Water (2006: 2), "[b]etween 1991 and 2000 over 665,000 people died in 2,557 natural disasters of which 90% were water-related events . . . Losses stemming from disasters have greater impact in developing countries as compared to developed countries. More than 95% of all deaths caused by disaster occur in the developing countries." As is the case with many environmental disasters, flooding hits vulnerable populations first (Mirza et al. 2003).

Floods often have different impacts on women compared with men. "The restricted mobility of women and their particular responsibilities mean that the main problems they report in floods are cooking, collecting drinking water and toilet facilities. There is also shame where women have to move to public places to shelter from floods. Female-headed households are particularly badly affected and vulnerable in severe floods" (Thompson and Sultana 1996: 7). Another gender issue is the different medical needs that women have in disaster situations. There were reports of pregnant women without access to medical help delivering babies after the 2008 floods in Bihar in India (Gupta et al. 2008). This is an explicit example of a unique human security need of women. Mishra et al. (2004: 226) argue that "the circumstances of women's lives determine how they are affected by disasters and their options for responding. Poor people are generally at greater risk during natural disasters, and women are disproportionately represented among the poor." These issues demonstrate that there are gendered differences in the ways men and women can experience environmental insecurity. These types of differences need to be incorporated into larger debates on security and environment. Additionally, there needs to be increased awareness of these differences by policymakers and relief organizations if disaster relief is going to adequately ensure the security of all populations.

If we want to understand environmental disasters as a security issue, then it is essential that we explore the reasons why people experience these disasters differently. Many understand structural inequalities of income, access to opportunity, and political power as determinate of vulnerability to natural disasters. This is because of undiversified and fragile livelihoods, and poor housing among other things. Gender is said to be one dimension of these structural differences, as evidenced by relief workers only recognizing male heads of households or impediments in transferring land title to female survivors (Rajagopalan and Parthib 2006; Oswald Spring 2008). If we treat environmental insecurity as a gender-neutral phenomenon, we miss important elements of the different experiences humans have regarding environmental change.

Food security is another element of environmental insecurity that is widely discussed in security and environment debates. Food insecurity has been connected to both state security issues and human security issues (Shiva 2000). However, like discussions of natural disasters, gender is often underexplored by the environment and security debates on food security. There is a great deal of evidence that during times of food scarcity it is women and children who suffer most (Steans 2006). In 2007–2008 there were startling hikes in food prices worldwide, prompting several studies on the impacts on these types of price hikes for vulnerable populations. There are several factors that have been linked to the food price hikes including naturally occurring events like drought, and human-created phenomena like falling food stocks, increased use of grains for feedstock and bio-fuels, and changes in consumption patterns in emerging economies around the world. Zenebe Uraguchi (2010) examined households in Bangladesh and Ethiopia and found that gender inequality makes women more vulnerable to increases in food prices. In particular, it matters whether a household is headed by a man or a woman, with female-headed households at a greater risk for lacking access to and control over resources that can cope with external shocks like price spikes. Additionally, women in both male- and female-headed households were found to be more likely than men during times of food shortages to adopt coping mechanisms which reduced their personal intake of food, leading in some cases to food insecurity for those women. At the same time, the study also found that women in the areas studied were resourceful in devising ways to cope with food scarcity. A range of mechanisms were employed, including reducing the number of meals eaten per day, borrowing money from relatives to buy food, sending children to eat with relatives or neighbors, and begging as the most serious option.

Women are vital providers of food security for whole communities, a fact that is acknowledged by the various UN initiatives that make gender central to our understanding of food security. For example, the Food and Agriculture Organization of the UN (FAO) has undertaken a number of projects specifically designed to promote gender equality in agriculture and food security policies. Despite this, women disproportionately belong to the category of marginal farmers in rural areas around the globe, and particularly in Africa. In many parts of this region, women are traditionally expected to produce food to feed their families but are simultaneously excluded from many credit opportunities and left out of much of the decision-making on agricultural policy. FAO (2010) claims:

> Rural women suffer systematic discrimination in the access to resources needed for socio-economic development. Credit, extension, input and seed supply services usually address the needs of male household heads. Rural women are rarely consulted in development projects that may increase men's production and income, but add to their own workloads. When work burdens increase, girls are removed from school more often than boys, to help with farming and household tasks.

This shows that elements of the international community have recognized the differential gender impacts of food insecurity and the agricultural policy employed to achieve food security. As always, it is important to examine these issues in a context-specific manner in order to get a clear picture of the insecurities populations face, however there appear to be wider connections between food insecurity and gender.

Gender and Proposed Causes of Environmental Insecurity

Examining the connections between security and environment through gender lenses also requires questioning some of the typical associations made between human behavior and environmental insecurity. It must be acknowledged that by pointing to a single factor as causing environmental insecurity, that factor also becomes the subject of proposed solutions. Factors therefore must be examined with a specific attention given to the gender differences embedded within them. Issues of increased consumption often associated with accelerating globalization, growing population, and migrating populations are all cited as phenomena contributing to environmental degradation by scholars concerned with the environment. What must be realized is that while these factors might in fact produce environmental insecurities, they must not be taken as straightforward targets for solutions if these solutions do not examine any potential imbalanced impacts they may have for segments of the population – women in particular. Thus far, none of the discourses on security and the environment have engaged in determining the particular impacts that solutions targeting the above-mentioned issues may have on women. Population is likely the issue with the clearest gender ties. Both the environmental conflict and environmental security discourses associate population growth with the potential for environmental damage. Many feminists criticize population limitation development strategies that otherwise ignore or exploit poor women, yet make them the main target of population programs (Sen 2004; Urban 2007). These scholars feel population control should not be made a substitute for directly addressing the poor economic situation many of the world's women face. In the words of Jessica Leann Urban (2007: 251) "[r]ather than the simplistic analyses and crass solutions associated with the 'greening of hate,' whereby poor populations of color are blamed for ecological devastation, intersectional analyses and activism, including especially anti-racist and anti-imperialist feminist solidarities across borders, are critical to transformative social change."

Scholars who focus on these issues argue that population policies should be critically assessed in order to expose why they are introduced, and who benefits from them. Questions like this raise the point that in some cases the health of women may benefit from family planning measures or other population related policies. At the same time, however, an uncritical link between women's health and population control, or population reduction and development, masks the potential problems these policies raise for women. Some feminist scholars also highlight the unequal negative ramifications population-reduction policies have on women and girls, including high levels of female child abandonment or abortion (Dalsimer and Nisonoff 1997; Hudson and den Boer 2005). Issues like these reveal the significant policy implications wrapped up in security and the environment discourses. These decisionmaking impacts are a practical reason for why gender must be addressed in these areas. This shows that whether or not gender concerns are incorporated into security and environment discourses is not merely a theoretical exercise, but rather has policy implications which affect people's lives.

There is some tendency within the environmental security discourse to treat potential sources of environmental insecurity as more problematic variables. In terms of increases in population growth, Simon Dalby (2002) suggests that scholars look at the specific context of population increases, such as increases in urban populations, rather than make general statements about population pressure and environmental damage. Similarly, Jon Barnett (2001: 59) claims that "to focus on the conflict potential inherent in population growth is to ignore the real causes of poverty and vulnerability, namely the economic disadvantages people in the industrializing world experience from their exposure to global capital." This shows that this perspective is more critical than the environmental conflict discourse; however, the fact that population pressure is still not assessed through gender analysis suggests that the approach has further to go toward gaining a fuller understanding of human security and environment.

Migration is another topic discussed as a potential contributor to environmental conflict or insecurity. Those who use an environmental conflict discourse in particular claim that human migration can potentially contribute to environmental degradation, resource scarcity, and therefore violent conflict over resources. As the resources of an area become depleted, the population of that area may be forced to migrate to an area with better environmental health (Homer-Dixon 1994). Úrsula Oswald Spring (2008: 30) calls attention to the many causes of migration by arguing that it "has complex roots because people flee from disasters, socio-economic crises, poverty, marginalization, public insecurity, famines, internal conflicts, and wars. The people in the host country often become xenophobic, sometimes aggravated by conflicts over land, water, jobs, and houses." This quote is consistent with the environmental conflict discourse linking perceived resource scarcity and conflict at multiple levels.

It is also important to realize that men and women often face different challenges as migrants or refugees (DeJong 2000; Enloe 1990; Indra 1999; Kofman 2004). Kofman (2004: 657) explains that women's international migrations are often shaped by their migration through family routes and power relationships in the household. "Immigration regulations may place women in a position of dependency, but their trajectories and strategies are also influenced by power relations within the household, in both countries of origin and destination." For example, in the particular case of environmental displacement in Sudan, women face unique challenges in their new lives – including being at risk for violence by male members of the household, and being at risk for social harassment and rape outside their homes as traditional forms of the marriage institution dissolve (Babiker Mahmoud 1999).

Gender and Environmental Governance

Another feature of each of the security and environment discourses is to offer potential solutions to their various images of environmental insecurity. Examining security and environment connections through gender lenses requires assessing these proposed solutions for potential gendered implications. One of the most widely discussed policy options for addressing environmental damage is sustainable development. Sustainable development, or "development that meets the needs of the present without compromising the ability of future generations to meet their own needs," was introduced in the late 1980s as a compromise position between those that wanted to draw attention to global environmental damage and those that wanted to ensure that Southern states could continue to develop their economies in ways consistent with the development process of Northern states (World Commission on Environment and Development 1987). Sustainable development became an international buzzword that came to mean almost everything and nothing. Actors used the term either with a focus on the "sustainable" or the "development" to mean very different things. Nonetheless, it remains an often-used concept within discussions of environmental change.

Within the security and environment discourses, sustainable development has been envisioned as a way to avoid large-scale environmental scarcity and thus avoid environmental conflict, as well as a more general way to avoid environmental damage and the human insecurities that go along with it (Barnett 2001; Pirages and DeGeest 2004). Sustainable development is typically discussed in ways that do not reflect the gendered nature of either of its key terms. Those concerned with women's typical situation of being on the fringes of development are not satisfied with the traditional conceptualization of the term sustainable development (Harcourt 1994). Since different paths to development often have survival implications for its population, a gender-sensitive approach to sustainable development that takes into account the needs of women, the ecosystem, and future generations within a particular setting appear necessary to ensure security. This means that if sustainable development is advocated as providing security, then the specific needs of women also need to be addressed within that framework.

Another critique of sustainable development is that it allows change to come in the form of the current structures of society rather than calling for substantial change (Worster 1995). Advocating for change through sustainable development does not require a challenge to either the dominant economic or political structures or discourses, both of which are identified as patriarchal by various feminists. If sustainable development policies designed to correct environmental damage do not address the marginalization of many people within society, then some environmental insecurities may be avoided but a number of additional insecurities will remain.

Both men and women are routinely impacted negatively by environmental damage. Because of this, there has been a call to view both men and women as stakeholders in environmental decisionmaking (Nellemann et al. 2011). This inclusive approach to the policy process has not always been implemented in practice, however. Women are often underrepresented, or unrepresented, in environmental decisionmaking. For example, Andrea Moraes and Patricia Perkins (2007: 487) point out that although Brazil has a series of participatory water management laws, women are underrepresented at all levels of decisionmaking. They explain that water law in the country "establishes Watershed Committees composed of representatives from government agencies and civil society, which are responsible for all water-related issues. In legal terms this means poor women can act as civil society representatives on the Watershed Committees for rivers close to their houses." They found that poor women are especially excluded as these types of committees have become more and more dominated by professionals. They view this as problematic because it is the poor and racialized women that are the ones most likely to suffer directly from water-related problems. This speaks to larger issues of who has the right to speak about environmental issues and where "expertise" comes from. Environmental issues have tended to be viewed as "science" issues rather than as human security issues (O'Brien 2006). This tendency can lead to limiting the voices deemed legitimate to speak about environmental issues.

There are some global and local organizations that specifically seek to incorporate local knowledge into environmental decisionmaking. One example is the M.S. Swaminathan Research Foundation, located in Chennai, India, which combines human health, food security, and gender concerns. The organization stresses all that can be gained by consulting women's knowledge in order to ensure food security, particularly in India. It is acknowledged that women play a unique role in the production of food in many parts of the world, and thus have much to offer those making policy in this issue area. This may be an example of the way that these sets of (overlapping) concerns can be explored in the future. There appears to be an awareness within NGOs of the connections between these areas, and perhaps scholars and policymakers will be convinced of the connections as well.

Climate Change as a Security Issue

An interesting place to more fully explore the connections between environment, security, and gender is by examining the on-going tendency to link climate change and security. Discussions of climate change have exploded in recent years. It is difficult to go for very long without hearing something new about climate change science or policy in the news. Climate change is predicted to have a range of impacts on humanity, including but not limited to rising sea levels, worsening natural disasters like floods and hurricanes, increased range for diseases, and disruptions of growing seasons leading to food insecurity (IPCC 2007). Because of the predicted scale of these problems and their impacts on human relations and organizations as well as environmental systems, climate change has been increasingly discussed using security discourses.

In the past few years there has been a large number of publications that specifically link climate change and security in multiple ways (Detraz 2011; Detraz and Betsill 2009). The securitization of climate change has been understood as a way to grant additional attention and resources to climate change, and to get the public to take it seriously. For example, Liotta and Shearer (2007: 5) claim that "to better understand impacts of climate change on human needs, we focus them through the conceptual lens of security." Similarly, Geoffrey Dabelko (2008: 39) explains that "Japan, Canada, and a wide range of UN bodies now commonly use [a human security] frame, and small island states commonly invoke it to dramatize the threat to survival posed by climate change-induced sea-level rise." These statements illustrate the strategic usage of security discourses to raise awareness of environmental issues, and climate change in particular.

The links between climate change and security are by no means new. As far back as the late 1980s there were people discussing a number of ways climate change might negatively impact humans and the globe, including imperil human health and well being, diminish global food security, increase political instability and the potential for international conflict, and accelerate the extinction of animal and plant species upon which human survival depends (Gore 1989; World Conference on the Changing Atmosphere: Implications for Global Security 1988). More recently the issue has been addressed by security institutions across the international community. For example, the UN Security Council has taken up the topic of climate change in both 2007 and 2011. Several states, particularly those predicted to be the hardest hit by climate change impacts, have claimed that the Security Council has a responsibility to address the threats to international peace and security that will accompany a changing climate (MacFarquhar 2011).

Security and Environment Discourses in Climate Debates

Each of the security and environment discourses outlined above show up in debates about whether climate change is a security issue, although in differing degrees. By and large, the environmental conflict and environmental security discourses have dominated discussions of climate change and security. Ecological security shows up in a much more limited fashion. Additionally, there are only scattered references in the climate security debate about gender and gendered impacts of climate change. While organizations like UNEP and Oxfam have been explicit in making these connections, scholars, policymakers, and the media have not made gender a central part of their understanding of climate security. Part of our task, therefore, is trying to understand how gender fits into these debates.

We can think of the different security and environment discourses as varying on whether they focus on threats or vulnerabilities, and how they conceptualize those sources of insecurity. The *environmental conflict* discourse is concerned with threats in a traditional sense. This discourse appears in discussions about climate change and security through discussions of a concern about climate-induced resource scarcity sparking violent conflicts, environmental migration, state instability due to climate impacts, and the threats that each of these elements poses for the international security in general. In particular, there have been discussions of climate change causing increased resource scarcity and competition over basic resources like water, energy sources, and food at a sub-state level. Many scholars and policymakers have focused particular attention on Africa as a region at risk for resource conflict as a result of climate-induced resource scarcity (Baldauf 2006; Hendrix and Glaser 2007). Several scholars and policymakers have asked whether the conflict in Darfur is evidence of climate conflict. Despite this, most analysts do not go so far as to suggest that we will see all-out resource wars because of climate change. Instead, most scholars predict that climate-induced scarcity will exacerbate existing tensions and potentially inflame resource conflicts. For this reason, climate change is often deemed a "threat multiplier."

Select states, particularly Northern states, have become some of the most vocal actors on the link between climate change and security. There have been a series of widely publicized incidents of Northern policymakers making the link between climate change and security. In 2004, U.K. Science Adviser David King claimed "climate change is the most severe problem that we are facing today – more serious even than the threat of terrorism" (Quoted in Sawin 2005). Bodies within the US government have also strongly made the connection between national security and climate change in recent years. In the Pentagon's 2010 Quadrennial Defense Review, several connections between climate change and security are raised, including the role for the US military in climate-induced humanitarian crises, threats to US military bases, US need for energy security (Department of Defense 2010b: 85). The report claimed "[w]hile climate change alone does not cause conflict, it may act as an accelerant of instability or conflict, placing a burden to respond on civilian institutions and militaries around the world." At the same time, some states within the international community challenge whether security institutions are the appropriate location for discussions of issues like climate change. For example, in UN Security Council debates in July 2011 China and Russia challenged the idea that climate change is something for the council to address (MacFarquhar 2011).

In contrast, when the *environmental security* discourse is used to discuss climate change, there is a concern about both threats and vulnerabilities. This discourse tends to focus on the human security implications of climate change. A clear example of the environmental security discourse is the statement "the impacts of climate change are expected to be widespread and felt in a range of systems and sectors including water resources, health, and food production" (McDonald 2010: 65). Each of these sectors has implications for human survival and well being, and goes beyond merely a concern for the security of the state. At the same time, they all trace back to the environmental processes associated with a changing climate and are thus a specific set of human security concerns.

The concept of vulnerability is an important one for climate change scholarship (Adger 2006; Eakin and Luers 2006). Scholars who write about environmental vulnerability call attention to the fact that people experience environmental change differently depending on current and historical patterns of resource allocation and the complex feedbacks inherent in coupled human-environment systems (Folke 2006; O'Brien and Leichenko 2000). This concern with vulnerability echoes some of the arguments about human security versus state security raised in Chapter 5. Liotta and Shearer (2007: 9) argue that expanding our concern beyond threats is essential if we are to tackle climate change effectively. They defined these vulnerabilities as "inherent limitations or disadvantages in the material conditions and social structures that otherwise allow individuals to subsist (if not thrive) and communities to function (if not prosper)." According to this position, climate change is a complex phenomenon that will result in both threats and vulnerabilities. Each of these are important to understand and address in order to ensure security in the face of a changing climate. Climate change is predicted to negatively impacts people's ability to live, an immediate threat to human security. This loss of life is directly related to the condition of vulnerability. Vulnerabilities associated with climate change include loss of livelihoods, food insecurity, health concerns, and increased poverty. These vulnerabilities stem from the range of predicted impacts of climate change and are direct threats to human security.

Finally, the *ecological security* discourse focuses on threats to and vulnerability of the environment itself. This discourse is largely absent from discussions of climate change and security. Climate change is typically discussed as a threat to humans and to states. According to Gaillard (2010: 224) "[t]he contemporary focus on climate change thus reinforces a paradigm where Nature is the danger sources (even if exacerbated by human activity . . .) and where people have had to adjust/adapt to that threat." Rather than the environment being presented as something whose security is in jeopardy, it is often the case that the environment is presented as the threat to act against.

There are very few examples of scholars, policymakers or the media discussing the negative security implications of climate change for the environment. When these are mentioned, it is typically part of a larger discussion of the range of impacts of climate change. For example, Sawin (2005) claims that:

> Already, there is growing evidence that climate change is affecting the life-support systems on which humans and other species depend . . . Recent studies have revealed changes in the breeding and migratory patterns of animals worldwide, from sea turtles to polar bears. Mountain glaciers are shrinking at ever-faster rates, threatening water supplies for millions of people and plant and animal species.

This passage exhibits the ecological security discourse in that it treats humans as a part of ecosystems, but not necessarily dominant over other elements of those ecosystems. However, the majority of works that connect climate change and security do not use this particular discourse. When the needs of the environment are mentioned, it tends to be a peripheral concern to human needs and insecurities.

Gender and Climate Change

Because climate change is an issue with direct implications for human security and is such a salient issue within the international community, it is essential that we understand the implications of a changing climate through gender lenses. There has been increasing attention paid to the connections between gender and predicted climate impacts in recent years, in particular by the NGO and policy communities. Organizations like the Gender CC network and the Global Gender and Climate Alliance have publicized the connections between gender and climate change. When feminist academics have studied gender and climate change they have tended to be gender, environment and development (GED) scholars or feminist researchers working for the UN, government ministries, and women's environmental organizations (MacGregor 2009). Despite this lag in academic scholarship, there are a number of specific contributions that understanding climate change and security through gender lenses offers. These include exploring gendered differences in environmental vulnerability, rethinking our understanding of climate change, and recognizing the contributions that gender makes to climate policymaking.

As is evident from the discussion above, there is a great deal of attention paid to the idea of vulnerability within climate change debates. For example, Clionadh Raleigh (2010: 71) claims that vulnerability is only partly tied to physical exposure to environmental damage and its effects. The root of vulnerability "stems from location and social disadvantages, including poverty and political marginalization. Limited assets and political power reduces access to resources and, in turn, narrows the range of options available in times of stress." There are a range of social factors that shape vulnerability, including dimensions of marginalization, like class, ethnicity, gender, and age. Those elements of society that contribute to groups being less valued as members also contribute to acute vulnerability in the face of environmental damage like that predicted to accompany climate change. This means when we discuss climate vulnerability we must understand that there are important social dimensions included in the concept. Food insecurity, livelihood insecurity, or increased environmental disasters will not be experienced the same ways by all members of society, and gender is an important component of differential implications of environmental vulnerability.

It is important to point out that when global environmental politics scholars and policymakers discuss vulnerability it is not to suggest that it is a "natural" or unproblematic condition. We can explore the condition of vulnerability while still recognizing agency. In fact, many feminist scholars and gender NGOs highlight how women are not "victims" or inactive political agents, but often display creative adaptation tendencies in the face of environmental damage. That being said, it is important to understand that because women often find themselves on the margins of society they will sometimes experience environmental problems differently from, and more severely than, non-marginalized groups.

There is a danger in simplistically linking women with poverty and thereby with vulnerability to climate change impacts. While it is true that estimates suggest up to 70 percent of the world's poor are women there are key differences in how climate change is predicted to look on the ground which will impact vulnerability (MacGregor 2009). It is important to unpack these relationships in order to understand where vulnerability stems from.

> Considering gender divisions of labour in agriculture, fisheries, the informal sector, the household, and the community, can assist us in pinpointing where vulnerability to ecological threats lies. Women's dependence on communal tree and plant resources, and their responsibility for fetching water, can place them under increasing strain as they trek further in search of firewood, and face diminishing plant resources and water shortages. Trekking long distances for water and fuel also affects the academic performance of young girls (Masika 2002: 5).

Examining the concept of vulnerability through gender lenses can help us understand the complexity inherent in the predicted future impacts of climate change.

We have already seen that men and women tend to experience food insecurity and natural disasters differently. Predictions suggest that climate change will result in an increase in both food insecurity and natural disasters (IPCC 2007). This means that even more attention must be paid to the particular ways that groups in society, particularly women, experience these kinds of insecurities. Climate change is expected to cause dramatic shifts in growing seasons and drought patterns. In terms of food security, which can also have implications on livelihood security for those who are agricultural workers, research suggests that women receive a smaller share of credit and assistance in agriculture. For example, recent studies have found that less than 10 percent of the credit granted to small farmers in Africa goes to women. Without credit, female farmers cannot buy the types of inputs needed to adapt to agriculture in a changed climate. These inputs include new agricultural technologies that use less water, as droughts may become more common, and new varieties of plant types and animal breeds intended for higher drought or heat tolerance (Demetriades and Esplen 2010).

Similarly, examining climate security through gender lenses will prompt us to pay attention to the unique security needs of men and women during natural disasters. Climate models predict that natural disasters will worsen as weather patterns change around the world (IPCC 2007). Women tend to die in higher numbers in certain disasters, and may be at greater risk as refugees or in relief camps. A recent study of the disasters that occurred between 1981 and 2002 in 141 countries found that more women than men die in disasters where women's economic and social rights are not ensured (Neumayer and Plümper 2007 cited in Sasvari 2010). Additionally, women may face unique problems in the aftermath of disasters. Justina Demetriades and Emily Esplen (2010: 135) explain that

> Gender inequalities also may be exacerbated in the aftermath
> of disasters. For example, there is some evidence to suggest that
> women and girls are more likely to become victims of domestic
> and sexual violence after a disaster, particularly when families
> have been displaced and are living in overcrowded emergency
> or transitional housing where they lack privacy. Adolescent girls
> report especially high levels of sexual harassment and abuse in the
> aftermath of disasters, and they complain of the lack of privacy
> they encounter in emergency shelters.

It is essential that these issues are incorporated into discussions of climate change as a security issue because they are very real security issues for those who experience them in the wake of environmental disasters.

For each of these areas of vulnerability it is essential to incorporate gender in such a way that rejects the false dichotomy of vulnerable women/invulnerable men. While gender is one important component of vulnerability that needs to be explored, there are other intersecting inequalities that contribute to increased environmental vulnerability. "So rather than discounting men in gender analyses of climate change as if they are somehow nongendered and impervious to the harsh impacts of environmental degradation in contexts of economic or social marginalization, we need to find spaces within gender and climate change frameworks to acknowledge and communicate the vulnerabilities that some men also experience" (Demetriades and Esplen 2010: 140). This kind of analysis includes recognizing multiple types of marginalization that both men and women can face that contributes to insecurity.

Another contribution of gender lenses to climate change and security debates is to rethink our understanding of climate change as well as its impacts. Some scholars suggest that climate change is a masculine issue area because of the domination of scientific discourses and "expertise," as well as the recent securitizing moves made in climate change discussions (MacGregor 2009). Environmental issues in general tend to be heavily influenced by scientific discourses in ways not seen in other IR issue areas. This is potentially problematic for scholars like Sandra Harding (1993: 39) who wish to problematize the idea of the sacredness of science. She claims that "[t]he project that science's sacredness makes taboo is the examination of science in just the ways any other institution or set of social practices can be examined." She argues that it is not that there is a fundamental problem with scientific objectivity, but instead that knowledge which is purported to be objective is often the subjective knowledge of privileged voices. Instead we must have a "strong objectivity," including the perspectives of the marginalized in the methodological and substantive concept of science (Harding 1998; Sylvester 2002). Science is often assumed to be correct and beyond questioning in today's society. Relying on an institution that is both dominated by males and is a part of the patriarchal social structure of society may be questioned by those that wish to call attention to its potential problems as well as benefits.

The world of science is often (mistakenly) imagined to be a world of male scientists. When we see scientists or hear stories of science in the media it is often male voices that are represented. For example, a recent report on the science coverage of the BBC found there was a notable lack of women who either covered or appeared in science stories (Sample 2011). This picture of the scientific community may be responsible for the tendency for women to express doubts about scientific comprehension. An interesting recent study by Aaron McCright (2010) on gender and climate change knowledge and concern found that women conveyed a greater assessed scientific knowledge of climate change than did men, yet were less confident about their scientific comprehension than were men. The study used eight years of Gallup data on climate change knowledge and concern in the US general public to conclude that women in the US are more likely to express concern about climate change and know more about scientific information about climate change, but also more likely to question their scientific knowledge. This lack of confidence may stem from a pervasive image of scientific expertise being associated with masculinity. Even beyond scientific expertise, the most recognizable voices on climate change also tend to be male. The Nielsen Company and Oxford University conducted an online survey in 2007 and found that 18 out of the 22 "most influential spokespeople on climate change" are men. The top of the list include Al Gore, Kofi Annan, Nelson Mandela, and Bill Clinton. There are five women on the list, but they are celebrities, like Oprah Winfrey and Angelina Jolie rather than policymakers or scientists (MacGregor 2009; Nielsen Company 2007). The women on the list do not hold positions that are strongly associated with political or professional expertise.

Additionally, authors like Karen O'Brien (2006: 2) claim that the current tendency in society to treat environmental concerns as issues of "science" rather than of human security fails to engage society in creating the transformations necessary to achieve sustainability. She claims that the framing of an issue shapes the types of questions that are asked, the research that takes precedence, and the solutions and policies that are suggested. "To reframe environmental change as an issue of human security involves asking some very relevant questions about equity, justice, vulnerability, power relations, and in particular, questions about whose security is actually threatened by environmental change." If we revise our understanding of climate change in a way that frames it as a human security issue, then we not only broaden the type of issues open for debate, but we may also broaden the range of voices considered to be legitimate actors to speak about climate change.

A final area of contribution that gender lenses makes to the climate security debate is through recognizing the contributions gender makes to governing climate change. At present, the major international climate change agreements contain little to no consideration of gender. Neither the 1994 United Nations Framework Convention on Climate Change, which was the first international treaty to address global warming, nor the Kyoto Protocol, which was the follow-up treaty, mention women or gender. Most recently, the Copenhagen Accord, the non-binding resolution that came out of the global climate conference in December of 2009, does not mention either gender or women. A report on long-term cooperative action that came from the Copenhagen Conference does mention gender in several places, but there is more emphasis on women "being vulnerable" to climate impacts than on the need to recognize women as stakeholders in climate policy. Additionally, women's share in the delegation of parties at the Copenhagen Conference was relatively small with about 30 percent of registered country delegates and about 10 percent heads of delegations being female (GenderCC 2010).

In addition to increasing the number of women present at global climate negotiations, there are specific questions about the kind of training deemed necessary for participation in these discussions. This is particularly true for discussions about areas like Clean Development Mechanisms (CDM), which are projects with a component that reduces or sequesters greenhouse gas emissions. Rachel Masika (2002: 7–8) argues that building capacity for women "in this area requires equal access to education, training, and technology in developing countries, and more female professionals and male experts who have received gender training in the fields of engineering and other technical areas, who could potentially contribute to a more gender-sensitive CDM policy." Also, there is debate about which strategies are most effective at getting gender incorporated in discussions. Should individuals and organizations seeking to incorporate gender into climate change discussions utilize insider strategies, and risk cooptation, or utilize outsider strategies and risk marginalization (Bretherton 2003)?

Finally, there is concern about what types of climate change policies should be privileged. This speaks to the distinction between mitigation and adaptation strategies. Using everyday language, mitigation refers to changing behavior in order to avoid the worst of the impacts of a changing climate. There has been a general trend in Northern states focusing a great deal of attention on mitigation strategies in global climate negotiations. At the same time, there has not been much attention paid to the particular expertise of women around the world in mitigation strategies at any level of policymaking. Adele Sasvari (2010: 16) claims that "[a]s women are traditionally responsible for biomass energy supply at the household level, they can also become key players in the adoption of new energy technologies that reduce greenhouse emissions."

Adaptation, on the other hand, refers to strategies designed to modify practices, infrastructure, policies, etc. in order to cope with the impacts of a changing climate. This includes paying particular attention to those groups that are expected to be the hardest hit by climate change. There has been a tendency for Southern states, at least in the last five years or so, to focus on adaptation strategies in global climate negotiations. This is perhaps unsurprising given the fact that states in the global South are expected to be particularly hard hit by climate change impacts, and the poor within all states are disproportionately expected to suffer from climate change impacts. The Intergovernmental Panel on Climate Change (IPCC), an international body of scientists who issue regular reports on climate change, includes a section on gender in their 2007 report on "impacts, adaptation and vulnerability." The report claims that:

> Climate change . . . has gender-specific implications in terms of both vulnerability and adaptive capacity. There are structural differences between men and women through, for example, gender-specific roles in society, work and domestic life. These differences affect the vulnerability and capacity of women and men to adapt to climate change. In the developing world in particular, women are disproportionately involved in natural resource-dependent activities, such as agriculture, compared to

salaried occupations. As resource-dependent activities are directly dependent on climatic conditions, changes in climate variability projected for future climates are likely to affect women through a variety of mechanisms: directly through water availability, vegetation and fuelwood availability and through health issues relating to vulnerable populations (especially dependent children and elderly). Most fundamentally, the vulnerability of women in agricultural economies is affected by their relative insecurity of access and rights over resources and sources of wealth such as agricultural land. (Adger et al. 2007: 730)

These points highlight the fact that while gender should be an important component in both mitigation and adaptation strategies, there is a clearer link between adaptation strategies and the on-the-ground experiences of insecurity in the face of climate change for both women and men. This means that there should be an even stronger focus on gender in adaptation policies than is currently the case.

Emancipation and Environmental Security

Including gender as a fundamental element of analysis in security and environment discourses represents an important opportunity for scholars to gain essential perspective on the security of both humans and the environment. Some important steps have been made thus far by scholars in terms of highlighting connections between security and the environment. It is now time to bring out the gendered elements both of these scholarly debates, as well as gendered elements of the topic of security and the environment itself for people's daily lives. If we are to understand the ins and outs of these links, gender must be a focus of analysis due to its ever-present impact on how this topic is understood and its impacts on how environmental insecurity is experienced. At present, this is still lacking. This is particularly troubling given the important policy implications of security and environment discourses. The fact that they lack an inclusion of gender concerns makes the process of formulating policies to address security and environment links incomplete.

Understanding the connections between gender, security, and

environment is even more important in an issue area like climate change. Climate change is predicted to have severe consequences that will impact a huge number of individuals across the globe. There are important social factors that can shape climate vulnerability, including gender. Climate vulnerability has been recognized as a security issue by many voices in the international community. The challenge now is to understand the numerous ways both climate vulnerability and climate policymaking are gendered. As a community of scholars, we should be asking which strategies contribute to both environmental sustainability and gender emancipation.

Emancipation is connected with environmental issues in several ways. Environmental degradation can severely limit the freedoms of those who live within marginalized environments. A report issued by UNEP claims that environmental damage has a range of potential impacts on women – "it limits their time that could be spent on income generation, alternative livelihood activities, training, education, participating in institutional and governing fora, engaging in social and developmental opportunities and maintaining their health" (Nellemann et al. 2011: 38). The report goes on to suggest that increased workloads for women, including having to walk farther and farther from home to collect water or fuelwood, leads to increased frequency of parents or guardians taking girls out of school in order to carry out these tasks. Additionally, men and women who experience environmental vulnerability may be forced to migrate to avoid natural disasters or ensure food security. Each of these is instances where choice will be limited due to daily experiences of environmental insecurity.

While these examples are documented in cases around the world, it is the task of critical scholars to contemplate the gendered sources of environmental insecurity without making essentialist claims about the needs or experiences of men or women. It is important that both sources of environmental vulnerability and the agency of marginalized communities are acknowledged. For example, this chapter discussed the various strategies that were utilized to cope with food insecurity in Bangladesh and Ethiopia (Uraguchi 2010). This is a reflection of the fact that those faced with environmental insecurity often come up with impressive coping mechanisms in the face of environmental change. That being said, the process of emancipation can be furthered if environment-related sources of threats and vulnerabilities are identified and removed. This task coincides with larger strategies of promoting and ensuring human security. Betty Reardon (2010) identifies several elements necessary for the achievement of human security, including the meeting of basic physical and survival needs, respect for personal and group dignity and identity, protection from avoidable harm, and access to a sustaining and sustainable environment. This illustrates the close ties between the fate of humans and the fate of the environment. The process of emancipation entails identifying the multiple obstacles to freedom that people face, whether these relate to war or conflict, economic marginalization, or environmental destruction.

Conclusion – The Contributions of Gender Lenses to Security

Security is an incredibly complex concept that is understood to have uniquely high stakes for actors in the international community. Security has been a principal concern for both scholars and policymakers and will continue to have an important place on global agendas. Judging by the number of book series, journals/journal articles, and conferences on security topics, it is clear that security studies occupies a central place within IR in particular. Using gender lenses to evaluate key topics within security studies allows for a greater level of exchange between feminists and non-feminist security scholars. It also brings feminist scholarship into a pivotal area of study within International Relations. This inclusivity is desirable to encourage fruitful dialogue across different "camps" of IR (Sylvester 2010). While this inclusivity is certainly important, it is not the most vital contribution of this exercise. Instead, using gender lenses to evaluate security illustrates that security studies misses out when gender is absent. Militarization, peacekeeping/peacebuilding, terrorism, human security, and environmental security are all topics that have shaped the terrain of both security scholarship and policymaking. Each of these are gendered, and it is therefore necessary to bring this to the forefront of analysis. Failing to do this ignores essential issues like the gendered consequences of militarization, the insecurity women can face through their interactions with peacekeepers, the policy implications of assuming that women cannot be violent, the unique sources of insecurity at a personal level that men and women may face because of being associated with a particular gender, and the unique contributions women and men can make to reversing environmental insecurity. These are just a few examples of what is gained by making gender a central element of security studies.

One of the goals of this book has been to illustrate that terms and ideas that are often considered to be natural or unproblematic within security scholarship and policymaking look different through the lenses of gender. Concepts like peacebuilding or environmental conflict, which have been widely used by security scholars, tend to be used as if they are gender neutral. Attention may be paid to the differences between the processes of peacekeeping and peacebuilding, or the range of impacts states face if there is a risk of environmental conflict within their borders, but these concerns only tell part of the story of security. The chapters in the book show that incorporating gender into security studies broadens our analysis of key concepts and fundamentally challenges the scope of analysis of much existing scholarship.

A second goal of the book is to demonstrate the central place gender has in security topics, whether this is recognized in most security scholarship or not. The current security discourses used by scholars and policymakers are gendered, which impacts how we understand and react to topics like terrorism or peacekeeping. It is therefore important to evaluate the gendered nature of these discourses in order to achieve reflexive scholarship and effective policymaking. In this way, gender analysis functions as a way to critically evaluate the numerous issues linked to the idea of security in order to reveal inconsistencies, power relations, marginalization, and emancipatory potential. We can use gender to reflect on the various sources of vulnerabilities and threats that contribute to insecurity. People experience insecurity in some instances because they are a man or woman, or because they don't comfortably fit into either category. An example of this is the perpetration of hate crimes against gays, lesbians, and transgender individuals. These acts often result from people reacting violently when individuals do not conform to the labels that we are all faced with.

It is not enough to take traditional concepts like security and conflict and lay gender on top of them. Feminist analysis involves recognizing the impossible fit between gendered identity and gendered assumptions and the way that many dominant security ideas have been conceptualized. For instance, state security is typically understood as an unproblematic public good. Feminist analysis challenges this assumption by asking about the disconnect between the provision of state security, militarization, and issues like sexual abuse or other forms of human insecurity. It challenges the role of the state and military institutions that do not always behave in ways that advance the security of all within their borders. It challenges the longstanding prioritization of state security over human security. It challenges the lack of women in positions of authority who are seen as legitimate voices to speak about security.

It is also essential that we use gender lenses that reflect the complexity of gendered socialization in society. We cannot simply say that men experience insecurity in these ways and women experience insecurity in these other ways. Gender identity is intricately tied to other identities including class, sexuality, race, ethnicity, etc. Therefore it is essential that we problematize the experiences of people while at the same time trying to identify patterns of insecurity. Chapter 4 examined the ways that gendered assumptions which are prevalent in the international community confuse our understanding of terrorism. Assuming that terrorists are necessarily male or that the presence of female terrorists requires unique explanation is an over-simplification with important implications. Terrorist organizations have already used these assumptions to avoid detection. When these organizations dress male terrorists like women or actively recruit women into their cause because it is easier for them to avoid detection, they are using gender stereotypes strategically. It is essential that these assumptions are critically evaluated in order to determine who is served by them and how they contribute to insecurity.

Likewise, we do not advance scholarship much if we adopt essentialist understandings of gender and rape, or gender and trafficking. As discussed in Chapter 2, many feminist scholars have studied rape as a security issue. This includes examining the power dynamics, processes of othering an enemy, and assumptions about masculinity and femininity that all contribute to rape being a relatively widespread phenomenon within society, particularly during times of conflict. Studying rape as a security issue using gender lenses requires exploring the societal processes that make this phenomenon persist, but also understanding the fact that essentialist assumptions about rape can blind us to the experiences of those that do not fit dominant views of who is most likely to suffer rape. This latter category includes men who are raped in both times of war and peace. Men who are raped experience a traumatic event, and in many cases are unlikely to report it because of assumptions about masculinity. Additionally, many rape crisis centers do not have resources to counsel male victims (Rabin 2012). At the same time, essentialist notions of human trafficking often result in conceptualization of the issue only involving white women as the victims of sexual trafficking. These reductionist ideas fail to capture the complexity of these issues, but more importantly, they cast certain individuals as more worthy of attention than others. This process does nothing to consider the insecurity experienced by multiple groups, often because of their associations with genders, races, ethnicities, etc. Critical scholarship must engage in reflexive scholarship to avoid this potential for essentialism.

The Process of Emancipation

The need for reflexive scholarship extends to examining emancipation and security. Emancipation is about removing obstacles to choice, and the threats and vulnerabilities associated with insecurity are important obstacles in people's lives. Throughout the book, emancipation has been described as a process. Regarding emancipation as a process does not suggest a definite, knowable end point, but rather implies that it must be the subject of continual evaluation. This evaluation needs the input of multiple voices – including those who experience insecurity, study conceptualizations of security, and make policy designed to remove threats and vulnerabilities. Feminists concerned with emancipation are not necessarily seeking to "give voice" in these contexts, but rather to evaluate multiple perspectives and provide space for them in their analysis.

Two concepts associated with emancipation are development and empowerment. Each of these ideas is regarded as linked to people's ability to make choices, and are also tied to security discourses. Chapter 5 claimed that development is often seen as a strategy for emancipation. This speaks to removing multiple obstacles to choice – including economic and physical constraints. Development is also tied to human security in those discourses that stress "freedom from want" either along with or prioritized over "freedom from fear." Caroline

Thomas (2001: 160) explains "human insecurity results directly from existing structures of power that determine who enjoys the entitlement to security and who does not. Such structures can be identified at several levels, ranging from the global, to the regional, the state and finally the local level." A lack of development is seen as resulting in vulnerability which undermines human security at a basic level.

Empowerment relates to enabling people to remove obstacles to choice. Shepherd (2010: xx) defines empowerment as "increased capacity for action." A form of empowerment that feminist scholars have studied is the ability to have a say in the political processes that impact people's daily lives. Chapter 3 addressed the international community's discussion of women at the peace-negotiation table. The UN, NGOs, states, and scholars have all suggested that it is necessary to include women in the peacebuilding process. This is so that gender equity is achieved, but also in order for the post-conflict phase to be shaped by a broad group with a stake in its future. Similarly, several actors have stressed that women should be understood as stakeholders in environmental issues like disaster relief (Enarson and Morrow 1998; Mishra et al. 2004). As stakeholders they should be incorporated into decisionmaking and policy implementation. When women have been significantly incorporated in environmental projects the results have ranged from improving their leadership qualities, confidence, self-reliance, and gaining more power in their communities (Aladuwaka and Momsen 2010). Each of these is important for achieving an increased capacity for action.

Development and empowerment are not unproblematic concepts. Each can be approached in an essentialist manner. Critically considering emancipation requires thinking reflexively about potential strategies for removing obstacles to choice. It also involves recognizing that there will be different interpretations of what people will ultimately be free to do, once obstacles have been removed. It must be acknowledged that people's choices will differ. Saba Mahmood (2005: 1–2) considers this issue with regard to women's participation in urban mosque movements in Egypt. She claims:

> Women's participation in, and support for, the Islamist
> movement provokes strong responses from feminists across a

broad range of the political spectrum. One of the most common reactions is the supposition that women Islamist supporters are pawns in a grand patriarchal plan, who, if freed from their bondage, would naturally express their instinctual abhorrence for the traditional Islamic mores used to enchain them. Even those analysts who are skeptical of the false-consciousness thesis underpinning this approach nonetheless continue to frame the issue in terms of a fundamental contradiction: why would such a large number of women across the Muslim world actively support a movement that seems inimical to their "own interests and agendas," especially at a historical moment when these women appear to have more emancipatory possibilities available to them?

This tension highlights differences within feminism in general (Sylvester 2010). Some feminists express a strong commitment to recognizing women's agency and choice, even if it manifests in channels like participation in religious movements which are often regarded as patriarchal. Other feminists have argued it has been impossible for women to freely make choices as long as they have existed in patriarchal systems. These differing perspectives highlight the ongoing conversations that take place among feminists, and further illustrate that there is not a single feminist perspective on security or emancipation.

If emancipation is conceptualized as removing constraints to choice, then we must consider cases where emancipation may result in some form of insecurity. The case of terrorism illustrates that some women who choose to engage in militancy view it as a means of empowerment. Likewise, we must contemplate the fact that freeing people to make their own choices may result in environmental insecurity. People may choose to use resources unsustainably or otherwise engage in behavior that contributes to environmental degradation. So, how can these tensions between emancipation and security be resolved? There is not an easy answer to that question, but any move towards this end would need to address underlying motivations for people's choices. In the case of environmental behaviors, this may require asking questions about how people conceptualize scarcity and abundance. How do they understand the relationship between humans and the environment? Exploring these underlying factors is necessary in a reflexive approach to security.

Shifting Away from Militarization

A goal many feminists share is that the international community move away from the processes of militarization and militarism. Militarization guides what is considered legitimate behavior, and Chapter 2 illustrated that this can have very real, negative consequences for people in their daily lives. Additionally, militarization privileges state security over human security and presents serious challenges to the achievement of human security. Reardon (2010: 7) strongly states the case by claiming "human security never can be achieved within the present highly militarized, war prone, patriarchal nation state system." The US wars in Iraq and Afghanistan were incorporated into several chapters of this book. This is because of the fact that these conflicts are widely understood as offering important examples of the consequences of militarization for multiple actors, and tied to multiple issues. These two conflicts involved large numbers of people playing a variety of roles – soldiers, civilians, humanitarians, private security contractors, government officials, peace protestors, etc. They have been the subject of a great deal of feminist analysis because of their scale and the range of impacts they have had on numerous states across the international system. As the conflicts "officially" come to an end, feminists will continue to ask questions about the implications of militarization for multiple forms of security.

Women's organizations have been some of the most strident advocates of the position that security can only be achieved through a rejection of militarization and a focus on peace. These organizations argue that war, conflict, and militarization are not an avenue to peace, but rather are the key obstacles to peace. This relates to the issue of peacekeeping as it has traditionally been approached in the international community. Many critical perspectives question whether peace can truly be achieved through the deployment of militarized bodies. Even if soldiers are given specific training as peacekeepers/peacebuilders, they are representatives of militaries – institutions that are routinely considered to further militarized masculinities which both men and women are expected to live up to. If peace (as well as war) is the purview of soldiers, then how much will militarization be absorbed in a post-conflict society? At the same time, what does this do for opening up space for female voices and the consideration of human security issues?

Critical perspectives like feminism also reject the idea of using human insecurity to justify military intervention. As seen in Chapter 5, if actors highlight human insecurity in the pre-conflict phase, it is not necessarily an indication of the policies that will be put in place during and after the conflict. Human security concerns can easily slip down the list of priorities, or be left to deal with after the "real business" of the country is finished. This is not to say that there are not pressing human security concerns across the planet, but rather that military intervention may not be the best way to address these urgent concerns. A militarized response to human insecurity may inadvertently lead to additional vulnerabilities and threats that actually worsen insecurity for both women and men.

Many of the issues discussed in this section directly relate to the state as the dominant actor in today's international system. The state is an actor that security scholars must include in their analysis. State actions have direct consequences for issues of security. The state is a central actor in processes of militarization and in drafting and implementing policies that have impacts on both state security and human security. States craft security policy according to how they understand the concepts associated with security. In this way, states are guided by differing security discourses. For example, in the days after 9/11 the US made policy through a state security discourse which included a specific definition of terrorism. The guiding discourse led to the "war on terror" which included both domestic and international components. Domestically it included increased surveillance authorized under the Patriot Act, and internationally it was directed at first Afghanistan and later, Iraq. Had the US been guided by different security discourses, policymaking would have looked different. Norway had a markedly different response to the terrorist attack in their country in July of 2011. The government's reaction was to reaffirm a commitment to a culture of openness, which was one of the specific complaints of the attacker. Prime Minister Jens Stoltenberg told reporters "It's absolutely possible to have an open, democratic, inclusive society, and at the same time have security measures and not be naïve . . . I think what we have seen is that there is going to be one Norway before and one Norway after July 22 . . . but I hope and also believe that the Norway we will see after will be more open, a more tolerant society than what we had before" (Schwirtz 2011). While it is absolutely true that the context of these two sets of attacks differs, it is also true that the states in question were operating under different security discourses.

This shows that it is possible for states to be guided by alternative security discourses. For instance, some states have strongly adopted environmental protection as a security issue. Small island states and others that are understood to be particularly vulnerable to the impacts of climate change have compared it to warfare. They have likened chimney stacks and exhaust pipes to weapons like guns and bombs (Detraz and Betsill 2009). This is an example of *broadening* security discourses to include a wide range of threats, in this case to state security. Alternatively, actors can *deepen* approaches to security by expanding the referents of security to include human beings. States like Canada, Norway, and Japan played a lead role in popularizing the idea of human security and laying some groundwork for how specific versions of human security could be incorporated into policymaking. While many proponents of human security argue that these states adopted conceptualizations of human security that were too narrowly tied to freedom from fear over freedom from want, or that their policies have not gone far enough to promote human security, the fact is that these and other states have demonstrated that state security is not the only legitimate concern for states in the international community.

This list illustrates that states operate under very different conceptualizations of security. Many critical perspectives have challenged the ways that states have historically carried out security policy. However, despite the fact that states have not always acted in ways that ensure security for those on the margins of society, they remain the most powerful actor in the international system. Engagement with the state, as well as other high-profile institutions like the UN, is necessary for those who actually want their work to translate into policy guidance. This may not be an easy task, but it is essential if we want our scholarship to have policy relevance. It is possible for states to make security policy in ways that reflect security discourses not associated with militarization, and reflecting on how gender changes security discourses is an important component in finding alternative ways to approach security.

In addition to states and international institutions, NGOs can play important roles in efforts to reconceptualize security. There are numerous organizations working to broaden and deepen security discourses. An example is Women in Security Conflict Management and Peace (WISCOMP), an organization that actively promotes redefining security in ways that incorporate gender, and encourages actors to rethink security policy in South Asia. One of their missions is to "[c]ontribute to an inclusive, people-oriented discourse on issues of security, which respects diversity and which foregrounds the perspectives of women and the hitherto marginalized" (WISCOMP 2011). The organization strives to demonstrate that security issues go beyond state security in South Asia and elsewhere. Another example of an organization which challenges dominant security narratives is the Okinawa Women Act Against Military Violence (OWAAMV). This organization was established in 1995 by women who spoke out against military violence in Okinawa, Japan. The group specifically targets gender-based violence committed by US soldiers, and the environmental destruction of military preparations and activities around military bases. They provide a human security and environmental security critique of military bases which contrasts with arguments that establishing bases abroad is necessary for state and international security (Akibayashi and Takazato 2010). Initiatives like these work towards a recognition that human security is an essential goal in its own right, and that gender is an essential component of attempts to rethink security. They are premised on the idea that how we understand security matters for how we are likely to address it.

International Security and Gender in the Future

Feminist security scholarship is a vibrant and expanding area of research. It is recognized as providing important insights into the complexity of the security terrain by critical scholars, but is increasingly influencing more mainstream security scholarship as well (Buzan and Hansen 2009). Much feminist security scholarship specifically seeks to understand the unique security situations of women and men. Most of these scholars acknowledge that both women and men are often negatively impacted by war and conflict, environmental insecurity, or human insecurity – however these impacts are typically gendered. In terms of a traditional security issue like war, feminist security scholars conclude that all stages of conflict are gendered – and that this often serves to make women more vulnerable than men to security threats. There is a tendency in this literature to look at what happens during wars as well as being concerned with their causes and endings. Feminist security studies also concentrate on the ways world politics can contribute to the insecurity of people, especially people who are marginalized and disempowered. This is in contrast to traditional security approaches that have typically evaluated security issues as narrowly confined to state security.

It is this focus on the insecurity of people that makes narratives like human security and environmental security appealing for much feminist scholarship. Discourses of human security and environmental security are useful ways to shift security discourses away from narratives that at best ignore gender, and at worst reinforce gender inequality. Each offers important space to think about the connections between the removal of threats/vulnerabilities and the process of emancipation. Both human security and environmental security are admittedly limited ideas with a great deal of conceptual baggage, but they have retained some of the revolutionary element that made them unique when they were first introduced into security scholarship and policymaking. They are useful tools for shifting the dominant security discourse to more accurately reflect the insecurity that people face in their daily lives.

At the same time, it is unhelpful for human security and environmental security to simply become subsumed under the idea of state security. It is often the case that both ideas are linked to state security because it remains a salient frame for not only security scholarship but also policymaking. In this way, proponents of both human security and environmental security make claims that the promotion of human security/environmental security actually enhances state security as well. While there are many instances where these various discourses work together and mutually support each other, human security and environmental security are valid goals in their own right without being linked to the security of states. Chapter 5 illustrated that attempts to combine state security and human security objectives may result in a prioritization of state security goals. When the rights and human security of women are linked to state security objectives they do not have a permanent place on policy agendas.

A similar picture emerges when we consider the multitude of security and environment discourses. The environmental conflict discourse is largely concerned with the security and stability of the state. If scholarship and policymaking is guided by this discourse alone, little attention or resources will be diverted to the vulnerabilities and threats to human beings or the environment itself. One of the shifts in discourse that the feminist community should strive for is to delink the concepts of human security and environmental security from state security. We should think of *security* as a broad umbrella, and military security/conflict should be subsumed under the umbrella along with things like insecurity in the face of natural disaster, insecurity due to loss of livelihood, etc.

Along these lines, it is necessary to reprioritize our standards of security. Arundhati Roy (2004) has asked:

> What does peace mean in a world in which the combined wealth of the world's 587 billionaires exceeds the combined gross domestic product of the world's 135 poorest countries? . . . What does peace mean to the poor who are being actively robbed of their resources and for whom everyday life is a grim battle for water, shelter, survival and, above all, some semblance of dignity? For them, peace is war.

This quote calls to mind ideas like economic security and livelihood security. Roy is highlighting North/South divisions here, but the sentiment also relates to divisions within wealthy societies. For example, there are important sources of insecurity within every country on the planet, including those which have a great deal of economic and military security as a state. Within many Northern states, large numbers of people experience insecurity in their daily lives through things like poverty, high crime rates, etc. For this reason, it is not enough to conceptualize security as simply state security, or to assume that the condition of security does not vary greatly within communities. To do so hides the complex picture of international security. The ways we conceptualize security need to be reflexive in both scholarship and policymaking. Understanding (in)security requires looking across multiple levels and recognizing the sources of insecurity in each.

We also must think about security in ways that recognize both vulnerability and agency. Vulnerability stems from societal structures and assumptions – not from weakness or inability. It is essential to keep this in mind when we consider women's vulnerability to security threats. This is not a book about big bad men and innocent little women. It is about the various sources of insecurity in the global community and how our understanding and policymaking about those sources of insecurity have changed over time and continue to change into the future.

We must also be aware of the gendered impacts of security policymaking. When scholars and policymakers identify issues or phenomena as security issues, then they become the target for solutions, but these solutions can have a range of (intended and unintended) gendered consequences. The discussions of population and environmental change in Chapter 6 highlight this. When population is linked to environmental change and its resulting insecurity, there are inevitably calls from multiple sectors for policies to decrease population. Within environmental politics scholarship there is a continual back-and-forth between people who want to put population on policy agendas because of its environmental consequences, and those that argue that to do so opens the door for repressive policies that have a range of unintended outcomes (Hartmann 2010). These debates are sure to heat up as the global population continues to increase past seven billion. The fact remains that proposed solutions to security issues must be carefully examined before they are implemented and justified based on crisis or emergency arguments. One unintended consequence of population policies in China is their link to human trafficking as discussed in Chapter 5. Traditional ideas about the preference for male children rather than female children in China contributes to the vulnerable position many girls find themselves in (LaFraniere 2011). This and other side-effects should convince us that all security issues are complicated and require careful examination.

The way we understand the world around us changes. In other words, discourses change. Security was once associated almost exclusively with war and conflict, but now space has been created for the inclusion of topics like peacekeeping/peacebuilding, terrorism, human security, and environmental security. This process of shifting discourses occurs continually in our daily lives. Whereas the world once thought of witches and wizards as old, mystical, somewhat dangerous creatures, we are now more prone to thinking of them as school children learning spells and playing sports on broomsticks. Referencing Harry Potter may seem trivial, but it illustrates both that concepts are not set in stone, and that popular culture, the media, and other agents of socialization have an important role to play in shaping how we understand the world around us. The discourses we use are shaped by the information we are exposed to. Chapter 4 argued that the media reinforce the idea that terrorists should be men because they are the violent ones while women are the beautiful souls. This assumption is spread to a wide number of people, and has negative implications for our conceptualizations of security.

This influence is not inconsequential, because policymakers are exposed to the same discourses and norms as the rest of us. This means that security discourses are as important for policymaking as they are for academic scholarship. Policymakers base their decisions on how they understand the world. Existing security discourses that privilege state security and ignore gender have been used to justify and encourage militarized responses to threats in the international system. These militarized responses have gendered impacts and blind us to an entire universe of alternative insecurities. Rethinking security through the lenses of gender encourages us to contest simplistic assumptions about threats, vulnerabilities, enemies, etc. It challenges both policymakers and academics to think about whose security is threatened. It problematizes existing narratives and discourses, and reveals that security studies without gender analysis can offer only partial understandings of security issues and incomplete frameworks for policymaking.

References

Abrahms, Max. 2006. "Why Terrorism Does Not Work." *International Security.* 31(2): 42–78.

Adger, W. Neil. 2006. "Vulnerability." *Global Environmental Change.* 16: 268–281.

Adger, W. Neil et al. 2007. *Assessment of Adaptation Practices, Options, Constraints and Capacity.* Intergovernmental Panel on Climate Change.

Agathangelou, Anna M., and L. H. M. Ling. 2004. "Power, Borders, Security, Wealth: Lessons of Violence and Desire from September 11." *International Studies Quarterly.* 48(3): 517–538.

Akibayashi, Kozue, and Suzuyo Takazato. 2010. "Gendered Insecurity under Long-Term Military Presence: The Case of Okinawa." In Reardon and Hans 2010, pp. 38–60.

Aladuwaka, Seela, and Janet Momsen. 2010. "Sustainable Development, Water Resources Management and Women's Empowerment: The Wanaraniya Water Project in Sri Lanka." *Gender and Development.* 18(1): 43–58.

Alexander, Ronni. 2010. "Seeking Human Security in a Militarized Pacific: Struggles for Peace and Security by Pacific Island Women." In Reardon and Hans 2010, pp. 197–229.

Alvarez, Lizette. 2008. "Despite Army's Assurances, Violence at Home." *New York Times.* http://www.nytimes.com/2008/11/23/us/23abuse.html?scp=1&sq=Despite%20Army%27s%20Assurances,%20Violence%20at%20Home.&st=cse (Accessed September 25, 2010).

Alvarez, Lizette, and Deborah Sontag. 2008. "When Strains on Military Families Turn Deadly." *New York Times.* http://www.nytimes.com/2008/02/15/world/americas/15iht-15vets.10076087.html?scp=2&sq=When%20Strains%20on%20Military%20Families%20Turn%20Deadly.&st=cse (Accessed September 25, 2010).

Anderlini, Sanam Naraghi. 2007. *Women Building Peace: What They Do, Why It Matters.* Boulder, CO: Lynne Rienner Publishers.

Anderson, Marion. 1999. "A Well-Kept Secret: How Military Spending

Costs Women's Jobs." In *Gender Camouflage: Women and the US Military*, eds Francine D'Amico and Laurie Weinstein. New York: New York University Press, pp. 247–252.

Andreas, Peter. 2003. "Redrawing the Line: Borders and Security in the Twenty-first Century." *International Security*. 28(2): 78–111.

Andrieu, Kora. 2010. "Civilizing Peacebuilding: Transitional Justice, Civil Society and the Liberal Paradigm." *Security Dialogue*. 41(5): 537–558.

Awumbila, Mariama, and Janet Henshall Momsen. 1995. "Gender and the Environment: Women's Time Use as a Measure of Environmental Change." *Global Environmental Change*. 5(4): 337–346.

Baaz, Maria Eriksson, and Maria Stern. 2009. "Why Do Soldiers Rape? Masculinity, Violence, and Sexuality in the Armed Forces in the Congo (DRC)." *International Studies Quarterly*. 53: 495–518.

Babiker Mahmoud, Fatima. 1999. "The Gender Impact of War, Environmental Disruption and Displacement." In *Ecology, Politics and Violent Conflict*, ed. Mohamed Suliman. New York: Zed Books, pp. 45–75.

Bäckstrand, Karin, and Eva Lövbrand. 2006. "Planting Trees to Mitigate Climate Change: Contested Discourses of Ecological Modernization, Green Governmentality and Civic Environmentalism." *Global Environmental Politics*. 6(1): 50–75.

Baldauf, Scott. 2006. "Africans Are Already Facing Climate Change." *Christian Science Monitor*. 4.

Balko, Radley. 2011. "A Decade After 9/11, Police Departments Are Increasingly Militarized." *The Huffington Post*. http://www. huffingtonpost.com/2011/09/12/police-militarization-9-11-september-11_n_955508.html (Accessed November 11, 2011).

Bank of Canada. 2012. "Canadian Journey." http://www.bankofcanada. ca/banknotes/bank-note-series/canadian-journey/ (Accessed January 4, 2012).

Barnett, Jon. 2001. *The Meaning of Environmental Security: Ecological Politics and Policy in the New Security Era*. New York: Zed Books.

Basu, Soumita. 2011. "Security as Emancipation: A Feminist Perspective." In *Feminism and International Relations: Conversations About the Past, Present and Future*, eds J. Ann Tickner and Laura Sjoberg. New York: Routledge, pp. 98–114.

Battersby, Paul, and Joseph M. Siracusa. 2009. *Globalization and*

Human Security. New York: Rowman and Littlefield Publishers, Inc.

Bellamy, Alex J., and Matt McDonald. 2002. "'The Utility of Human Security': Which Humans? What Security? A Reply to Thomas and Tow." *Security Dialogue.* 33(3): 373–377.

Bellamy, Alex J., Paul Williams, and Stuart Griffin. 2009. *Understanding Peacekeeping.* Malden, MA: Polity.

Berkowitz, Dan. 2005. "Suicide Bombers as Women Warriors: Making News Through Mythical Archetypes." *Journalism and Mass Communication Quarterly.* 82(3): 607–622.

Bhandari, Meena. 2011. "Health Check for Sierra Leone." *Guardian.* http://www.guardian.co.uk/global-development/poverty-matters/2011/jun/24/sierra-leone-free-heatlh-care-one-year-on-missing-drugs/print (Accessed July 18, 2011).

Billon, Philippe Le. 2001. "The Political Ecology of War: Natural Resources and Armed Conflicts." *Political Geography.* 20: 561–584.

Bloom, Mia. 2005. *Dying to Kill: The Allure of Suicide Terror.* New York: Columbia University Press.

Booth, Ken. 1991. "Security and Emancipation." *Review of International Studies.* 17(4): 313–326.

——. 2005. "Critical Explorations." In *Critical Security Studies and World Politics,* ed. Ken Booth. Boulder, CO: Lynne Rienner Publishers, pp. 1–20.

——. 2007. *Theory of World Security.* New York: Cambridge University Press.

Brandt, Patrick T., and Todd Sandler. 2010. "What Do Transnational Terrorists Target? Has It Changed? Are We Safer?" *Journal of Conflict Resolution.* 54: 214.

Bretherton, Charlotte. 2003. "Movements, Networks, Hierarchies: A Gender Perspective on Global Environmental Governance." *Global Environmental Politics.* 3(2): 103–119.

Brison, Susan J. 2002. "Gender, Terrorism, and War." *Signs: Journal of Women in Culture and Society.* 28(1): 435–437.

Broadbent, Lucy. 2011. "Rape in the US Military: America's Dirty Little Secret." *Guardian.* http://www.guardian.co.uk/society/2011/dec/09/rape-us-military (Accessed December 12, 2011).

Bromley, Mark, and Carina Solmirano. 2012. *Transparency in Military Spending and Arms Acquisitions in Latin America and the Caribbean.* SIPRI.

Browne, Kingsley. 2007. *Co-ed Combat: The New Evidence that Women Shouldn't Fight the Nation's Wars*. New York: Sentinel.

Brownmiller, Susan. 1975. *Against Our Will: Men, Women and Rape*. New York: Fawcett Books.

Buckingham-Hatfield, Susan. 2000. *Gender and Environment*. New York: Routledge.

Bumiller, Elisabeth. 2010. "Sex Assault Reports Rise in Military." *New York Times*: p.14. http://www.nytimes.com/2010/03/17/us/17assault.html?scp=1&sq=sexual%20assault%20reports%20rise%20in%20military&st=cse (Accessed: 8/14/2010).

———. 2011. "Raid Account, Hastily Told, Proves Fluid." *New York Times*: A1.

Buruma, Ian, and Avishai Margalit. 2002. "Occidentalism." *New York Review of Books*. http://www.nybooks.com/articles/archives/2002/jan/17/occidentalism/ (Accessed June 18, 2011).

Buzan, Barry. 1991. 2nd edition. *People, States and Fear: An Agenda for International Security Studies in the Post-Cold War Era*. Boulder, CO: Lynne Rienner Publishers.

Buzan, Barry, and Lene Hansen. 2009. *The Evolution of International Security Studies*. New York: Cambridge University Press.

Buzan, Barry, Ole Wæver, and Jaap de Wilde. 1998. *Security: A New Framework for Analysis*. Boulder, CO: Lynne Rienner Publishers.

Campbell, David. 1998. *Writing Security: United States Foreign Policy and the Politics of Identity*. Minneapolis: University of Minnesota Press.

Campbell, Howard. 2008. "Female Drug Smugglers on the US-Mexico Border: Gender, Crime, and Empowerment." *Anthropological Quarterly*. 81(1): 233–267.

Carnahan, Michael, Scott Gilmore, and William Durch. 2007. "New Data on the Economic Impact of UN Peacekeeping." *International Peacekeeping*. 14(3): 384–402.

Carpenter, R. Charli. 2006. "Recognizing Gender-Based Violence Against Civilian Men and Boys in Conflict Situations." *Security Dialogue*. 37(1): 83–103.

Carver, Terrell. 2003. "Gender/Feminism/IR." *International Studies Review*. 5(2): 288–290.

Chandler, David. 2008. "Human Security: The Dog That Didn't Bark." *Security Dialogue*. 39(4): 427–438.

Chandler, David, and Nik Hynek, eds. 2011. *Critical Perspectives on Human Security: Rethinking Emancipation and Power in International Relations*. New York: Routledge.

Chant, Sylvia. 2008. "The 'Feminisation of Poverty' and the 'Feminisation' of Anti-Poverty Programmes: Room for Revision?" *Journal of Development Studies.* 44(2): 165–197.

Chopra, Tanja. 2009. "When Peacebuilding Contradicts Statebuilding: Notes from the Arid Lands of Kenya." *International Peacekeeping.* 16(4): 531–545.

Christie, Ryerson. 2010. "Critical Voices and Human Security: To Endure, to Engage or to Critique?" *Security Dialogue.* 41(2): 169–190.

Cockburn, Cynthia. 2010. "Gender Relations as Causal in Militarization and War: A Feminist Standpoint." *International Feminist Journal of Politics.* 12(2): 139–157.

CODEPINK. 2011. "About Us." http://www.codepink4peace.org/article.php?list=type&type=3 (Accessed October 16, 2010).

Cohn, Carol. 1993. "Wars, Wimps, and Women: Talking Gender and Thinking War." In *Gendering War Talk*, eds Miriam Cooke and Angela Woollacott. Princeton, NJ: Princeton University Press, pp. 225–246.

Cole, Alyson M. 2008. "The Other V-word: The Politics of Victimhood Fueling George W. Bush's War Machine." In Riley et al. 2008, pp. 117–130.

Collins, Alan. 2007. *Contemporary Security Studies.* New York: Oxford University Press.

Commission on Human Security. 2003. *Human Security Now.* New York: Commission on Human Security. http://www.policyinnovations.org/ideas/policy_library/data/01077/_res/id=sa_File1/ (Accessed February 15, 2011).

Conca, Ken. 1994. "In the Name of Sustainability: Peace Studies and Environmental Discourse." In *Green Security or Militarized Environment*, ed. J. Kakonen. Dartmouth: Aldershot, pp. 7–24.

Confortini, Catia Cecilia. 2011. "Doing Feminist Peace: Feminist Critical Methodology, Decolonization and the Women's International League for Peace and Freedom (WILPF), 1945–75." *International Feminist Journal of Politics* 13(3): 349–370.

Connell, R. W. 1995. *Second Masculinities.* Los Angeles: University of California Press.

Coulter, Chris. 2008. "Female Fighters in the Sierra Leone War: Challenging the Assumptions?" *Feminist Review.* 88: 54–73.

Cronin, Audrey Kurth. 2003. "Behind the Curve: Globalization and International Terrorism." *International Security.* 27(3): 30–58.

Cunningham, Karla. 2003. "Cross-Regional Trends in Female Terrorism." *Studies in Conflict and Terrorism.* 26: 171–195.
——. 2008. "The Evolving Participation of Muslim Women in Palestine, Chechnya, and the Global Jihadi Movement." In Ness 2008, pp. 84–99.

D'Amico, Francine. 2000. "Citizen-Soldier? Class, Race, Gender, Sexuality and the US Military." In *States of Conflict: Gender, Violence and Resistance,* eds Susie Jacobs, Ruth Jacobson, and Jennifer Marchbank. New York: Zed Books, pp. 105–122.

D'Amico, Francine, and Peter R. Beckman. 1994. "Introduction." In *Women, Gender, and World Politics: Perspectives, Policies, and Prospects,* eds Peter R. Beckman and Francine D'Amico. Westport, CN: Bergin and Garvey, pp. 1–14.

D'Costa, Bina. 2006. "Marginalized Identity: New Frontiers of Research for IR?" In *Feminist Methodologies for International Relations,* eds Brooke A. Ackerly, Maria Stern, and Jacqui True. New York: Cambridge University Press, pp. 129–152.

Dabelko, Geoffrey D. 2008. "An Uncommon Peace: Environment, Development, and the Global Security Agenda." *Environment.* 50(3): 32–45.

Dalby, Simon. 2002. *Environmental Security.* Minneapolis: University of Minnesota Press.
——. 2009. *Security and Environmental Change.* Malden, MA: Polity.

Dalsimer, Marlyn, and Laurie Nisonoff. 1997. "Abuses against Women and Girls under the One-Child Family Plan in the People's Republic of China." In *The Women, Gender and Development Reader,* ed. Lynn Duggan and Nalini Visvanathan. New Jersey: Zed Books, pp. 284–292.

Davies, Sara E. 2009. *Global Politics of Health.* Malden, MA: Polity.

DeJong, Gordon F. 2000. "Expectations, Gender, and Norms in Migration Decision-Making." *Population Studies.* 54(3): 307–319.

DeLarrinaga, Miguel, and Marc G. Doucet. 2008. "Sovereign Power and the Biopolitics of Human Security." *Security Dialogue.* 39(5): 517–537.

Demetriades, Justina, and Emily Esplen. 2010. "The Gender Dimensions of Poverty and Climate Change Adaptation." In *Social Dimensions of Climate Change: Equity and Vulnerability in a Warming World,* eds Robin Mearns and Andrew Norton. Washington, DC: The World Bank, pp. 133–144.

Denov, Myriam S. 2006. "Wartime Sexual Violence: Assessing a
    Human Security Response to War-Affected Girls in Sierra Leone."
    Security Dialogue. 37(3): 319–342.
Denov, Myriam, and Richard MacLure. 2006. "Engaging the Voices
    of Girls in the Aftermath of Sierra Leone's Conflict: Experiences
    and Perspectives in a Culture of Violence." *Anthropologica.* 48(1):
    73–85.
Department of Defense. 2010a. *Female Active Duty Military Personnel
    by Rank/Grade.* United States Government. http://siadapp.dmdc.
    osd.mil/personnel/MILITARY/rg1009f.pdf (Accessed August 4,
    2011).
——. 2010b. *Quadrennial Defense Review Report.* Washington, DC:
    United States Government. http://www.defense.gov/qdr/qdr%20
    as%20of%2029jan10%201600.PDF (Accessed October 16, 2010).
Der Derian, James. 1995. "The Value of Security: Hobbes, Marx,
    Nietzsche and Baudrillard." In *On Security*, ed. Ronnie D.
    Lipschutz. New York: Columbia University Press, pp. 24–45.
Detraz, Nicole. 2009. "Environmental Security and Gender: Necessary
    Shifts in an Evolving Debate." *Security Studies.* 18(2): 345–369.
——. 2011. "Threats or Vulnerabilities? Assessing the Link Between
    Climate Change and Security." *Global Environmental Politics.*
    11(3).
Detraz, Nicole, and Michele M. Betsill. 2009. "Climate Change
    and Environmental Security: For Whom the Discourse Shifts."
    International Studies Perspectives. 10(3): 304–321.
Deudney, Daniel. 1990. "The Case Against Linking Environmental
    Degradation and National Security." *Millennium: Journal of
    International Studies.* 19(3): 461–476.
DFAIT. 1999. *Human Security: Safety for People in a Changing World.*
    Ottawa: Department of Foreign Affairs and International Trade.
    http://summit-americas.org/Canada/HumanSecurity-english.htm
    (Accessed July 20, 2011).
Dowell, Leilani. 2008. "Violence against Women: The US War on
    Women." In Riley et al. 2008, pp. 219–223.
Duffield, Mark. 2007. *Development, Security and Unending War:
    Governing the World of Peoples.* Malden, MA: Polity.
Dugger, Celia W. 2011. "Uganda Lacks Resources to Prevent Maternal
    Deaths." *New York Times.* http://www.nytimes.com/2011/07/30/
    world/africa/30uganda.html&_r=1&hp (Accessed August 1, 2011).
Duncanson, Claire. 2009. "Narratives of Military Masculinity in

Peacekeeping Operations." *International Feminist Journal of Politics* 11(1): 63–80.

Eakin, Hallie, and Amy L. Luers. 2006. "Assessing the Vulnerability of Social-Environmental Systems." *Annual Review of Environment and Resources.* 31: 365–394.

Edberg, Mark. 2004. *El Narcotraficante: Narcocorridos and the Construction of a Cultural Persona on the US-Mexican Border.* Austin: University of Texas Press.

Eisenstein, Zillah. 2007. *Sexual Decoys: Gender, Race and War in Imperial Democracy.* New York: Zed Books.

——. 2008. "Resexing Militarism for the Globe." In Riley et al. 2008, pp. 27–46.

Elbe, Stefan. 2010. *Security and Global Health.* Malden, MA: Polity.

Elshtain, Jean Bethke. 1987. *Women and War.* Chicago: The University of Chicago Press.

Emmanuel, Sarala. 2002. "The Female Militant Romanticised." *Women in Action.* 1(April): 15–18.

Enarson, Elaine, and Betty Hearn Morrow. 1998. *The Gendered Terrain of Disaster: Through Women's Eyes.* Westport, CT: Praeger.

Enloe, Cynthia. 1990. *Bananas, Beaches and Bases: Making Feminist Sense of International Politics.* Berkeley: University of California Press.

——. 2000. *Maneuvers: The International Politics of Militarizing Women's Lives.* Berkeley: University of California Press.

——. 2002. "Untitled." *International Feminist Journal of Politics.* 4(1): 103.

——. 2004. *The Curious Feminist: Searching for Women in a New Age of Empire.* Berkeley: University of California Press.

——. 2007. *Globalization and Militarism: Feminists Make the Link.* New York: Rowman and Littlefield Publishers.

——. 2010. *Nimo's War, Emma's War: Making Feminist Sense of the Iraq War.* Berkeley: University of California Press.

FAO. 2010. "Why Gender?" ed. United Nations. *Food and Agriculture Organization.* http://www.fao.org/gender/gender-home/gender-why/why-gender/en/ (Accessed January 26, 2011).

Ferber, Abby L., and Michael S. Kimmel. 2008. "The Gendered Face of Terrorism." *Sociology Compass* 2(3): 870–887.

Fluri, Jennifer L. 2008. "'Rallying Public Opinion' and Other Misuses of Feminism." In Riley et al. 2008, pp. 143–160.

Folke, Carl. 2006. "Resilience: The Emergence of a Perspective for Social-Ecological Systems Analysis." *Global Environmental Change.* 16: 253–267.

Friedman, Barbara. 2008. "Unlikely Warriors: How Four US News Sources Explained Female Suicide Bombers." *Journalism and Mass Communication Quarterly.* 85(4): 841–859.

Friesendorf, Cornelius. 2007. "Pathologies of Security Governance: Efforts Against Human Trafficking in Europe." *Security Dialogue.* 38(3): 379–402.

Gaillard, Jean-Christophe. 2010. "Vulnerability, Capacity and Resilience: Perspectives for Climate and Development Policy." *Journal of International Development.* 22: 218–232.

Galey, Margaret E. 1986. "The Nairobi Conference: The Powerless Majority." *PS.* 19(2): 255–65.

GenderCC. 2010. "In Retrospect: Gender in COP15." http://www. gendercc.net/fileadmin/inhalte/Dokumente/UNFCCC_conferen ces/COP15/Gender_in_the_Copenhagen_outcomes_final.pdf (Accessed November 10, 2010).

Gentry, Caron E. 2009. "Twisted Maternalism: From Peace to Violence." *International Feminist Journal of Politics* 11(2): 235–52.

Gentry, Caron E., and Laura Sjoberg. 2011. "The Gendering of Women's Terrorism." In Sjoberg and Gentry 2011, pp. 57–80.

Gentry, Caron E., and Kathryn Whitworth. 2011. "The Discourse of Desperation: The Intersections of Neo-Orientalism, Gender and Islam in the Chechen Struggle." *Studies in Conflict and Terrorism.* 4(2): 145–161.

Gilmore, Jonathan. 2011. "A Kinder, Gentler Counter-Terrorism." *Security Dialogue.* 42(1): 21 -37.

Giroux, Henry A. 2008. "The Militarization of US Higher Education after 9/11." *Theory, Culture and Society.* 25(5): 56–82.

Gizelis, Theodora-Ismene. 2009. "Gender Empowerment and United Nations Peacebuilding." *Journal of Peace Research.* 46(4): 505–523.

Gleditsch, Nils Petter. 1998. "Armed Conflict and the Environment: A Critique of the Literature." *Journal of Peace Research.* 35(3): 381–400.

Goldenberg, Suzanne. 2005. "US Soldiers Accused of Sex Assaults." *Guardian.* http://www.guardian.co.uk/world/2005/mar/08/iraq. suzannegoldenberg?INTCMP=SRCH (Accessed June 19, 2011).

Goldstein, Joshua S. 2001. *War and Gender: How Gender Shapes the War System and Vice Versa.* New York: Cambridge University Press.

Goldsworthy, Heather. 2010. "Women, Global Environmental Change, and Human Security." In *Global Environmental Change and Human Security,* eds Richard A. Matthew et al. Cambridge, MA: MIT Press, pp. 215–236.

Gore, Al. 1989. "Our Global Eco-Blindness; Earth's Fate Is the No. 1 National Security Issue." *The Washington Post.* 14 May.

Grewal, Inderpal. 2003. "Transnational America: Race, Gender and Citizenship After 9/11." *Social Identities.* 9(4): 535–561.

Groskop, Viv. 2004. "Chechnya's Deadly 'Black Widows.'" *New Statesman.* 6 September 2004: 32–33.

Gunning, Jeroen. 2007. "A Case for Critical Terrorism Studies." *Government and Opposition.* 43(3): 363–393.

Gupta, Alok, Arnab Pratim Dutta, and Savvy Soumya Misra. 2008. "That sinking feeling." *Down to Earth.* September 16–30: 22–30.

Haas, Peter M. 2002. "Constructing Environmental Conflicts from Resource Scarcity." *Global Environmental Politics.* 2(1): 1–11.

Haddad, Simon. 2009. "Lebanese and Palestinian Perspectives on Suicide Bombings: An Empirical Investigation." *International Studies.* 46(3): 295–318.

Hajer, Maarten. 1995. *The Politics of Environmental Discourse: Ecological Modernization and the Policy Process.* London: Oxford University Press.

Hamilton, Carrie. 2007. "The Gender Politics of Political Violence: Women Armed Activists in ETA." *Feminist Review.* 86: 132–148.

Hansen, Lene. 2000. "The Little Mermaid's Silent Security Dilemma and the Absence of Gender in the Copenhagen School." *Millennium: Journal of International Studies.* 29(2): 285–306.

——. 2001. "Gender, Nation, Rape." *International Feminist Journal of Politics.* 3(1): 55–75.

——. 2006. *Security as Practice: Discourse Analysis and the Bosnian War.* New York: Routledge.

Harcourt, Wendy. 1994. "Negotiating Positions in the Sustainable Development Debate: Situating the Feminist Perspective." In *Feminist Perspectives on Sustainable Development,* ed. Wendy Harcourt. Atlantic Highlands, NJ: Zed Books.

Harding, Luke. 2004. "The Other Prisoners." *Guardian*. http://www.
guardian.co.uk/world/2004/may/20/iraq.gender?INTCMP=SRCH
(Accessed June 19, 2011).

Harding, Sandra. 1993. *The Science Question in Feminism*. Ithaca:
Cornell University Press.

——. 1998. *Is Science Multicultural?* Indianapolis: Indiana University
Press.

Harrington, Carol. 2005. "The Politics of Rescue: Peacekeeping and
Anti-Trafficking Programmes in Bosnia-Herzegovina and Kosovo."
International Feminist Journal of Politics. 7(2): 175–206.

Hartmann, Betsy. 2010. "Rethinking the Role of Population in Human
Security." In *Global Environmental Change and Human Security*,
eds Richard A. Matthew et al. Cambridge, MA: MIT Press, pp.
193–214.

Hasso, Frances S. 2005. "Discursive and Political Deployments by/of
the 2002 Palestinian Women Suicide Bombers/Martyrs." *Feminist
Review*. (81): 23–51.

Hendessi, Mandana. 1986. "Fourteen Thousand Women Meet: Report
from Nairobi, July 1985." *Feminist Review*. 23: 147–156.

Hendrix, Cullen S., and Sarah M. Glaser. 2007. "Trends and Triggers:
Climate, Climate Change and Civil Conflict in Sub-Saharan
Africa." *Political Geography*. 26: 695–715.

Herdy, Amy, and Miles Moffeit. 2003. "Betrayal in the Ranks."
Denver Post. http://extras.denverpost.com/justice/tdp_betrayal.pdf
(Accessed November 15, 2010).

Herring, Eric. 2008. "Critical Terrorism Studies: An Activist
Scholar Perspective." *Critical Studies on Terrorism*. 1(2):
197–211.

Heupel, Monika. 2007. "Adapting to Transnational Terrorism: The
UN Security Council's Evolving Approach to Terrorism." *Security
Dialogue*. 38: 477.

Higate, Paul. 2003. "'Soft Clerks' and 'Hard Civvies': Pluralizing
Military Masculinities." In *Military Masculinities: Identity and the
State*, ed. Paul Higate. Westport, CT: Praeger, pp. 27–42.

Higate, Paul, and Marsha Henry. 2004. "Engendering (In)security
in Peace Support Operations." *Security Dialogue*. 35(4):
481–498.

Hillier, Debbie, and Benedict Dempsey. 2012. *A Dangerous Delay: The
Cost of Late Response to Early Warnings in the 2011 Drought in the
Horn of Africa*. Oxford, UK: Oxfam and Save the Children.

Holt, Maria. 2010. "The Unlikely Terrorist: Women and Islamic Resistance in Lebanon and the Palestinian Territories." *Critical Studies on Terrorism*. 3(3): 365–382.

Homer-Dixon, Thomas. 1994. "Environmental Scarcities and Violent Conflict: Evidence from Cases." *International Security*. 19(1): 5–40.

——. 1999. *Environment, Scarcity, and Violence*. Princeton, NJ: Princeton University Press.

Hoogensen, Gunhild, and Svein Vigeland Rottem. 2004. "Gender Identity and the Subject of Security." *Security Dialogue*. 35(2): 155–171.

Hoogensen, Gunhild, and Kirsti Stuvøy. 2006. "Gender, Resistance and Human Security." *Security Dialogue*. 37(2): 207–228.

Hopton, John. 2003. "The State and Military Masculinity." In *Military Masculinities: Identity and the State*, ed. Paul Higate. Westport, CT: Praeger, pp. 111–124.

Hua, Julietta, and Holly Nigorizawa. 2010. "US Sex Trafficking, Women's Human Rights and the Politics of Representation." *International Feminist Journal of Politics*. 12(3): 401–423.

Hudson, Heidi. 2005. "'Doing' Security as Though Humans Matter: A Feminist Perspective on Gender and the Politics of Human Security." *Security Dialogue*. 36(2): 155–174.

——. 2010. "Peace Building Through a Gender Lens and the Challenges of Implementation in Rwanda and Côte d'Ivoire." In Sjoberg 2011, pp. 256–279.

Hudson, Valerie M., and Andrea M. den Boer. 2005. *Bare Branches: The Security Implications of Asia's Surplus Male Population*. Cambridge, MA: MIT Press.

Hynes, H. Patricia. 2004. "On the Battlefield of Women's Bodies: An Overview of the Harm of War to Women." *Women's Studies International Forum*. 27: 431–445.

ICISS. 2001. *The Responsibility to Protect*. Ottawa: International Development Research Centre. http://www.iciss.ca/pdf/Commission-Report.pdf (Accessed July 25, 2011).

Indra, Doreen. 1999. *Engendering Forced Migration: Theory and Practice*. New York: Berghahn Books.

IOM. 2011. "Counter-Trafficking." *International Organization for Migration*. http://www.iom.int/jahia/Jahia/counter-trafficking (Accessed July 21, 2011).

IPCC. 2007. "Summary for Policymakers" eds S. Solomon et al. http://www.ipcc.ch/pdf/assessment-report/ar4/wg1/ar4-wg1-spm.pdf (Accessed April 23, 2010).

Iqbal, Zaryab. 2006. "Health and Human Security: The Public Health Impact of Violent Conflict." *International Studies Quarterly.* 50(3): 631–649.

Jackson, Nicole J. 2006. "International Organizations, Security Dichotomies and the Trafficking of Persons and Narcotics in Post-Soviet Central Asia: A Critique of the Securitization Framework." *Security Dialogue.* 37(3): 299–317.

Jackson, Richard. 2009. "Knowledge, Power and Politics in the Study of Political Terrorism." In Jackson et al. 2009, pp. 66–83.

Jackson, Richard, Lee Jarvis, Jeroen Gunning, and Marie Breen Smyth. 2011. *Terrorism: A Critical Introduction.* New York: Palgrave Macmillan.

Jackson, Richard, Marie Breen Smyth, and Jeroen Gunning, eds. 2009. *Critical Terrorism Studies: A New Research Agenda.* New York: Routledge.

Jennings, Kathleen M. 2010. "Unintended Consequences of Intimacy: Political Economies of Peacekeeping and Sex Tourism." *International Peacekeeping.* 17(2): 229–243.

Jones, Jane Clare. 2011. "Anders Breivik's Chilling Anti-Feminism." *Guardian.* http://www.guardian.co.uk/commentisfree/2011/jul/27/breivik-anti-feminism (Accessed January 16, 2012).

Judt, Tony. 2001. "America and the War." *New York Review of Books.* http://www.nybooks.com/articles/archives/2001/nov/15/america-and-the-war/ (Accessed June 18, 2011).

Just, Sine Nørholm. 2006. "Embattled Agencies – How Mass Mediated Comparisons of Lynndie England and Jessica Lynch Affect the Identity Positions Available to Female Soldiers in the US Army." *Scandinavian Journal of Management.* 22: 99–119.

Kaldor, Mary. 2010. "A Different Kind of War." *Guardian.* http://www.guardian.co.uk/commentisfree/2010/may/26/afghanistan-human-security-withdrawal?INTCMP=SRCH (Accessed July 13, 2011).

Kanetake, Machiko. 2010. "Whose Zero Tolerance Counts? Reassessing a Zero Tolerance Policy against Sexual Exploitation and Abuse by UN Peacekeepers." *International Peacekeeping.* 17(2): 200–214.

Katzenstein, Peter J. 2003. "Same War: Different Views: Germany, Japan, and Counterterrorism." *International Organization.* 57(4): 731–760.

Kelly, Liz. 2000. "Wars Against Women: Sexual Violence, Sexual Politics and the Militarised State." In *States of Conflict: Gender,*

Violence and Resistance, eds Susie Jacobs, Ruth Jacobson, and Jennifer Marchbank. New York: Zed Books, pp. 45–65.

Kent, Alexandra. 2006. "Reconfiguring Security: Buddhism and Moral Legitimacy in Cambodia." *Security Dialogue*. 37(3): 343–361.

King, Gary, and Christopher J. L. Murray. 2001. "Rethinking Human Security." *Political Science Quarterly*. 116(4): 585–610.

Kinsella, Helen. 2003. "For a Careful Reading: The Conservatism of Gender Constructivism." *International Studies Review*. 5(2): 294–297.

Kirk, Gwyn. 2008. "Contesting Militarization: Global Perspectives." In *Security Disarmed: Critical Perspectives on Gender, Race, and Militarization,* eds Barbara Sutton, Sandra Morgen, and Julie Novkov. New Brunswick: Rutgers University Press, pp. 30–55.

Koch, Michael T., and Sarah A. Fulton. 2011. "In the Defense of Women: Gender, Office Holding, and National Security Policy in Established Democracies." *Journal of Politics*. 73(1): 1–16.

Kofman, Eleonore. 2004. "Gendered Global Migrations." *International Feminist Journal of Politics*. 6(4): 643–665.

Kovitz, Marcia. 2003. "The Roots of Military Masculinity." In *Military Masculinities: Identity and the State*, ed. Paul R. Higate. Westport, CT: Praeger, pp. 1–14.

Krause, Keith, and Michael C. Williams. 1996. "Broadening the Agenda of Security Studies: Politics and Methods." *Mershon International Studies Review*. 40(2): 229–254.

Kronsell, Annica. 2005. "Gendered Practices in Institutions of Hegemonic Masculinity." *International Feminist Journal of Politics*. 7(2): 280–298.

Kvammen, Julie Platou. 2011. "Different Forms of Exploitative Labour – How to Draw the Line?" *Global Eye on Human Trafficking*. Issue 10: 8.

LaFraniere, Sharon. 2011. "81 Children Rescued in Raids on Trafficking Ring, Chinese Officials Say." *New York Times*. http://www.nytimes.com/2011/07/28/world/asia/28china.html?ref=world (Accessed July 28, 2011).

Leander, Anna. 2005. "The Market for Force and Public Security: The Destabilizing Consequences of Private Military Companies." *Journal of Peace Research*. 42(5): 605–622.

Lee, Barbara. 2008. "Gender, Race, and Militarism: Toward a More Just Alternative." In *Security Disarmed: Critical Perspectives on Gender,*

Race, and Militarization, eds Barbara Sutton, Sandra Morgen, and Julie Novkov. New Brunswick: Rutgers University Press, pp. 56–64.

Lee, Na Young. 2007. "The Construction of Military Prostitution in South Korea during the US Military Rule, 1945–1948." *Feminist Studies*. 33(3): 453–481.

Levy, Marc A. 1995. "Is the Environment a National Security Issue?" *International Security*. 20(2): 35–62.

Liotta, P. H. 2002. "Boomerang Effect: the Convergence of National and Human Security." *Security Dialogue*. 33(4): 473–488.

——. 2005. "Through the Looking Glass: Creeping Vulnerabilities and the Reordering of Security." *Security Dialogue*. 36(1): 49–70.

Liotta, P. H., and Allan W. Shearer. 2007. *Gaia's Revenge: Climate Change and Humanity's Loss*. Westport, CT: Praeger.

Lipschutz, Ronnie D. 1995. "On Security." In *On Security*, ed. Ronnie D. Lipschutz. New York: Columbia University Press, pp. 1–23.

Litfin, Karen T. 1999. "Constructing Environmental Security and Ecological Interdependence." *Global Governance*. 5(3): 359–378.

Lobasz, Jennifer K. 2008. "The Woman in Peril and the Ruined Woman: Representations of Female Soldiers in the Iraq War." *Journal of Women, Politics and Policy*. 29(3): 305–334.

——. 2010. "Beyond Border Security: Feminist Approaches to Human Trafficking." In Sjoberg 2011, pp. 214–234.

Lutz, Catherine. 2008. "Living Room Terrorists." In *Security Disarmed: Critical Perspectives on Gender, Race, and Militarization*, eds Barbara Sutton, Sandra Morgen, and Julie Novkov. New Brunswick: Rutgers University Press, pp. 223–230.

McCright, Aaron M. 2010. "The Effects of Gender on Climate Change Knowledge and Concern in the American Public." *Population and Environment*. 32(1): 66–87.

McDonald, Bryan L. 2010. *Food Security*. Malden, MA: Polity.

McDonald, Matt. 2009. "Emancipation and Critical Terrorism Studies." In Jackson et al. 2009, pp. 109–123.

McEvoy, Sandra. 2010. "Loyalist Women Paramilitaries in Northern Ireland: Beginning a Feminist Conversation about Conflict Resolution." In Sjoberg 2011, pp. 129–150.

MacFarlane, S. Neil, and Yuen Foong Khong. 2006. *Human Security and the UN. A Critical History*. Bloomington: Indiana University Press.

MacFarquhar, Neil. 2011. "U.N. Deadlock on Addressing Climate

Shift." *New York Times.* http://www.nytimes.com/2011/07/21/world/21nations.html?_r=1&scp=2&sq=security%20council&st=cse (Accessed July 21, 2011).

MacGregor, Sherilyn. 2009. "A Stranger Silence Still: The Need for Feminist Social Research on Climate Change." *The Sociological Review.* 57: 124–140.

MacKenzie, Megan. 2010. "Securitizing Sex? Towards a Theory of the Utility of Wartime Sexual Violence." *International Feminist Journal of Politics.* 12(2): 202–221.

Mackey, Robert. 2011. "Newspaper 'Regrets' Erasing Hillary Clinton." *New York Times.* http://thelede.blogs.nytimes.com/2011/05/10/newspaper-regrets-erasing-hillary-clinton/?scp=3&sq=hillary%20clinton&st=cse http://thelede.blogs.nytimes.com/2011/05/10/newspaper-regrets-erasing-hillary-clinton/?scp=3&sq=hillary%20clinton&st=cse, 5/23/2011 (Accessed May 13, 2011).

MacLean, Sandra J. 2008. "Microbes, Mad Cows and Militaries: Exploring the Links Between Health and Security." *Security Dialogue.* 39(5): 475–494.

Mahmood, Saba. 2005. *Politics of Piety: The Islamic Revival and the Feminist Subject.* Princeton, NJ: Princeton University Press.

Masika, Rachel. 2002. *Gender, Development, and Climate Change.* Oxford: Oxfam GB.

Masters, Cristina. 2009. "Femina Sacra: The 'War on/of Terror', Women and the Feminine." *Security Dialogue.* 40(1): 29–49.

Mazurana, Dyan. 2005. "Gender and the Causes and Consequences of Armed Conflict." In Mazurana et al. 2005, pp. 29–42.

Mazurana, Dyan, Angela Raven-Roberts, and Jane Parpart. 2005. *Gender, Conflict, and Peacekeeping.* New York: Rowman and Littlefield Publishers.

MEED. 2004. "Violence Returns to Gaza After New Year Lull." *Middle East Economic Digest.* 48(3): 3.

Melzer, Patricia. 2009. "'Death in the Shape of a Young Girl': Feminist Responses to Media Representations of Women Terrorists During the 'German Autumn' of 1977." *International Feminist Journal of Politics* 11(1): 35–62.

Mies, Maria, and Vandana Shiva. 1993. *Ecofeminism.* Halifax, Nova Scotia: Fernwood Publications.

Ministry of Water Resources. 1999. "National Water Policy." http://www.mowr.gov.bd/Documents/National%20Water%20Policy%20%28English%29.pdf (Accessed February 2, 2012).

Mirza, M. Monirul Qader, R. A. Warrick, and N. J. Ericksen. 2003. "The Implications of Climate Change on Floods of the Ganges, Brahmaputra and Meghna Rivers in Bangladesh." *Climatic Change.* 57(3): 287–318.

Mishra, Prafulla K., Shaheen Nilofer, and Sumananjali Mohanty. 2004. "Gender and Disasters: Coping with Drought and Floods in Orissa." In *Livelihood and Gender: Equity in Community Resource Management*, ed. Sumi Krishna. Thousand Oaks, California: SAGE Publications, pp. 226–247.

Mohanty, Chandra Talpade. 2003. *Feminism Without Borders: Decolonizing Theory, Practicing Solidarity.* Durham: Duke University Press.

Mookherjee, Nayanika. 2006. "'Remembering to Forget': Public Secrecy and Memory of Sexual Violence in the Bangladesh War of 1971." *Journal of the Royal Anthropoligical Institute.* 12: 433–450.

——. 2008. "Gendered Embodiments: Mapping the Body-Politic of the Raped Woman and the Nation in Bangladesh." *Feminist Review.* 88: 36–53.

Moon, Katharine. 1997. *Sex among Allies: Military Prostitution in US-Korea Relations.* New York: Columbia University Press.

Moraes, Andrea, and Patricia E. Perkins. 2007. "Women, Equity and Participatory Water Management in Brazil." *International Feminist Journal of Politics.* 9(4): 485–493.

Nacos, Brigitte L. 2008. "The Portrayal of Female Terrorists in the Media: Similar Framing Patterns in the News Coverage of Women in Politics and in Terrorism." In Ness 2008, pp. 217–235.

Nayak, Meghana. 2006. "Orientalism and 'Saving' US State Identity after 9/11." *International Feminist Journal of Politics.* 8(1): 42–61.

Nielsen Company, The. 2007. "Climate Change and Influential Spokespeople: A Global Nielsen online survey." http://lk.nielsen.com/documents/ClimateChampionsReportJuly07.pdf (Accessed January 19, 2011).

Nellemann, Christian, Ritu Verma, and Lawrence Hislop, eds. 2011. "Women at the Frontline of Climate Change: Gender Risks and Hopes." http://www.unep.org/pdf/rra_gender_screen.pdf (Accessed January 24, 2012).

NEPAD. 2005. "African Post-Conflict Reconstruction Policy Framework." http://www.africanreview.org/docs/conflict/PCR%20Policy%20Framework.pdf (Accessed February 15, 2011).

Ness, Cindy D. 2005. "In the Name of the Cause: Women's Work in Secular and Religious Terrorism." *Studies in Conflict and Terrorism.* 28(5): 353–373.

——. 2008. *Female Terrorism and Militancy: Agency, Utility and Organization.* New York: Routledge.

Newell, Peter. 2005. "Race, Class and the Global Politics of Environmental Inequality." *Global Environmental Politics.* 5(3): 70–94.

Newman, Edward. 2001. "Human Security and Constructivism." *International Studies Perspectives.* 2(3): 239–251.

Nishat, Ainun, and Islam M. Faisal. 2000. "An Assessment of the Institutional Mechanisms for Water Negotiations in the Ganges-Brahmaputra-Meghna System." *International Negotiation.* 5(2): 289–310.

Nivat, Anne. 2008. "The Black Widows: Chechen Women Join the Fight for Independence – and Allah." In Ness 2008, pp. 122–130.

Nordland, Rod. 2011. "For Soldiers, Death Sees No Gender Lines." *New York Times.* http://www.nytimes.com/2011/06/22/world/asia/22afghanistan.html?scp=1&sq=nordland%20sixty%20percent%20of%20those%20deaths%20are%20classified%20by%20the%20military&st=cse (Accessed June 21, 2011).

Nossiter, Adam. 2011. "In Sierra Leone, Heartening Progress for Pregnant Women." *New York Times.* http://www.nytimes.com/2011/07/18/world/africa/18sierra.html?_r=1&hp (Accessed July 18, 2011).

Nusair, Isis. 2008. "Gendered, Racialized, and Sexualized Torture at Abu Ghraib." In Riley et al. 2008, pp. 179–193.

Nye, Joseph S., and Sean M. Lynn-Jones. 1988. "International Security Studies: A Report of a Conference on the State of the Field." *International Security.* 12(4): 5–27.

O'Brien, Karen. 2006. "Are We Missing the Point? Global Environmental Change as an Issue of Human Security." *Global Environmental Change.* 16: 1–3.

O'Brien, Karen L., and Robin M. Leichenko. 2000. "Double Exposure: Assessing the Impacts of Climate Change Within the Context of Economic Globalization." *Global Environmental Change.* 10(3): 221–232.

O'Rourke, Lindsey. 2009. "What's Special about Female Suicide Terrorism?" *Security Studies.* 18(4): 681–718.

Oswald Spring, Úrsula. 2008. *Human, Gender and Environmental Security: A HUGE Challenge.* Bonn, Germany: UNU Institute for Environment and Human Security.

Outshoorn, Joyce. 2004. *Politics of Prostitution: Women's Movements, Democratic States, and the Globalisation of Sex Commerce.* New York: Cambridge University Press.

Owen, Taylor. 2008. "The Critique That Doesn't Bite: A Response to David Chandler's 'Human Security: The Dog That Didn't Bark.'" *Security Dialogue.* 39(4): 445–453.

Pape, Robert A. 2005. *Dying to Win: The Strategic Logic of Suicide Terrorism.* New York: Random House.

Pape, Robert A., Lindsey O'Rourke, and Jenna McDermit. 2010. "What Makes Chechen Women So Dangerous?" *New York Times.* http://www.nytimes.com/2010/03/31/opinion/31pape. html?scp=1&sq=what%20makes%20chechen%20women%20so%20 dangerous&st=cse (Accessed March 24, 2011).

Parashar, Swati. 2009. "Feminist International Relations and Women Militants: Case Studies from Sri Lanka and Kashmir." *Cambridge Review of International Affairs.* 22(2): 235–256.

——. 2010. "Women, Militancy, and Security: The South Asian Conundrum." In Sjoberg 2011, pp. 168–188.

——. 2011. "Gender, Jihad, and Jingoism: Women as Perpetrators, Planners, and Patrons of Militancy in Kashmir." *Studies in Conflict and Terrorism.* 34: 295–317.

Paris, Roland. 2001. "Human Security: Paradigm Shift or Hot Air?" *International Security.* 26(2): 87–102.

Paterson, Matthew. 2001. *Understanding Global Environmental Politics: Domination, Accumulation, Resistance.* New York: Palgrave.

Pérez, Gina M. 2006. "How a Scholarship Girl Becomes a Soldier: The Militarization of Latina/o Youth in Chicago Public Schools." *Identities: Global Studies in Culture and Power.* 13: 53–72.

Perlo-Freeman, Sam. 2011. *Budgetary Priorities in Latin America: Military, Health and Education Spending.* Stockholm: SIPRI.

Peterson, V. Spike, and Anne Sisson Runyan. 1999. 2nd edition *Global Gender Issues.* Boulder, CO: Westview Press.

——. 2010. *Global Gender Issues in the New Millennium.* Boulder, CO: Westview Press.

Phillips, Ruth. 2008. "Feminism, Policy and Women's Safety During Australia's 'War on Terror.'" *Feminist Review.* 89: 55–72.

Pirages, Dennis Clark, and Theresa Manley DeGeest. 2004. *Ecological*

Security: An Evolutionary Perspective on Globalization. Boulder, CO: Rowman and Littlefield Publishers, Inc.

Puechguirbal, Nadine. 2010. "Discourses on Gender, Patriarchy and Resolution 1325: A Textual Analysis of UN Documents." *International Peacekeeping.* 17(2): 172–187.

Pugh, Michael, Neil Cooper, and Mandy Turner. 2008. *Whose Peace? Critical Perspectives on the Political Economy of Peacebuilding.* New York: Palgrave Macmillan.

Qazi, Farhana. 2011. "The Mujahidaat: Tracing the Early Female Warriors of Islam." In Sjoberg and Gentry 2011, pp. 29–56.

Rabin, Roni Caryn. 2012. "Men Struggle for Rape Awareness." *New York Times.* http://www.nytimes.com/2012/01/24/health/as-victims-men-struggle-for-rape-awareness.html (Accessed January 24, 2012).

Rajagopalan, Swarna, and Nandhini Parthib. 2006. "Disasters and Security." ed. WISCOMP. http://www.wiscomp.org/Forum-Report.pdf (Accessed January 21, 2010).

Raleigh, Clionadh. 2010. "Political Marginalization, Climate Change, and Conflict in African Sahel States." *International Studies Review.* 12(1): 69–86.

Raleigh, Clionadh, and Henrik Urdal. 2007. "Climate Change, Environmental Degradation and Armed Conflict." *Political Geography.* 26: 674–694.

Ranstorp, Magnus. 2009. "Mapping Terrorism Studies After 9/11: An Academic Field of Old Problems and New Prospects." In Jackson et al. 2009, pp. 13–33.

Raven-Roberts, Angela. 2005. "Gender Mainstreaming in United Nations Peacekeeping Operations: Talking the Talk, Tripping over the Walk." In Mazurana et al. 2005, pp. 43–64.

RAWA. 2009. "Not All Feminists Love Escalation in Afghanistan." http://www.rawa.org/rawa/2009/12/06/not-all-feminists-love-escalation-in-afghanistan.html (Accessed July 25, 2011).

Reardon, Betty A. 2010. "Women and Human Security: A Feminist Framework and Critique of the Prevailing Patriarchal Security System." In Reardon and Hans 2010, pp. 7–37.

Reardon, Betty A., and Asha Hans, eds. 2010. *The Gender Imperative: Human Security vs State Security.* New Delhi, India: Routledge.

Rees, Wyn, and Richard J. Aldrich. 2005. "Contending Cultures of Counterterrorism: Transatlantic Divergence or Convergence?" *International Affairs.* 81(5): 905–923.

Richter-Montpetit, Melanie. 2007. "Empire, Desire and Violence: A Queer Transnational Feminist Reading of the Prisoner 'Abuse' in Abu Ghraib and the Question of 'Gender Equality.'" *International Feminist Journal of Politics.* 9(1): 38–59.

Riley, Robin, Chandra Talpade Mohanty, and Minnie Bruce Pratt, eds. 2008. *Feminism and War: Confronting US Imperialism.* New York: Zed Books.

Rome Statute. 1998. "Rome Statute of the International Criminal Court." http://untreaty.un.org/cod/icc/statute/romefra.htm (Accessed August 4, 2011).

Roy, Arundhati. 2004. "Peace and the New Corporate Liberation Theology." http://www.abc.net.au/rn/bigidea/stories/s1232956.htm (Accessed July 8, 2011).

Roy, Nilanjana S. 2010. "Bangladesh War's Toll on Women Still Undiscussed." *New York Times.* http://www.nytimes.com/2010/08/25/world/asia/25iht-letter.html (Accessed November 18, 2011).

Ruether, Rosemary Radford. 1997. "Ecofeminism: First and Third World Women." *Ecotheology.* 2: 72–83.

Sadler, Anne G., Brenda M. Booth, and Brian L. Cook. 2003. "Factors Associated With Women's Risk of Rape in the Military Environment." *American Journal of Industrial Medicine.* 43: 262–273.

Said, Edward. 1978. *Orientalism.* New York: Pantheon.

Sample, Ian. 2011. "BBC Gives Too Much Weight to Fringe Views on Issues Such as Climate Change." *Guardian.* http://www.guardian.co.uk/science/2011/jul/20/bbc-climate-change-science-coverage (Accessed July 20, 2011).

Sandilands, Catriona. 1999. *The Good-Natured Feminist: Ecofeminism and the Quest for Democracy.* Minneapolis: University of Minnesota Press.

Sasson-Levy, Orna. 2003. "Feminism and Military Gender Practices: Israeli Women Soldiers in 'Masculine' Roles." *Sociological Inquiry.* 73(3): 440–465.

Sasvari, Adele Anna. 2010. "Changes in Climate Negotiations: Gender Equality Towards Copenhagen." *Global Social Policy.* 10(1): 15–18.

Saul, Ben. 2007. *Terrorism.* Sydney, Australia: Legal Information Access Centre. http://www.legalanswers.sl.nsw.gov.au/hot_topics/pdf/terrorism_58.pdf (Accessed January 16, 2012).

Sawin, Janet L. 2005. "Climate Change Poses Greater Security Threat Than Terrorism." *Global Security Brief #3.* http://www.worldwatch. org/node/77 (Accessed October 13, 2010).

Schweitzer, Yoram. 2008. "Palestinian Female Suicide Bombers: Virtuous Heroines or Damaged Goods?" In Ness 2008, pp. 131–145.

Schwirtz, Michael. 2011. "Norway's Premier Vows to Keep an Open Society." *New York Times.* http://www.nytimes.com/2011/07/28/ world/europe/28norway.html?ref=norway (Accessed August 18, 2011).

Seager, Joni. 1999. "Patriarchal Vandalism: Militaries and the Environment." In *Dangerous Intersections: Feminist Perspectives on Population, Environment, and Development,* eds Jael Silliman and Ynestra King. Cambridge, MA: South End Press, pp. 163–188.

Sedghi, Hamideh. 1994. "Third World Feminist Perspectives on World Politics." In *Women, Gender, and World Politics: Perspectives, Policies, and Prospects,* eds Peter R. Beckman and Francine D'Amico. Westport, CT: Bergin and Garvey, pp. 89–108.

Seelye, Katharine Q. 1995. "Gingrich's 'Piggies' Poked." *New York Times.* http://www.nytimes.com/1995/01/19/us/gingrich-s-piggies-poked.html?scp=1&sq=Gingrich%27s%20%27Piggies%27%20 Poked.&st=cse (Accessed January 19, 2011).

Seger, Paul. 2011. "Interactive Panel Debate 1: A Possible Approach for Defining Human Security." http://www.eda.admin.ch/etc/medialib/ downloads/edazen/topics/intorg/un/missny/other.Par.0072.File. tmp/e%2020110415spu_HSN%20Statement_P1.pdf (Accessed July 11, 2011).

Selin, Henrik, and Stacy D. VanDeveer. 2003. "Mapping Institutional Linkages in European Air Pollution Politics." *Global Environmental Politics.* 3(3): 14–46.

Sen, Gita. 2004. "Women, Poverty, and Population: Issues for the Concerned Environmentalist." In *Green Planet Blues: Environmental Politics From Stockholm to Johannesburg,* eds Ken Conca and Geoffrey Dabelko. Boulder, CO: Westview Press, pp. 358–367.

——. 2006. "Reproductive Rights and Gender Justice in the Neo-conservative Shadow." In *Engendering Human Security: Feminist Perspectives,* eds Thanh-Dam Truong, Saskia Wieringa, and Amrita Chhachhi. New York: Zed Books, pp. 36–55.

Sharpe, Albie. 2010. "Gender, Health, Peace and Security." In Reardon and Hans 2010, pp. 351–383.

Shepherd, Laura J. 2006. "Veiled References: Constructions of Gender in the Bush Administration Discourse on the Attacks on Afghanistan Post-9/11." *International Feminist Journal of Politics* 8(1): 19–41.

——. 2008. *Gender, Violence and Security: Discourse as Practice.* New York: Zed Books.

——. 2010. *Gender Matters in Global Politics: A Feminist Introduction to International Relations.* New York: Routledge.

Shigematsu, Setsu, Anuradha Kristina Bhagwati, and Eli Paintedcrow. 2008. "Women-of-Color Veterans on War, Militarism, and Feminism." In Riley et al. 2008, pp. 93–102.

Shiva, Vandana. 2000. *Stolen Harvest: The Hijacking of the Global Food Supply.* Cambridge, MA: South End Press.

Siegel, Matt. 2011. "Australia Says It Will Open Combat Roles to Women." *New York Times.* http://www.nytimes.com/2011/09/28/world/asia/australia-will-allow-women-to-serve-in-frontline-combat.html?ref=world (Accessed September 28, 2011).

Silke, Andrew. 2009. "Contemporary Terrorism Studies: Issues in Research." In Jackson et al. 2009, pp. 34–48.

Simić, Olivera. 2010. "Does the Presence of Women Really Matter? Towards Combating Male Sexual Violence in Peacekeeping Operations." *International Peacekeeping.* 17(2): 188–199.

Simons, Marlise. 2011. "International Court Charges Qaddafi With War Crimes." *New York Times.* http://www.nytimes.com/2011/06/28/world/africa/28libya.html?_r=1&ref=world (Accessed June 28, 2011).

SIPRI. 2011. *Background Paper on SIPRI Military Expenditure Data, 2010.* Stockholm International Peace Research Institute. http://www.sipri.org/research/armaments/milex/factsheet2010 (Accessed August 3, 2011).

Sjoberg, Laura. 2007. "Agency, Militarized Femininity and Enemy Others." *International Feminist Journal of Politics* 9(1): 82–101.

——. 2009. "Feminist Interrogations of Terrorism/Terrorism Studies." *International Relations.* 23(1): 69–74.

——. 2011. "Emancipation and the Feminist Security Studies Project." In *Feminism and International Relations: Conversations About the Past, Present and Future,* eds J. Ann Tickner and Laura Sjoberg. New York: Routledge, pp. 115–122.

Sjoberg, Laura, Grace D. Cooke, and Stacy Reiter Neal. 2011. "Introduction: Women, Gender, and Terrorism." In Sjoberg and Gentry 2011, pp. 1–25.

Sjoberg, Laura, and Caron E. Gentry. 2007. *Mothers, Monsters, Whores: Women's Violence in Global Politics*. London: Zed Books.

——. eds. 2011. *Women, Gender, and Terrorism*. Athens, GA: University of Georgia Press.

Sjoberg, Laura, and Jessica Peet. 2011. "A(nother) Dark Side of the Protection Racket: Targeting Women in Wars." *International Feminist Journal of Politics*. 13(2): 163–182.

Slim, Hugo. 2012. "Why East Africa's Famine Warning Was Not Heeded." *Guardian*. http://www.guardian.co.uk/commentisfree/ 2012/jan/18/east-africa-famine-warning (Accessed January 19, 2012).

Sluka, Jeffrey A. 2009. "The Contribution of Anthropology to Critical Terrorism Studies." In Jackson et al. 2009, pp. 138–155.

Soh, Chunghee Sarah. 2001. "Prostitutes versus Sex Slaves: The Politics of Representing the 'Comfort Women.'" In *Legacies of the Comfort Women of World War II*, eds Margaret Stetz and Bonnie B. C. Oh. Armonk, NY: M. E. Sharpe, pp. 69–90.

Soroos, Marvin S. 2010. "Approaches to Enhancing Human Security." In *Global Environmental Change and Human Security*, eds Richard Matthew et al. Cambridge, MA: MIT Press, pp. 177–192.

Spearin, Christopher. 2008. "Private, Armed and Humanitarian? States, NGOs, International Private Security Companies and Shifting Humanitarianism." *Security Dialogue*. 39(4): 363–382.

Speckhard, Anne, and Akhmedova, Khapta. 2008. "Black Widows and Beyond: Understanding the Motivations and Life Trajectories of Chechen Female Terrorists." In Ness 2008, pp. 100–121.

Steans, Jill. 1998. *Gender and International Relations*. Brunswick, NJ: Rutgers University Press.

——. 2006. *Gender and International Relations: Issues, Debates and Future Directions*. Malden, MA: Polity.

——. 2010. "Body Politics: Human Rights in International Relations." In *Gender Matters in Global Politics: A Feminist Introduction to International Relations*, ed. Laura J. Shepherd. New York: Routledge, pp. 74–88.

Stone, Christopher D. 2000. "The Environment in Wartime: An Overview." In *The Environmental Consequences of War: Legal, Economic, and Scientific Perspectives*, eds Jay E. Austin and Carl E. Bruch. Cambridge: Cambridge University Press, pp. 16–37.

Stone, Jennie, and Katherine Pattillo. 2011. "Al-Qaeda's Use of Female Suicide Bombers in Iraq: A Case Study." In Sjoberg and Gentry 2011, pp. 159–175.

Street, Amy E., Dawne Vogt, and Lissa Dutra. 2009. "A New
    Generation of Women Veterans: Stressors Faced by Women
    Deployed to Iraq and Afghanistan." *Clinical Psychology Review*. 29:
    685–694.
Sturgeon, Noel. 1999. "Ecofeminist Appropriations and Transnational
    Environmentalisms." *Identities*. 6: 255–279.
Sutton, Barbara, and Julie Novkov. 2008. "Rethinking Security,
    Confronting Inequality: An Introduction." In *Security Disarmed:
    Critical Perspectives on Gender, Race, and Militarization*,
    eds Barbara Sutton, Sandra Morgen, and Julie Novkov. New
    Brunswick: Rutgers University Press, pp. 3–29.
Sylvester, Christine. 2002. *Feminist International Relations: An
    Unfinished Journey*. Cambridge: Cambridge University Press.
——. 2010. "Tensions in Feminist Security Studies." *Security Dialogue*.
    41(6): 607–614.
Sylvester, Christine, and Swati Parashar. 2009. "The Contemporary
    'Mahabharata' and the Many 'Draupadis': Bringing Gender to
    Critical Terrorism Studies." In Jackson et al. 2009, pp.
    178–193.
Takacs, Stacy. 2005. "Jessica Lynch and the Regeneration of American
    Identity and Power Post-9/11." *Feminist Media Studies*. 5(3):
    297–310.
Theohary, Catherine A., and John Rollins. 2011. "Terrorist Use
    of the Internet: Information Operations in Cyberspace." ed.
    Congressional Research Service. http://www.fas.org/sgp/crs/terror/
    R41674.pdf (Accessed June 15, 2011).
Thomas, Caroline. 2001. "Global Governance, Development and
    Human Security: Exploring the Links." *Third World Quarterly*.
    22(2): 159–175.
Thompson, Paul M., and Parvin Sultana. 1996. "Distributional and
    Social Impacts of Flood Control in Bangladesh." *The Geographical
    Journal*. 162(1): 1–13.
Tickner, J. Ann. 1992. *Gender in International Relations: Feminist
    Perspectives on Achieving Global Security*. New York: Columbia
    University Press.
——. 2001. *Gendering World Politics: Issues and Approaches in the Post-
    Cold War Era*. New York: Columbia University Press.
——. 2002. "Feminist Perspectives on 9/11." *International Studies
    Perspectives*. 3: 333–350.
Toros, Harmonie, and Jeroen Gunning. 2009. "Exploring a Critical

Theory Approach to Terrorism Studies." In Jackson et al. 2009, pp. 87–108.

Truong, Thanh-Dam, Saskia Wieringa, and Amrita Chhachhi, eds 2006. *Engendering Human Security: Feminist Perspectives*. New York: Zed Books.

UN. 1995. "Beijing Declaration." http://www.un.org/womenwatch/daw/beijing/platform/declar.htm (Accessed March 21, 2009).

——. 2002. "Gender Mainstreaming: An Overview." ed. Office of the Special Adviser on Gender Issues and Advancement of Women. http://www.un.org/womenwatch/osagi/pdf/e65237.pdf (Accessed June 25, 2010).

UN Conduct and Discipline Unit. 2010. "Frequently Asked Questions." http://cdu.unlb.org/FAQ3.aspx (Accessed February 3, 2011).

UN Department of Peacekeeping Operations. 2010. "Ten-year Impact Study on Implementation of UN Security Council Resolution 1325 (2000) on Women, Peace and Security in Peacekeeping." ed. Peacekeeping Best Practices Section. http://www.un.org/en/peace keeping/documents/10year_impact_study_1325.pdf (Accessed June 15, 2011).

UN News Service. 2011. "ICC issues arrest warrants for Libyan officials for alleged crimes against humanity." http://www.un.org/apps/news/story.asp?NewsID=38855&Cr=Libya&Cr1= (Accessed June 27, 2011).

UN Peacebuilding Commission. 2011. "Peacebuilding Commission." http://www.un.org/en/peacebuilding/ (Accessed January 6, 2012).

UN Peacekeeping. 2010. "DPKO/OMA Statistical Report on Female Military and Police Personnel in UN Peacekeeping Operations Prepared for the 10th Anniversary of the SCR 1325." http://www.un.org/en/peacekeeping/documents/gender_scres1325_chart.pdf (Accessed January 6, 2012).

——. 2011a. "Contributions to United Nations Peacekeeping Operations." http://www.un.org/en/peacekeeping/contribu-tors/2011/nov11_1.pdf (Accessed January 3, 2012).

——. 2011b. "Gender Statistics by Mission." http://www.un.org/en/peacekeeping/contributors/gender/2011gender/nov11.pdf (Accessed January 6, 2012).

UN Security Council. 2000. "Resolution 1325." http://www.un.org/events/res_1325e.pdf (Accessed August 9, 2011).

——. 2008. "Resolution 1820." http://daccess-dds-ny.un.org/doc/

UNDOC/GEN/N08/391/44/PDF/N0839144.pdf?OpenElement (Accessed August 9, 2011).

UN Water. 2006. "Gender, Water and Sanitation: A Policy Brief." http://www.unwater.org/downloads/unwpolbrief230606.pdf (Accessed December 13, 2008).

UNAIDS. 2010. *Global Report: UNAIDS Report on the Global AIDS Epidemic.* UNAIDS. http://issuu.com/unaids/docs/unaids_global report_2010?mode=embed&layout=http%3A%2F%2Fskin.issuu. com%2Fv%2Flight%2Flayout.xml&showFlipBtn=true (Accessed July 19, 2011).

UNDP. 1994. "New Dimensions of Human Security: Human Development Report 1994." http://hdr.undp.org/en/reports/global/hdr1994/chapters/ (Accessed June 22, 2011).

UNODC. 2004. "United Nations Convention Against Transnational Organized Crime and the Protocols Thereto." http://www. unodc.org/documents/treaties/UNTOC/Publications/TOC%20 Convention/TOCebook-e.pdf (Accessed July 22, 2011).

——. 2009. *Global Report on Trafficking in Persons.* United Nations Office on Drugs and Crime. http://www.unodc.org/documents/ Global_Report_on_TIP.pdf (Accessed July 21, 2011).

Uraguchi, Zenebe Bashaw. 2010. "Food Price Hikes, Food Security, and Gender Equality: Assessing the Roles and Vulnerability of Women in Households of Bangladesh and Ethiopia." *Gender and Development.* 18(3): 491–501.

Urban, Jessica Leann. 2007. "Interrogating Privilege/Challenging the 'Greening of Hate.'" *International Feminist Journal of Politics.* 9(2): 251–264.

US Department of State. 2008. "2007 Country Reports on Human Rights Practices – Haiti." http://www.unhcr.org/refworld/country,, USDOS,,HTI,,47d92c722,0.html (Accessed January 6, 2012).

Vargas, Virginia. 2006. "Globalisation, Social Movements and Feminism: Coming Together at the World Social Forum." In *Engendering Human Security: Feminist Perspectives,* eds Thanh-Dam Truong, Saskia Wieringa, and Amrita Chhachhi. New York: Zed Books, pp. 191–210.

Wæver, Ole. 1995. "Securitization and Desecuritization." In *On Security,* ed. Ronnie D. Lipschutz. New York: Columbia University Press, pp. 46–86.

Walsh, Declan. 2012. "Bombs Target Muslims at Service in Pakistan." *New York Times.* http://www.nytimes.com/2012/01/16/world/

asia/shiite-muslims-target-of-bomb-blast-in-southern-pakistan.
html?ref=terrorism (Accessed January 15, 2012).

Walt, Stephen M. 1991. "The Renaissance of Security Studies."
International Studies Quarterly. 35(2): 211–239.

Warren, Karen J. 1997. *Ecofeminism: Women, Culture, Nature.*
Bloomington: Indiana University Press.

Wheeler, Nicholas. 2000. *Saving Strangers: Humanitarian Intervention
in International Society.* Oxford: Oxford University Press.

Whitworth, Sandra. 2004. *Men, Militarism and UN Peacekeeping.*
Boulder, CO: Lynne Rienner Publishers.

——. 2008. "Militarized Masculinity and Post-Traumatic Stress
Disorder." In *Rethinking the Man Question: Sex, Gender and
Violence in International Relations*, eds Jane Parpart and Marysia
Zalewski. New York: Zed Books, pp. 109–126.

Wibben, Annick T. R. 2008. "Human Security: Toward an Opening."
Security Dialogue. 39(4): 455–462.

——. 2011. *Feminist Security Studies: A Narrative Approach.* New York:
Routledge.

Wilcox, Lauren. 2009. "Gendering the Cult of the Offensive." *Security
Studies.* 18(2): 214–240.

Willett, Susan. 2010. "Introduction: Security Council Resolution
1325: Assessing the Impact on Women, Peace and Security."
International Peacekeeping. 17(2): 142–158.

Williams, Paul D. 2008. *Security Studies: An Introduction.* New York:
Routledge.

Williams, Timothy. 2009. "80 Are Killed in 3 Suicide Bombings in
Iraq." *New York Times.* http://www.nytimes.com/2009/04/24/
world/middleeast/24iraq.html?scp=9&sq=female%20suicide%20
bomber&st=cse (Accessed June 15, 2011).

WISCOMP. 2011. "Overview." *WISCOMP.* http://www.wiscomp.org/
engendering_overview.asp (Accessed August 22, 2011).

Wolfendale, Jessica. 2006. "Terrorism, Security, and the Threat of
Counterterrorism." *Studies in Conflict and Terrorism.* 29(7):
753–770.

Wong, Edward. 2005. "Rebels Dressed as Women Attack Iraqi Police
Station." *New York Times.* http://www.nytimes.com/2005/11/05/
international/middleeast/05iraq.html?sq=rebels%20dressed%20
as%20women%20attack%20iraqi%20police%20stations&st=cse&
scp=1&pagewanted=print http://www.nytimes.com/2005/11/05/
international/middleeast/05iraq.html?sq=rebels%20dressed%20

as%20women%20attack%20iraqi%20police%20stations&st=cse&sc p=1&pagewanted=print, 5/24/11 (Accessed March 1, 2011).

World Commission on Environment and Development. 1987. "From One Earth to One World." In *Our Common Future*, Oxford: Oxford University Press, pp. 1–23.

World Conference on the Changing Atmosphere. 1988. *The Changing Atmosphere: Implications for Global Security*. Toronto, Canada: World Conference on the Changing Atmosphere. http://www. cmos.ca/ChangingAtmosphere1988e.pdf (Accessed August 29, 2010).

Worster, Donald. 1995. "The Shaky Ground of Sustainability." In *Deep Ecology for the 21st Century: Readings on the Philosophy and Practice of the New Environmentalism*, ed. George Sessions. Boston: Shambhala, pp. 417–427.

Wyn Jones, Richard. 1999. *Security, Strategy, and Critical Theory*, ed. Ken Booth. Boulder, CO: Lynne Rienner Publishers.

Zalewski, Marysia. 1995. "Well, What is the Feminist Perspective on Bosnia?" *International Affairs*. 71(2): 339–356.

Zarkov, Dubravka. 2001. "The Body of the Other Man: Sexual Violence and the Construction of Masculinity, Sexuality and Ethnicity in Croatian Media." In *Victims, Perpetrators or Actors? Gender, Armed Conflict and Political Violence*, eds Caroline O. N. Moser and Fiona C. Clark. New York: Zed Books, pp. 69–82.

Zedalis, Debra. 2008. "Beyond the Bombings: Analyzing Female Suicide Bombers." In Ness 2008, pp. 49–68.

Zimelis, Andris. 2009. "Human Rights, the Sex Industry and Foreign Troops: Feminist Analysis of Nationalism in Japan, South Korea and the Philippines." *Cooperation and Conflict*. 44(1): 51–71.

Index